First edition published 2006

ISBN 1-86976-228-2

Printed in New Zealand by JPNZ Internati

www.jpnz.co.nz

# CONTENTS

# INTRODUCTION

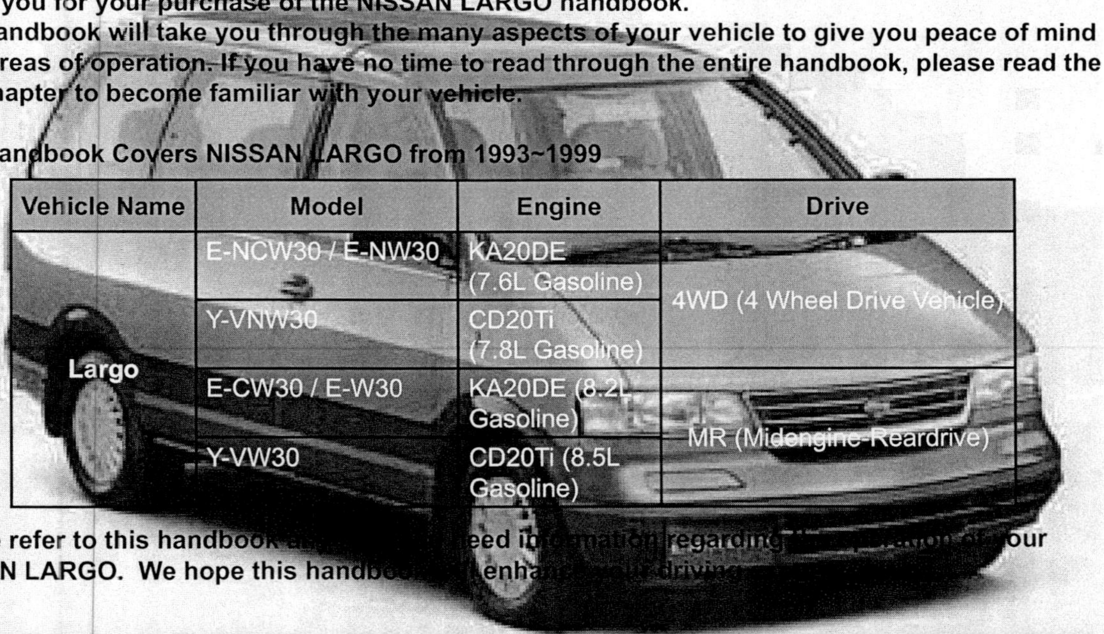

**Thank you for your purchase of the NISSAN LARGO handbook.**
**This handbook will take you through the many aspects of your vehicle to give you peace of mind in all areas of operation. If you have no time to read through the entire handbook, please read the first chapter to become familiar with your vehicle.**

This Handbook Covers NISSAN LARGO from 1993~1999

| Vehicle Name | Model | Engine | Drive |
|---|---|---|---|
| Largo | E-NCW30 / E-NW30 | KA20DE (7.6L Gasoline) | 4WD (4 Wheel Drive Vehicle) |
| | Y-VNW30 | CD20Ti (7.8L Gasoline) | |
| | E-CW30 / E-W30 | KA20DE (8.2L Gasoline) | MR (Midengine-Reardrive) |
| | Y-VW30 | CD20Ti (8.5L Gasoline) | |

**Please refer to this handbook [illegible] need information regarding [illegible] your NISSAN LARGO. We hope this handbook [illegible] enhance your driving [illegible]**

# NISSAN LARGO

# FRONT PANEL OVERVIEW

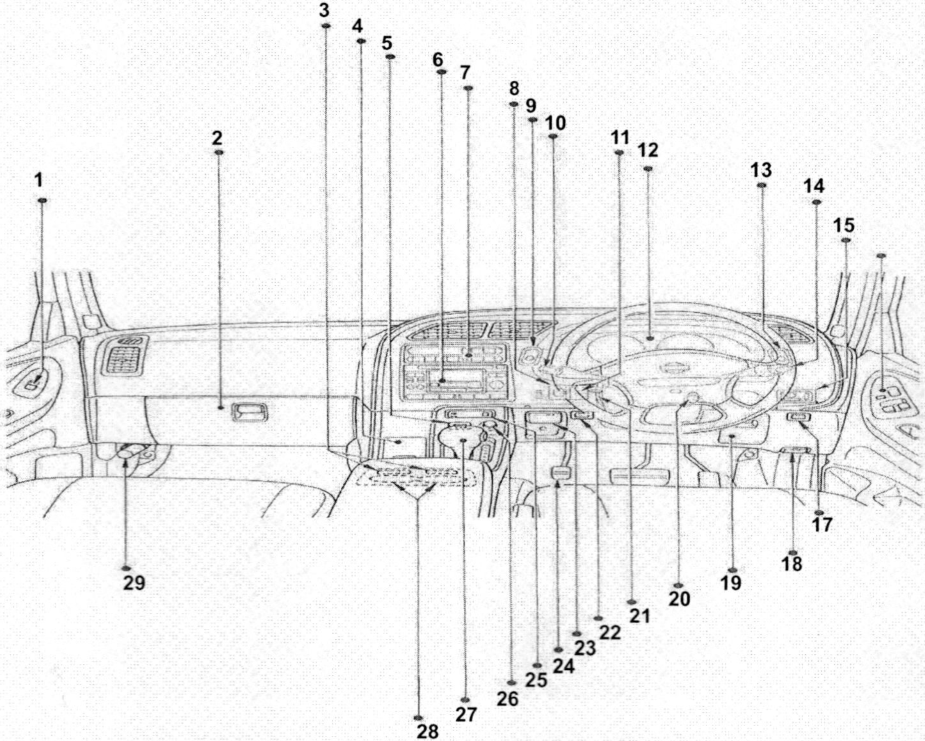

1. Power Window Switch (Passengers' Seat)
2. Glove Box
3. Coin Box
4. Ash Tray
5. Auto Mode Switch
6. Audio
7. Full Auto Air Conditioner
8. Adjustable Shock Absorber Switch
9. Hazard Light Switch
10. Wiper / Washer Switch
11. Coin Box
12. Meter
13. Rear Defogger Switch
14. Light Combination Switch
15. Power Door Mirror Switch
16. Power Window Switch
17. Auto Slide Door Switch
18. Front Hood Opener
19. Fuse Box
20. Key Switch
21. Handle Position Adjustment Lever
22. Corner & Back Sonar Switch
23. Unlock Parking Brake Switch
24. Parking Brake Pedal
25. Clock
26. Cigarette Lighter
27. Select Lever
28. Cup Holder
29. Flare

# INTERIOR OVERVIEW

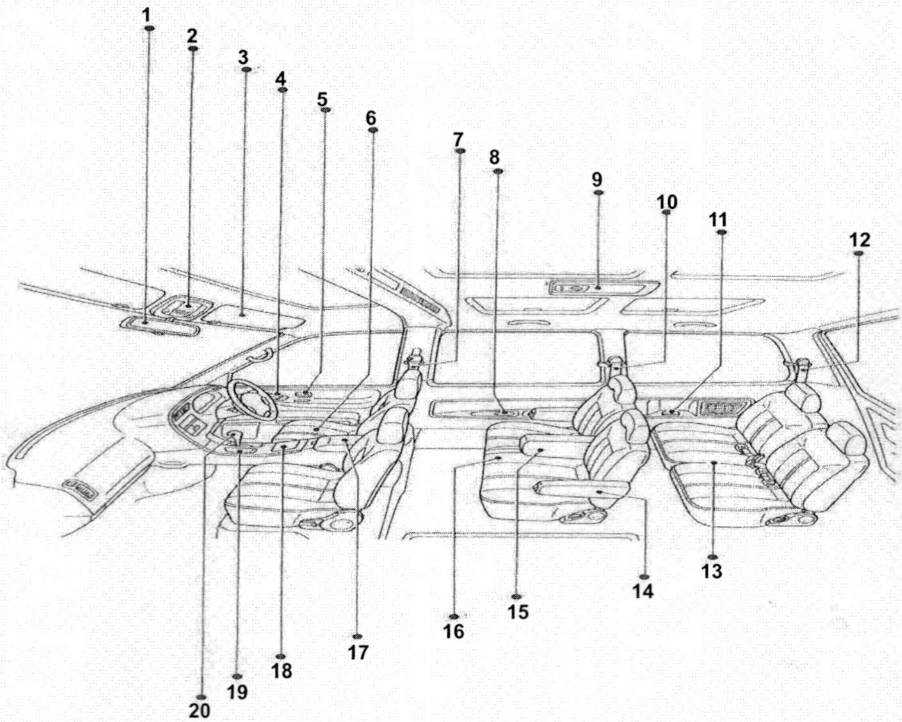

1. Rear View Mirror
2. Interior Light
3. Sun Visor
4. Power Window Switch
5. Door Lock
6. Front Seat
7. Seat Belt
8. Remote Control Switch (Rear Auto Air Conditioner)
9. Interior Light
10. Seat Belt
11. Ash Tray
12. Seat Belt
13. Third Seat
14. Side Arm Rest
15. Centre Arm Rest
16. Second Seat
17. Console Box With Lid
18. Cup Holder / Coin Box
19. Ash Tray
20. Select Lever

# EXTERIOR OVERVIEW

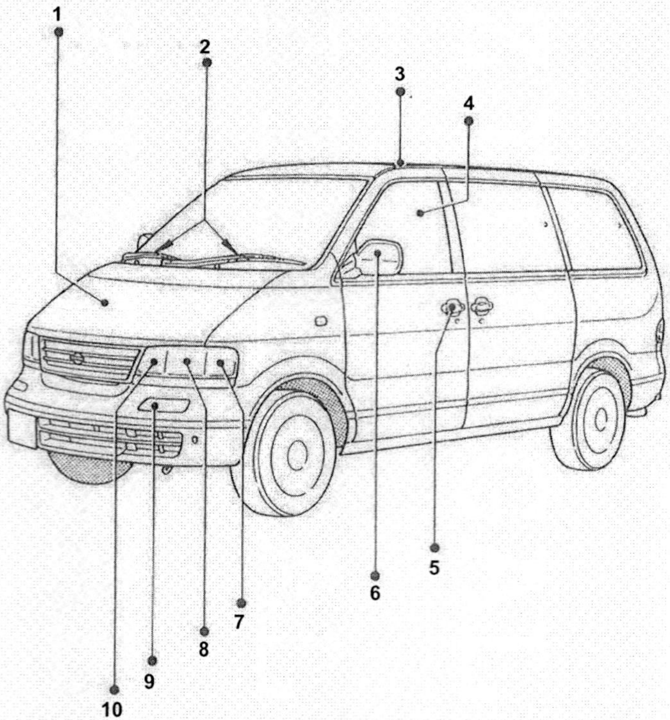

1. Front Hood
2. Front Wiper
3. Sun Roof
4. Window
5. Door
6. Door Mirror
7. Front Position Light
8. Head / Clearance Light
9. Indicator Light
10. Fog Light

# EXTERIOR OVERVIEW

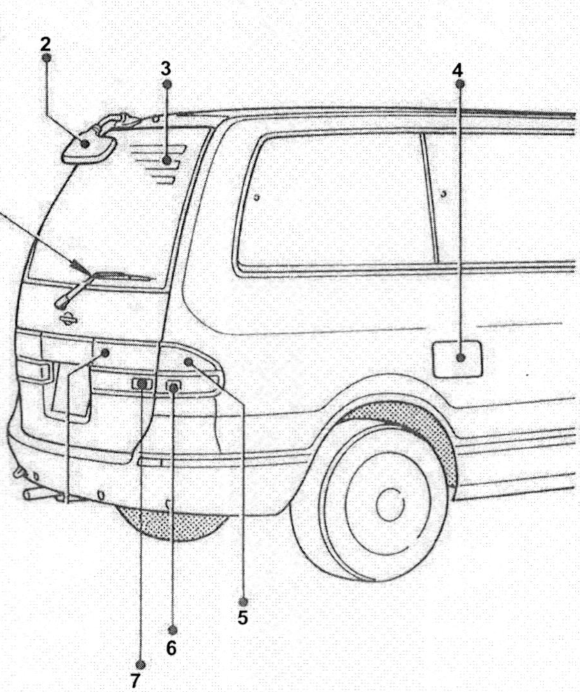

1. Rear Wiper
2. Rear Under Mirror
3. Rear Defogger
4. Fuel Lid
5. Tail / Stop Light
6. Indicator Light
7. Reverse Light

# SAFETY INFORMATION

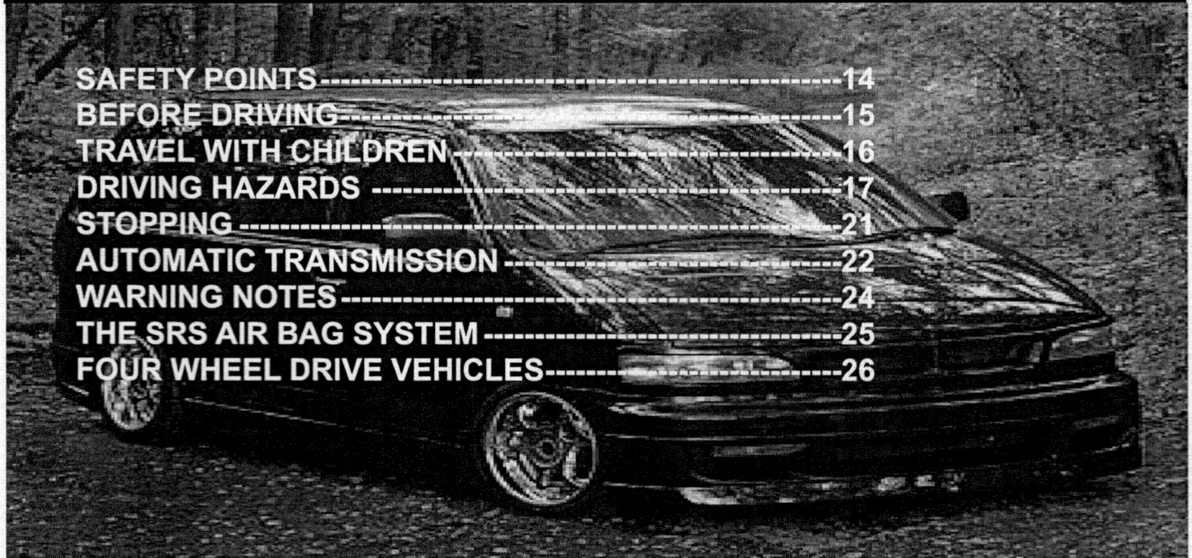



## NISSAN LARGO

# SAFETY POINTS

## KEYS

- Your vehicle has 2 keys, however the type of key may differ according to the vehicle model. Keep the spare key in a separate location.
- If you lose your key, contact Nissan with your key number to have another one made.

Write your key number here:

| |
|---|
| |

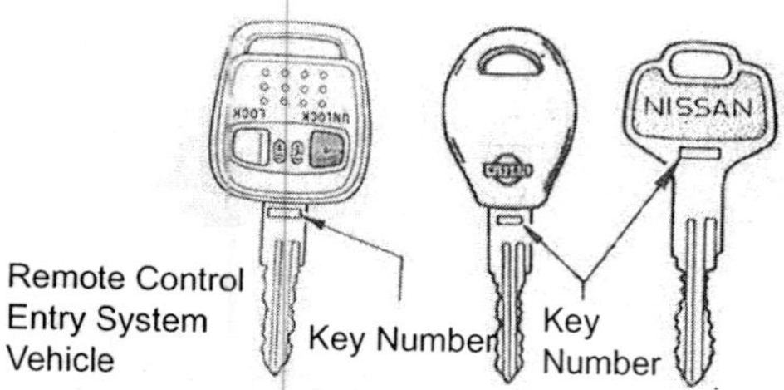


## CORRECT FUEL

- Be sure to only use fuel specified for your vehicle. Do not put inferior gasoline or diesel into your vehicle.

| ENGINE TYPE | FUEL |
|---|---|
| KA24DE | Unleaded Regular Gasoline |
| CD20ETi | Diesel |

## MAINTENANCE NOTE

- Keep your maintenance note with vehicle inspection certificate.
- Before diving the vehicle, please read the conditions of the inspection and maintenance book.
- Inspection and maintenance are required by law.
- Each time you get your vehicle inspected, write down the results in the maintenance note.

# BEFORE DRIVING

## DAILY CHECK

Daily checks are important for keeping your vehicle running safely. If you notice anything unusual (sound, vibrations, noise, water, oil leaks etc. ), have your vehicle checked by your Nissan dealer.

## PEDAL OBSTRUCTIONS

Do not place cans or other rubbish on the floor around your feet, and make sure the floor mats do not obstruct the pedals.

## CARBON NON OXIDE HAZARD

Do not have the engine running in a concealed area for an extended period of time as this will fill the area with carbon monoxide which is colourless and odourless. It is dangerous and may cause gas poisoning.

## FLAMMABLE OBJECTS

Do not carry flammable objects such as gasoline and flammable gas in spray cans in your vehicle. They may ignite or explode. These are very dangerous.

# TRAVELLING WITH CHILDREN

## Do not allow children to operate windows, doors, boot and Seats.

- Hands or Heads may get caught.
- Lock the electric windows so that children do not operate them accidentally.
- Use the child safety door lock.
- Be careful not to get children caught in the boot when they are PLAYING around the vehicle. It may result in a serious injury

## Seat children in the rear seat

Avoid letting a child sit in the front passenger seat as the child's actions may distract the driver, or the child may play with the switches and levers.

## Use safety belts for children

Always use a safety belt for children. In no circumstances should a child be held in a passenger's arms. In a collision it will be impossible to hold onto the child, and serious injury may result.

## Do not put hands or head out the sun roof

Make sure children do not put their hands or head out the sun roof. Sudden braking or striking an object outside the vehicle could result in serious injury.

## Do not leave children alone in the vehicle

Always take children with you when driving the vehicle. In sunny conditions, the interior of the vehicle can become extremely hot, endangering a child's life.
Children may also unintentionally move the car, start a fire or cause similar accidents.

# WHEN DRIVING

## Seat belts

- All passengers must always wear seat belts.
- If the seat belt is not worn correctly, its effectiveness may be reduced and may cause injuries in accident situations.
- SRS air bags are designed to complement the seat belts, not replace them. Wear the seat belt at all times while driving.

## Motorway Driving

- Check you have sufficient fuel before driving on a motorway or highway. It is dangerous to run out of fuel on a motorway.
- Check the tyre pressure before driving on a motorway. The tyre may blow if you drive at high speeds with low air pressure.
- If an accident were to occur, prepare the triangle reflector on your vehicle. (Sold separately)

## Do not turn off the engine or remove the key while driving

Turning off the engine will cause the boosters to cease functioning, which will cause the steering to grow heavy and the brakes to stop working properly.
Removing the key will cause the steering to lock, which is extremely dangerous.

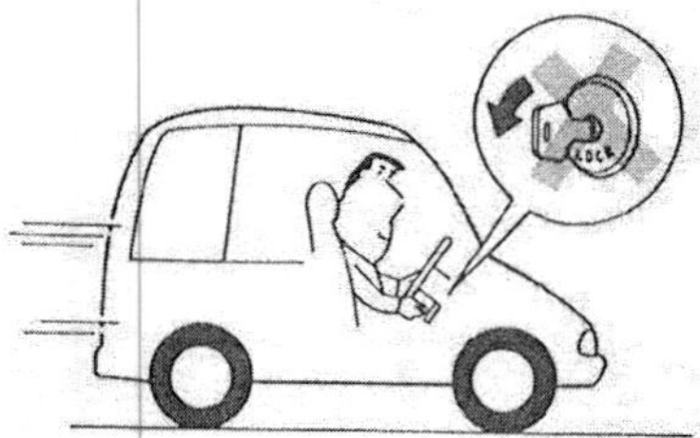

## Luggage

Do not over load the luggage in the front passenger seat or the rear seat. It may get thrown into you when braking suddenly.

## Wet Weather Driving

- Be extra careful when the road is wet as it becomes very slippery.
- Driving in puddles on the road at high speed can result in hydroplaning, which is where the tyres cannot maintain contact with the road. The brakes and steering wheel become ineffective as the vehicle skids on top of the water and slides out of control. Reduce speed when driving through rain and puddles. Hydroplaning occurs particularly when the tyres are worn.
- Do not drive into deep puddles as it causes damage to the engine and vehicle.

## Exercise caution when driving on slippery surfaces

On icy, wet or snow-covered roads, reduce speed and avoid sudden braking, acceleration and turning. Avoid harsh engine braking as this can also cause the tyres to slip.

## Combine the use of engine braking on long downhill slopes

Holding the brake pedal down continuously can cause the brakes to heat up, demisting their effect. Combine the use of the brakes with engine braking.

(Engine braking refers to the brake effect caused by removing the foot from the accelerator while driving. Refer to the latter part of this booklet for details.)

## Wet Brakes

When driving in wet conditions be careful of wet brakes. Occasionally test the brakes by applying them lightly several times. If the brakes are wet, keep lightly applying then until they dry out. Take extra care with following distance.

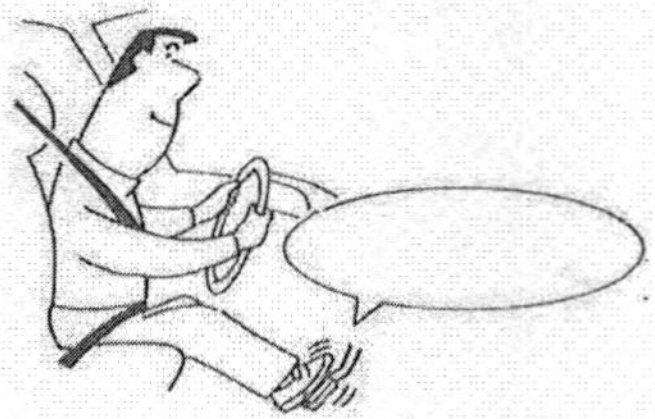

## Do not rest foot on brake pedal

Do not rest your foot on the brake pedal while driving as this will increase wear on the brakes, and may cause them to overheat and malfunction.

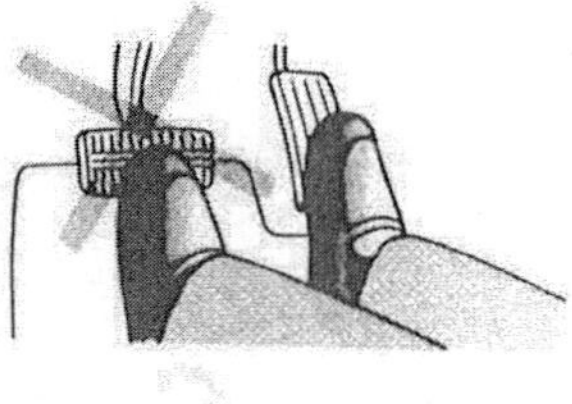

## In strong cross winds

If the car is buffeted by strong cross winds, hold the steering wheel firmly and gradually reduce speed. Take care at tunnel exits, on bridges and on sunken roads, as cross winds often develop in these areas .

## In the event of trouble while driving

If any warning lights come on, stop the vehicle promptly in a safe place and take suitable measures. Continuing to drive could lead to an accident.

In the event of a puncture or blow out, hold the steering wheel firmly, gradually reduce speed and stop in a safe place. Do not brake or change direction suddenly, as this may cause you to lose control of the vehicle. In cases where the undercarriage has been subjected to a strong impact, stop the vehicle in a safe place immediately and check for fuel and brake fluid leaks, or damage to parts on the underside of the vehicle, such as the muffler. If any damage has occurred, contact a Nissan dealer.

## When reversing pay attention to surrounding area

Rear view mirrors have blind spots. Check for people or obstacles by getting out of the vehicle.

# STOPPING

## Parking on a hill

- Always apply the parking brake firmly as the vehicle may start moving.
- Place the shift lever in P position.
- A wheel stopper will be effective in preventing the vehicle from moving.

## Do not stop the car on top of or near to flammable material

Do not park on top of or near to flammable material such as dry grass, paper, wood or oil, as the exhaust pipe and exhaust fumes can become very hot, which presents a fire risk.
Park the vehicle well clear of wood or painted wood, as the exhaust fumes may discolour or burn it.

## Steering Wheel

Do not hold the steering wheel fully right / left for a long time. This may damage the power steering.

## Moving The Vehicle

Always turn the engine on when moving the vehicle. If you utilise a downward sloping hill to move the vehicle without starting the engine, the brakes will not be effective and the steering will be very heavy.

## Sleeping In The Vehicle

Always turn the engine off if you are going to sleep inside the vehicle

- If the accelerator is depressed, or the shift lever is moved involuntarily when the engine is running, a serious accident could occur.
- If the accelerator is continuously pressed, the engine could overheat and a fire may result.
- Gas poisoning may also occur.

## When Leaving The Vehicle

When leaving the vehicle, always apply the parking brake, turn off the and take your keys with you. Do not leave children in the vehicle alone, or leave valuable objects in the vehicle.

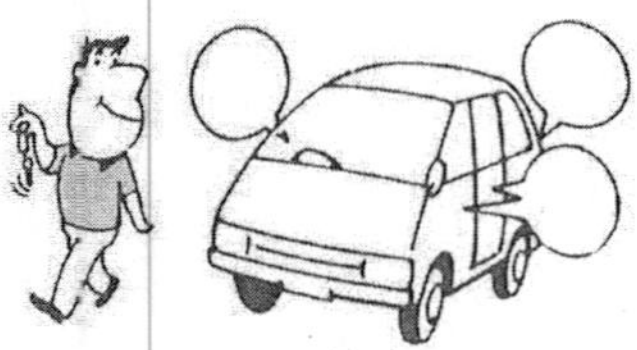

# AUTOMATIC TRANSMISSION

Vehicles fitted with automatic transmission are easier to drive for there is no need for gear changes or clutch operation. However, you should still familiarise yourself with the correct technique for driving automatic transmission vehicles.

## Pedal Position

Before starting the engine, check the position of the pedals. To avoid confusion, only use your right foot to press the accelerator and brake pedals.

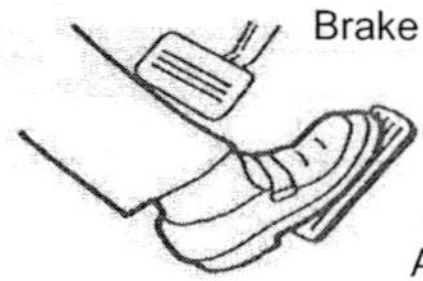


## Creep Motion

When the shift lever is in any position other than P or N, the vehicle may creep forward even when the accelerator pedal has not been depressed. Care must be taken not to cause a collision with another vehicle. When stationary, even when on level ground, apply the brake pedal or the vehicle may creep forward. In particular, immediately after the engine has been started or when the air conditioner is operating, creep motion will be stronger. Depress the brake firmly.

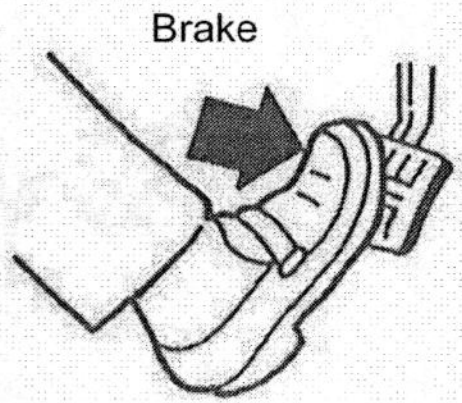


## Shift Lever Operation

When operating the shift lever when taking off, do not press the accelerator pedal, but have the brake pedal depressed. If the shift lever is moved with the accelerator depressed, the vehicle could move suddenly and an accident could result. After reversing, make a habit of moving the shift lever from R to N immediately.

## Place Shift Lever In P When Parking

When parking, place the shift lever in P. If the shift lever is not in P or N, the vehicle may move forward with the creeping motion, and if you press the accelerator by accident the vehicle will take off suddenly and an accident may occur.

## Shift Lock System

Automatic vehicles are fitted with a shift lock system to prevent the shift lever being moved accidentally.

- Unless the brake pedal is depressed, the shift lever cannot be moved out of P.
- If the ignition is in ACC or LOCK, the shift lever cannot be moved even with the brake pedal depressed.
- If the shift lever cannot be moved from P because of a flat battery etc., press the shift lock release button while shifting the lever.
- The key cannot be removed unless the shift lever is in P.
- If the shift lever is placed in R when the ignition is ON, a buzzer will sound to alert the driver that the shift lever is in R. The buzzer cannot be heard outside the vehicle.

## Depress Accelerator Slowly

Do not depress the accelerator quickly, as the vehicle will take off suddenly and an unexpected accident may occur.

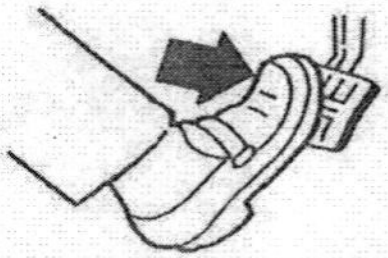

## Do Not Place Shift Lever Into 'N' While Driving

Do not place the shift lever into N when driving as the engine brake will completely cease to function, and it may damage the transmission.

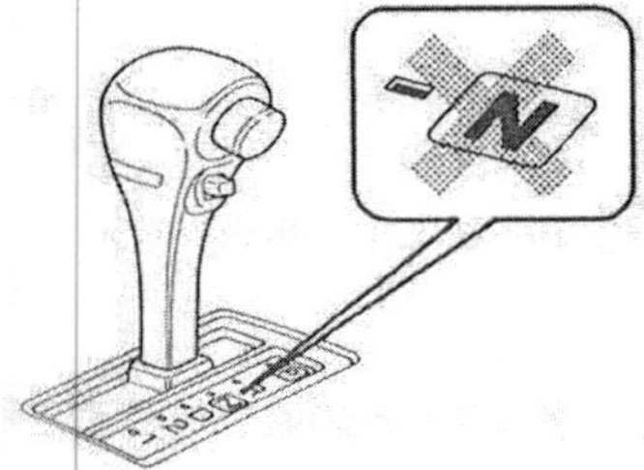

## Kick Down

When the shift lever is in D or 2, if the accelerator is pressed to a certain position the transmission will kick down to a lower gear, giving the vehicle instant power which is useful when overtaking or pulling onto a motorway.

# WARNING NOTES

## Accessories

Do not hang accessories on the front windscreen as it will obstruct your vision, or the suction caps could act as a lens and ignite. Accessories may get thrown into you if the air bag inflates.

## Ashtrays

Always put out tobacco and matches before putting them in the ashtray, and always keep the lid closed when not in use. Do not overfill ashtrays, or put flammable materials in the ashtrays.

## Gas lighters

Do not leave gas lighters in the vehicle as they may ignite and cause a fire.

## Radiator

Do not remove the cap when the radiator is hot. Hot water or steam may spurt out. Refill the coolant once the temperature has cooled down.

## Modifying the vehicle

Do not modify this vehicle. Only use Nissan genuine parts otherwise the vehicle may become unsafe, or damage may be caused to other vehicle parts. Do not change or repair the steering wheel by yourself as this will stop the air bags from operating.

# THE SRS AIR BAG SYSTEM

The SRS air bag system is activated Instantaneously in the event of the vehicle being subjected to a large frontal impact. The air bags act to absorb the collision impact on the driver or passenger's head areas. It is not designed to replace seat belts, which should still be worn.

The air bags alone cannot stop passengers being thrown from the vehicle or similar events. They must be combined with seat belts to work properly.
Always ensure both the driver and any passengers wear seat belts.

The SRS air bag system is operable when the ignition is in the ON position. The system is activated by a large Impact, such as a frontal collision with a moving or parked vehicle, or a wall.

Faults in the SRS air bag system will be indicated by the air bag warning light coming on.
If the air bag warning light does not go out after first coming on when the ignition is switched to ON, or if the light comes on or flashes while driving, have the vehicle checked at a Nissan dealer promptly.

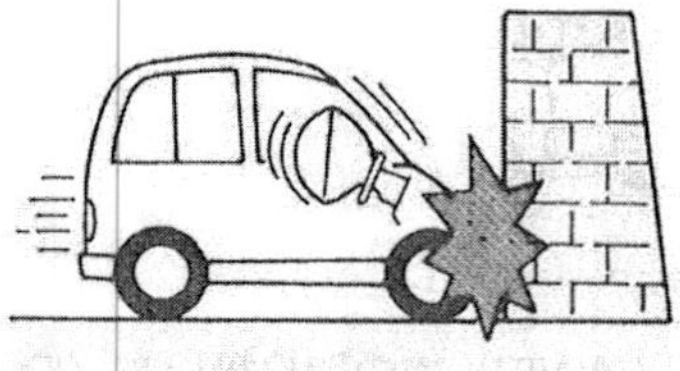

# FOUR WHEEL DRIVE VEHICLES

Four wheel drive vehicles operate well on surfaces that are wet, snowy, greasy and steep etc., because power is distributed to all four wheels. To better understand the performance of a 4WD vehicle it is important to read the following points below:

- A 4WD vehicle handles very well in various situations but it still has its limitations. The axles, steering wheel and brakes operate the same as a standard vehicle.
- If the vehicle becomes stuck, it is advised not to overuse the accelerator pedal as this will deepen the hole making it even more difficult to get out. Place a stone or a piece of wood behind the tyre and manoeuvre the vehicle backwards and forwards until the vehicle is free.
- When replacing the tyres or wheels, make sure they are replaced with the same recommended size, brand, type and tread pattern. Failure to do so will result in decreased performance.
- Rotate the tyres every 5,000 km, and check the tyre air pressure regularly. Consult your Nissan dealer for advice when rotating your tyres.

## When using chains

Always attach chains to the rear wheels, and only use on snow-covered roads to avoid damaging the drive mechanism. In cases where driving with chains is unavoidable, always switch to 2WD.

## Rotate tyres regularly

If the tyres are unevenly worn or tire pressure differs significantly from that specified, the vehicle may not function properly and safety may be impaired. Check tyre pressure regularly and rotate tires every 5,000 kilometres.

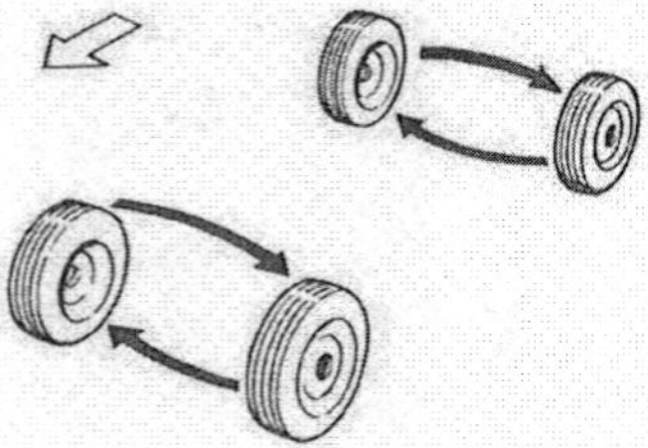

# METERS, DISPLAY LIGHTS, WARNING LIGHTS ECT

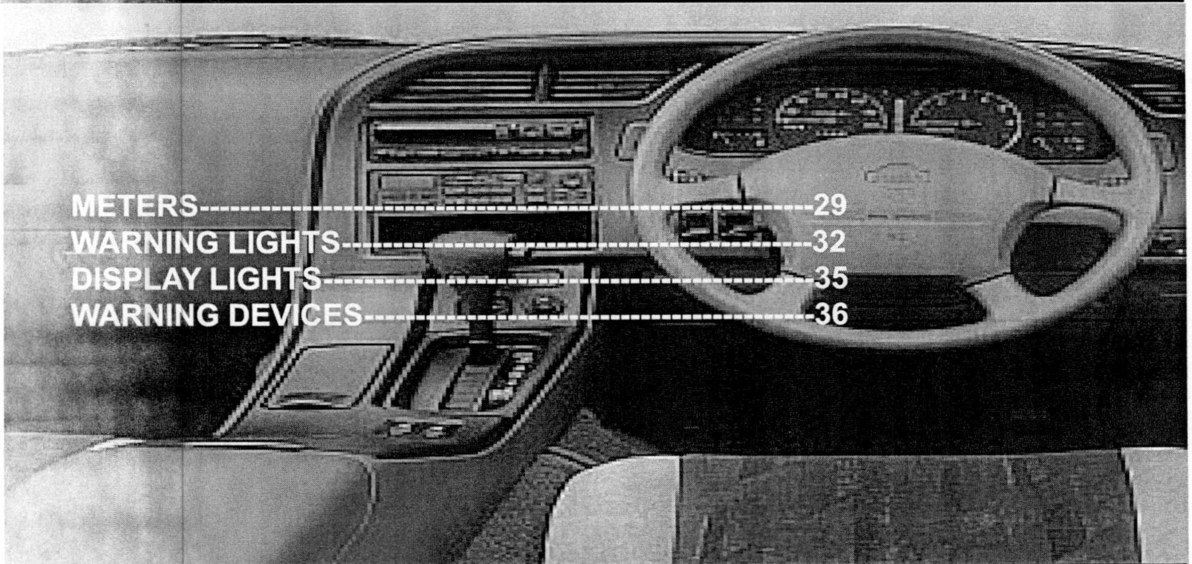



## NISSAN LARGO

# METERS

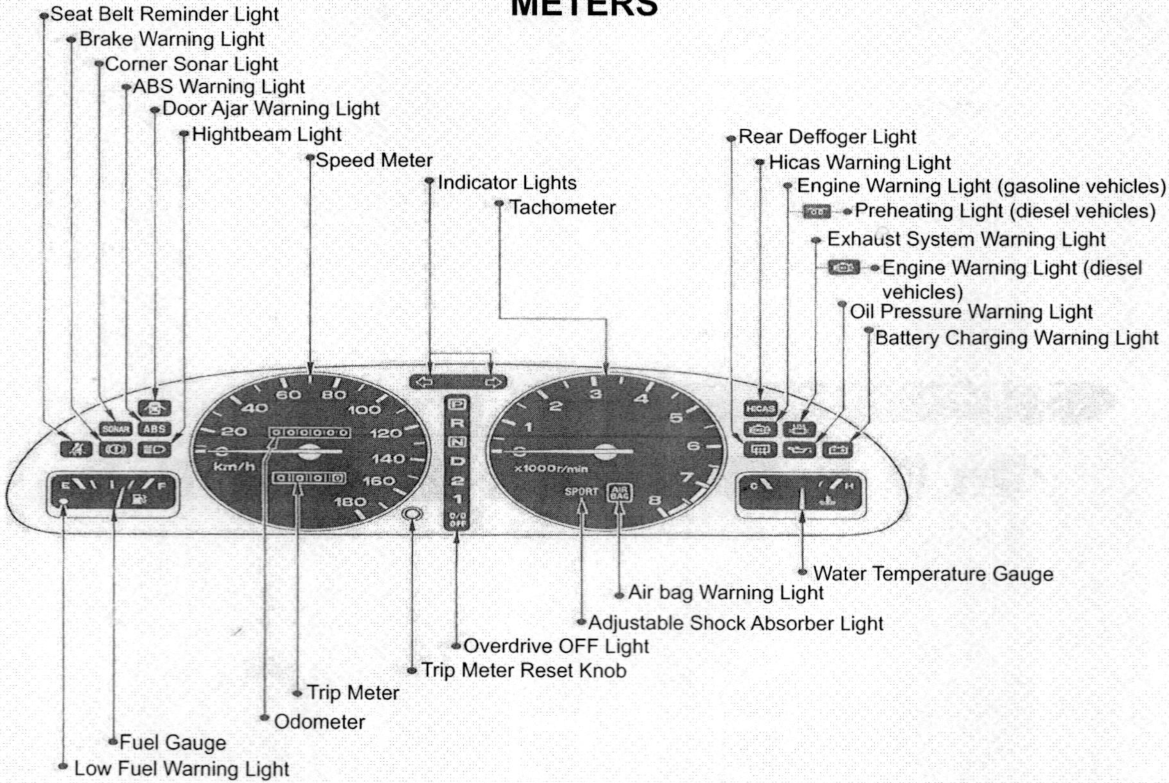
Seat Belt Reminder Light
Brake Warning Light
Corner Sonar Light
ABS Warning Light
Door Ajar Warning Light
Hightbeam Light
Speed Meter
Indicator Lights
Tachometer
Rear Deffoger Light
Hicas Warning Light
Engine Warning Light (gasoline vehicles)
Preheating Light (diesel vehicles)
Exhaust System Warning Light
Engine Warning Light (diesel vehicles)
Oil Pressure Warning Light
Battery Charging Warning Light
Water Temperature Gauge
Air bag Warning Light
Adjustable Shock Absorber Light
Overdrive OFF Light
Trip Meter Reset Knob
Trip Meter
Odometer
Fuel Gauge
Low Fuel Warning Light

# METERS

## Speed Meter

Shows the vehicle's travelling speed in kilometres per hour.

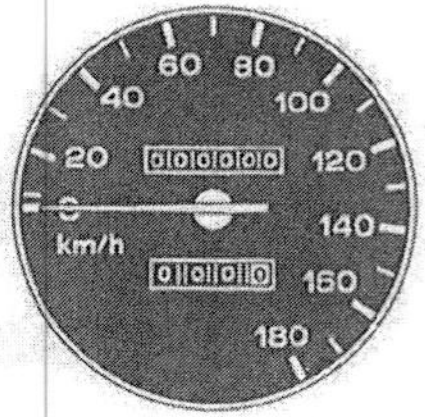


## Odometer

Shows the total distance travelled in kilometres.

## Trip Meter

Show the total distance travelled in kilometres since the last reset. The last number is in 100m units.

## Tachometer (rev meter)

Shows the engine revolutions per minute.

Caution:

Do not drive with the tachometer needle in the red zone. In this range the engine is over-reving, which can cause damage.

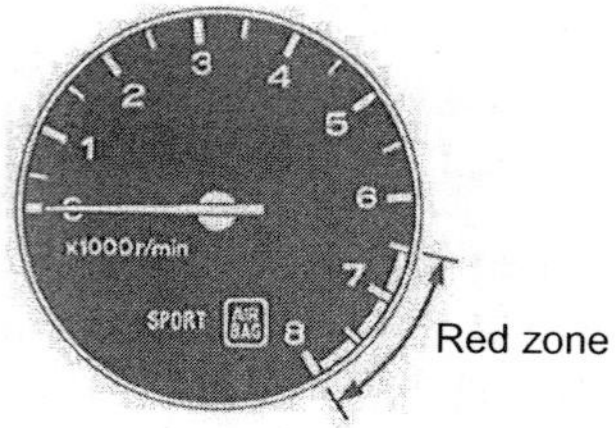


## Fuel gauge

The fuel gauge is independent of the ignition therefore it will sow the amount of fuel left regardless of the position of the ignition.

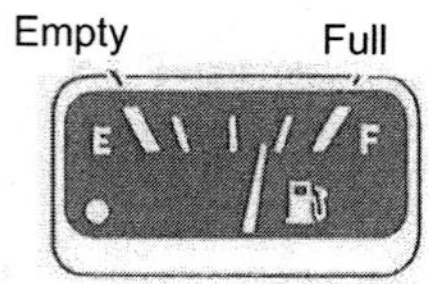

Advice:

- When the ignition has been turned OFF for a long time the needle may move, so be sure to check the fuel gauge when the ignition is ON.
- After refuelling and switching on the ignition, it will take some time for the fuel gauge to settle at the correct fuel level.
- The fuel gauge will move with movements of the fuel in the tank on curves or hills.

## Water Temperature Gauge

Shows the temperature of the engine coolant when the ignition is in ON position. Normally, the needle will be below H when driving.

Caution:

If the gauge shows "overheat", stop promptly in a safe place.

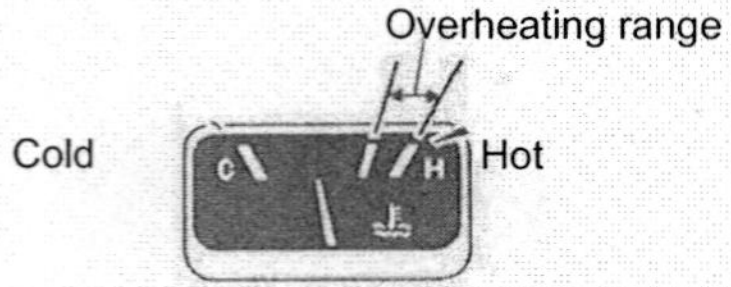


# WARNING LIGHTS

## Door Ajar Warning Light

This light will come on if a door is open or not closed properly. Ensure the light is off before starting to drive

## Seat Belt Reminder Light

This light will come on if the ignition is in the ON position and the driver's seat belt is not fastened.

## ABS Warning Light

This light will come on when there is a problem with the ABS electrical control system

## Brake Warning Light

This light will illuminate in the following situations when the ignition is ON:

- When the parking brake is on.
- When the brake fluid is low.

- When there is a problem with the brake booster (diesel vehicles).
  The fan belt might be broken or a fault in the vacuum pump, vacuum hose and booster is indicated.
- When the engine room fan is disconnected (diesel vehicles).
  The engine room fan is disconnected when the brake warning light and oil pressure warning light come on at the same time

Advice:

- If the light continues to show after the parking brake has been released, stop in a safe place and contact your Nissan dealer. In this situation the brakes may not be working effectively. Press the brake pedal hard to slow down the vehicle.
- Remember to release the parking brake when driving.
- If there is a metallic screeching sound coming from around the brakes, take the vehicle to your Nissan dealer as soon as possible.

## Low Fuel Warning Light

This light will come on when the ignition is ON and the fuel level has decreased to approximately 14 litres (2WD vehicles), 12 litres (4WD vehicles)

Advice:

Refuel as soon as possible

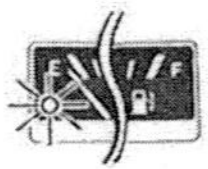

## Air bag Warning Light

This light will come on for  when the ignition is ON. There is a problem in the air bag system when this light stays on more than 7 seconds.

Advice:

If the light stays on or flashes, have your vehicles checked promptly at a Nissan dealer

## Hicas Warning Light

This light will come on when the engine is running, a fault in the hicas electric control system is indicated or the oil level has decreased.

Advice:

JPNZ recommends that have your vehicles checked promptly at a Nissan dealer.

## Engine Warning Light

This light will come on when the engine is running and a fault in the engine electric control system is indicated. (For gasoline vehicles, the light will illuminate: For diesel vehicles, this light will flash

**Diesel vehicles**
This light will flash when if water collects in the fuel filter when the engine is running.

Advice:

Drain water from the filter as soon as possible. After draining, have the vehicle checked at a Nissan dealer immediately.

## Exhaust Temperature Warning Light

This light will come on when the temperature of the exhaust gets extremely hot.

Advice:

- If the warning light comes on while driving, slow down until it goes off.
- Have your vehicle checked by a Nissan dealer

## Oil Pressure Warning Light

- This light will come on if the pressure of the oil that is used to lubricate the engine drops while the engine is running.
- **Engine Room Fan Disconnected Warning Light** (Diesel vehicles)
  This light and brake warning light come on at the same time, the engine room fan will be disconnected

Advice:

- If the light comes on while the engine is running pull over to a safe place, stop the engine and contact your Nissan dealer. Continuing to rung the engine may damage the engine.Have the vehicle checked by a Nissan dealer.

## Battery Charging Warning Light

- This lift will come on if a fault occurs in the battery's charging system while the engine is running.

Advice:

- If the light comes on while the engine is running pull over to a safe place, stop the engine and contact your Nissan dealer. Continuing to rung the engine may damage the engine.Have the vehicle checked by a Nissan dealer.

## Engine Bay Fan Disconnected Warning Light

This light and brake warning light come on at the same time, the engine room fan will be disconnected.

Advice:

Have your vehicles checked promptly at a Nissan dealer.

# DISPLAY LIGHTS

KEY ON The ignition must be in the ON position

## Corner Sonar Light

KEY ON

To operate this switch, simply push the "ON" switch. The light will flash when the corner sonar light switch is activated.

## High Beam Indicator

LIGHT ON

This light will come on when the headlights are on high beam.

## Indicator Lights

KEY ON

The lights will flash when the indicator switch or Hazard light switch is activated.

## Shift Lever Position Indicator

KEY ON

The position of the shift lever is shown.

## Overdrive Off (O/D OFF Light)

KEY ON

The light will come on when the overdrive switch is turned off.

## Adjustable Shock Absorber Light

KEY ON

This light will come on when the adjustable shock absorber light switch is activated, and the drive mode selected with the sports mode.

## Preheating Light (Diesel Vehicles)

KEY ON

This light will come on when the glow-plug is preheating. It will go out when the glow-plug preheating is complete.

## Rear Defforger Light

KEY ON

This light will come on when the rear deffoger light switch is activated.

## Power Mode light

KEY ON

To operate this light, simply press the AT mode switch.

This light also will come on when depressing the accelerator fully to change the drive mode to the power mode. ( The light will come on approx. 2 seconds)

- Its located in the AT mode switch

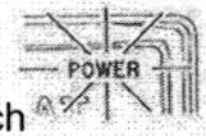


## Snow Mode Light

KEY ON

To operate this light, simply push the AT mode switch.

- Its located in the AT mode switch

# WARNING DEVICES

## Brake pad worn warning buzzer

A metallic clank will sound when the brake pad is worn.

Advice:

Have the vehicle checked by a Nissan dealer.

## Key reminder buzzer

A buzzer will sound if the driver's door is opened while the key is in the ignition.

Advice:

Remove the key from the ignition. (The buzzer will not sound when the ignition is ON. The buzzer sound is the same as that for the headlight reminder buzzer.)

## Reverse buzzer (Automatic vehicles)

If the shift lever is in R when the ignition is ON, a buzzer will sound inside the vehicle.

Advice:

The buzzer sounds as a warning to the driver, in order to protect against accidents and make the vehicle more user-friendly. The buzzer is not designed to warn people outside the vehicle.

## Headlight reminder buzzer

A buzzer will sound if the engine is turned off and the driver's door is opened while the headlights are still on.

Advice:

Turn off the headlights. (The buzzer will not sound when the ignition is ON. The buzzer sound is the same as that for the key reminder buzzer)

# SWITCHES

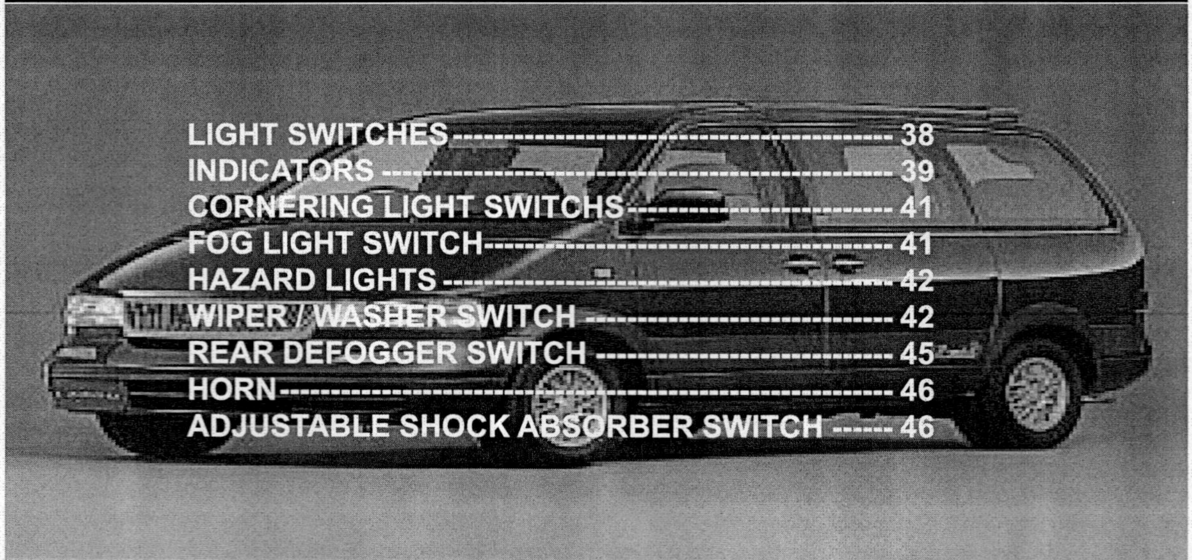



# NISSAN LARGO

# LIGHT SWITCH

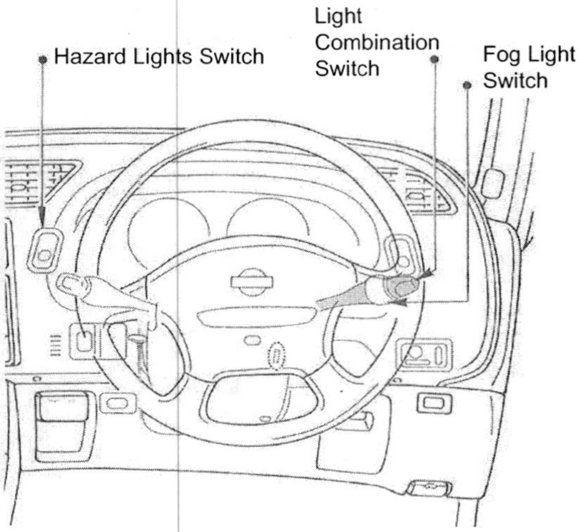


## LIGHT COMBINATION SWITCH

The light switch is independent of the ignition.

## LIGHT SWITCH OPERATION

Turn the light switch and align the position of the dot to either turn the lights on or off as shown below.

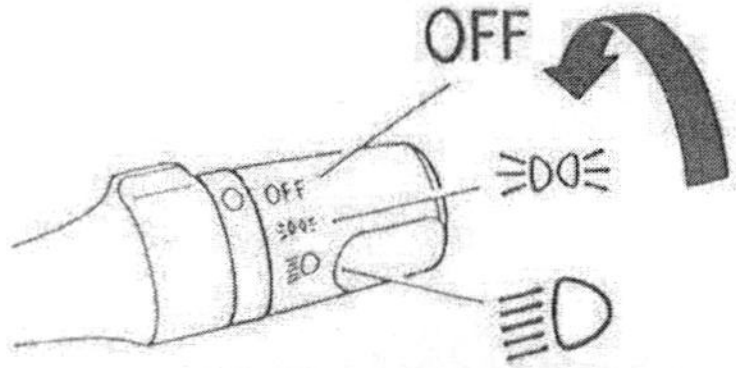


| Switch position | Headlights | Clearance / Tail / Licence Plate / Meter Lights |
|---|---|---|
| OFF | OFF | OFF |
| 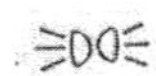 | OFF | ON |
|  | ON | ON |

Advice:

- Do not leave lights on when the engine is not running, as this will drain the battery.
- If the engine is running hot and the driver's door is opened while the headlights are still on, a buzzer will sound to warn the driver.

## Selecting high beam and low beam

LIGHT ON

Push the lever towards the front of the vehicle to select high beam and pull towards you to return to low beam.

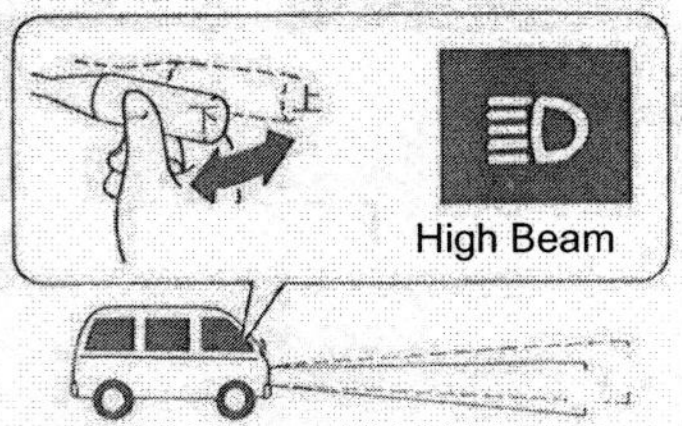


Advice:

- Use low beam when there are oncoming vehicles or vehicles in front of you, or when driving in the city.
- The high beam light will come on the display.

## Signalling intention to overtake

When the lights are on low beam, pull the lever lightly back towards you.

# INDICATORS

KEY ON

- If the lever is moved either up or down to the position shown in the diagram, the indicators and the indicator display light on the meter panel will flash.
- If the lever is lightly pushed up or down to the position shown in the diagram, the indicators will flash while the lever is held in that position. This is useful for changing lanes and so forth.

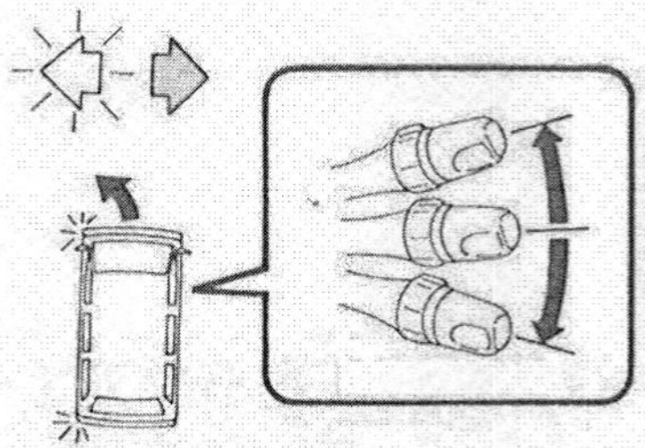

Advice:

- If the lever does not return after making a turn, push it back manually.
- If the indicators flash very quickly, a bulb may be blown. Contact your Nissan dealer to have it replaces.

## CORNERING LIGHT SWITCH

KEY ON

The cornering light illuminates the direction you are turning while driving at night. It will come on when you indicate left or right while the headlights and the ignition are on.

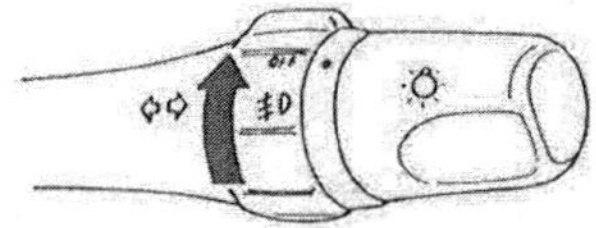

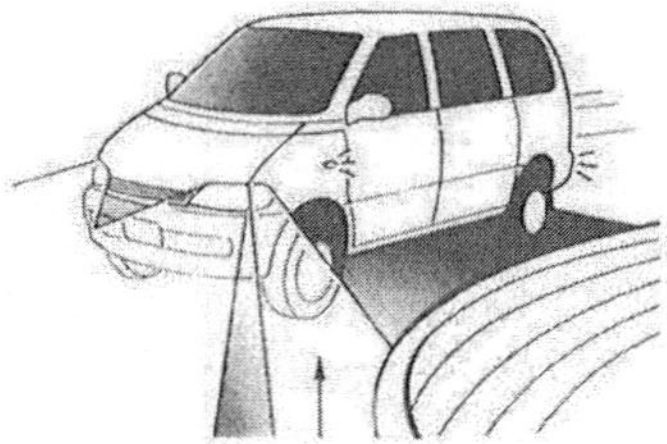

## FOG LIGHT SWITCH

The fog lights can be used regardless of the ignition position. They are useful when visibility is bad due to the fog.

- To turn on, align the mark with the dot.
- To turn off, turn the light switch to the OFF position.

For UMIBOZU LARGO vehicles,

Press I or II on the switch to illuminate the corresponding fog light as showing in the diagram.

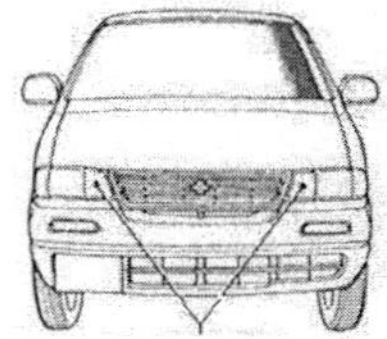

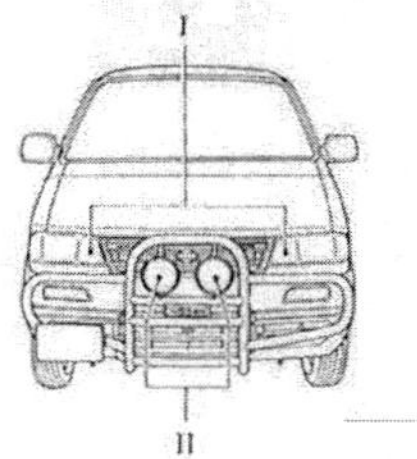

## HAZARD LIGHTS

Use the hazard lights in an emergency or breakdown situation when the vehicle has to be stopped on the road.

- Pressing the switch will make all indicators and both arrows on the meter panel flash simultaneously.
- Press the switch again to turn the hazard lights off.

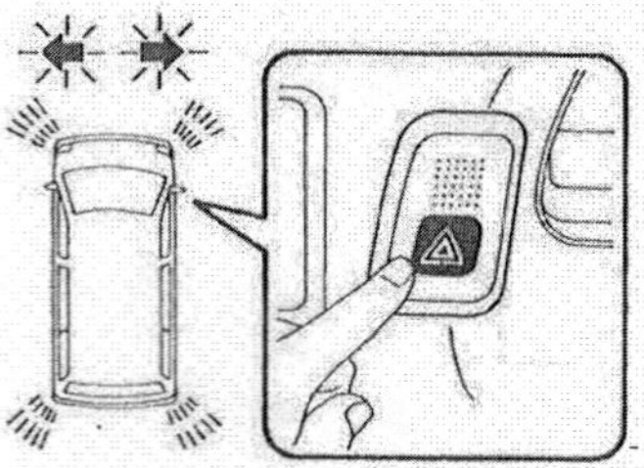

Advice:

Do not leave the hazard lights on for an extended period of time. This will drain the battery and the engine will not start again.

# WIPER / WASHER SWITCH

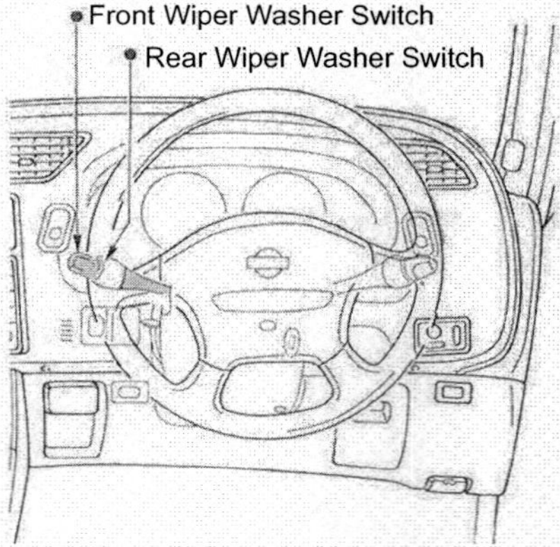


## WIPERS

The ignition must be in the ON position.

To operate the wipers push the lever down.

| Switch position | Wiper operation |
|---|---|
| OFF | Stopped |
| INT | Intermittent |
| LO | Low-speed continuous |
| HI | High-speed continuous |

## 2 Speed variable non intermittent type

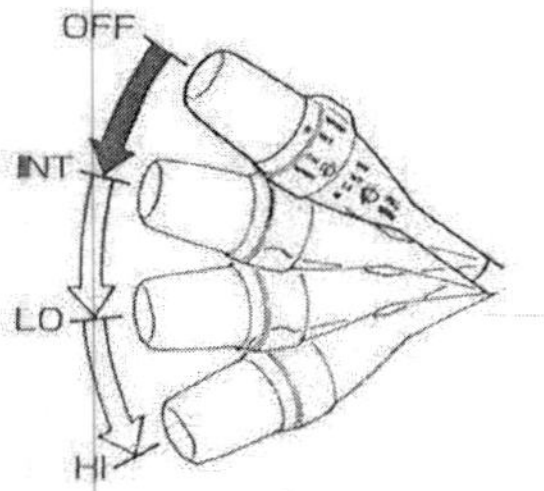


## 2 Speed variable non intermittent type

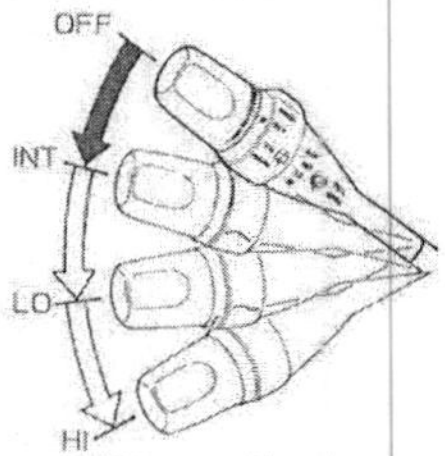


Non Grandege vehicles

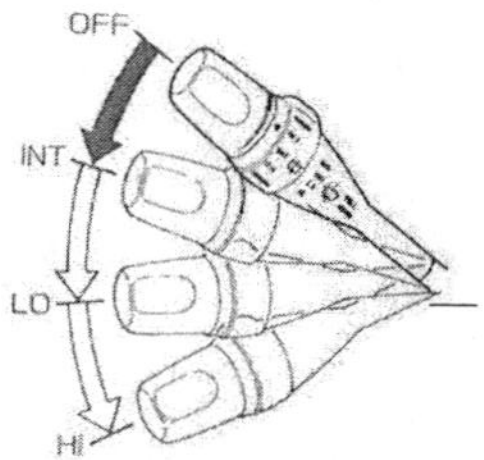


Grandege vehicles

<u>Advice:</u>

- Using the wipers on a dry windscreen may scratch the glass or damage the wiper blades. Operate the washer before using the wipers.
- Do not operate the wipers when the wiper blades are frozen or in any way stuck to the windscreen, as doing so may damage the wipers or the wiper motor. Warm up the windscreen with the heater first.
- Do not operate the washer continuously for more than thirty seconds, or when the washer tank is empty. It may cause damage to the washer motor.
- Do not operate the wipers while the wiper arms are standing upright.
- If there is snow on the windscreen, the wipers may stop. Turn the switch off and clear the snow off the windscreen before using the wipers again.
- Do not use the wipers for a long period of time when the engine is not running as it will drain the battery.

## Adjusting the front wiper interval

It is possible to vary the time interval of the intermittent wiper operation.

Turn the end of the lever to adjust.

Long interval

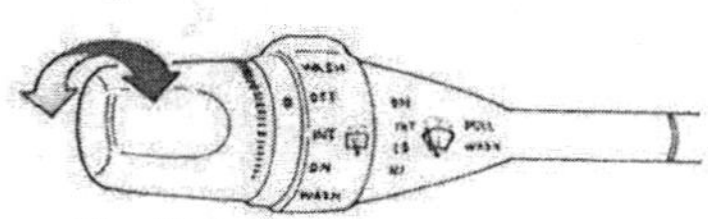

Short interval

# WASHER FLUID DISPERSION

## Front Washer Dispersion

The ignition must be in the ACC position.
Pull the lever towards you to spray washer fluid onto the windscreen. The wipers will operate several times.

Advice:

- Do not operate the washer for more than 30 seconds when the washer tank is empty. It may cause damage to the washer motor.
- If the washer fluid does not depress after refilling, contact your Nissan dealer.

# REAR WASHER SWITCH

The ignition must be in the ACC position.

| Switch Position | Rear Wiper Operation |
|---|---|
| WASH | Rear washer operation |
| OFF | Stopped |
| INT | Intermittent |
| ON | Continuous |

## Wiper

Turn the lever to the INT position to operate the wipers intermittently and turn the lever to the ON position to operate the wipers continuously.

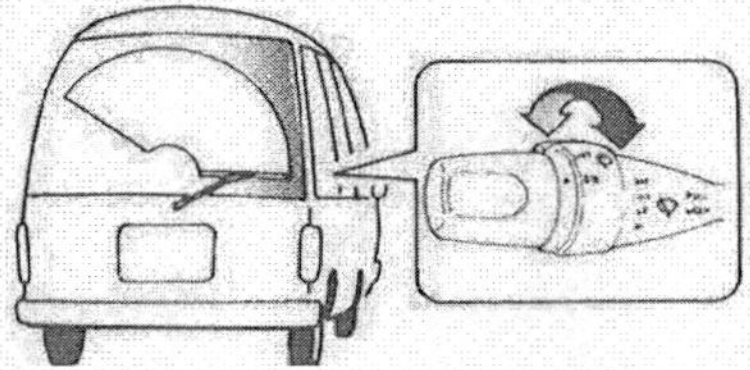

## Washer

While turning the lever to the WASH position, the washer fluid will be sprayed on to the rear windscreen.
Caution:

- When it is cold, the washer fluid sprayed onto the windscreen may freeze and obstruct vision. Use the heater to heat the windscreen before dispensing washer fluid.

Advice:

- Using the wipers on a dry windscreen may scratch the glass or damage the wiper blades. Operate the washer before using the wipers.
- Do not operate the wipers when the wiper blades are frozen or in any way stuck to the windscreen, as doing so may damage the wipers or the wiper motor. Warm up the windscreen with the heater first.
- Do not operate the washer continuously for more than thirty seconds, or when the washer tank is empty. It may cause damage to the washer motor.
- Do not operate the wipers while the wiper arms are standing upright.
- If there is snow on the windscreen, the wipers may stop. Turn the switch off and clear the snow off the windscreen before using the wipers again.
- Do not use the wipers for a long period of time when the engine is not running as it will drain the battery.

## REAR DEFOGGER SWITCH

The ignition must be in the ON position for the rear defogger to operate. The defogger heats the rear window to remove fogging. Press the switch to operate, and press again to turn off.When the rear defogger is operating, the operation light in the switch will illuminate.

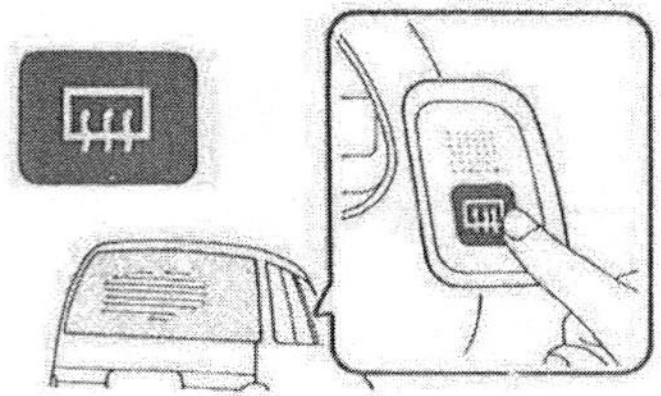

Advice:

- Do not use the defogger for an extended period of time, or for melting snow from the window, as it consumes a large amount of power.
- When cleaning inside the car, use a soft damp cloth and wipe gently to avoid damaging the heating lines on the inside of the rear windscreen. Do not use glass cleaner or detergent.

Note:

- Vehicles fitted with door mirrors with heaters, they will operate simultaneously when the rear defogger switch is pressed.

## HORN

The horn operates independently to the ignition. To sound the horn, press the padded panel in the centre of the steering wheel.

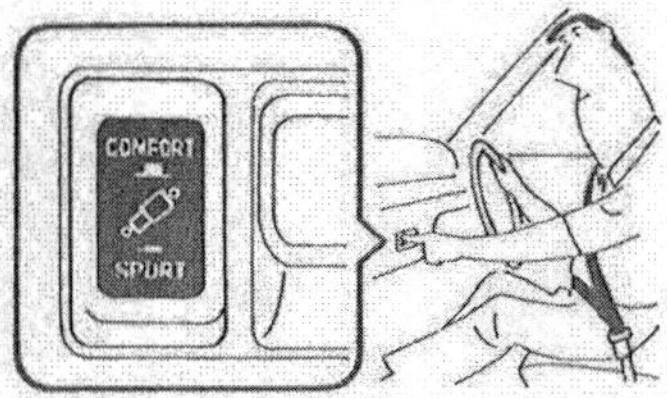


Note:
The horn will sound with easier operation, if the bottom side of the padded panel is pushed.

## ADJUSTABLE SHOCK ABSORBER SWITCH

The ignition must be in ON position.
The damping force of the shock absorbers can be selected by changing the switch according to driving conditions.

| Switch Position | Application |
|---|---|
| COMFORT | A soft ride quality for city driving. |
| SPORT | A stiff ride quality emphasizing handling stability for off-road or high-speed driving |

| Switch Position | Switch Operation | Display light on the meter panel |
|---|---|---|
| COMFORT |  | SPORT |
| SPORT |  | SPORT |

# DRIVING OPERATION

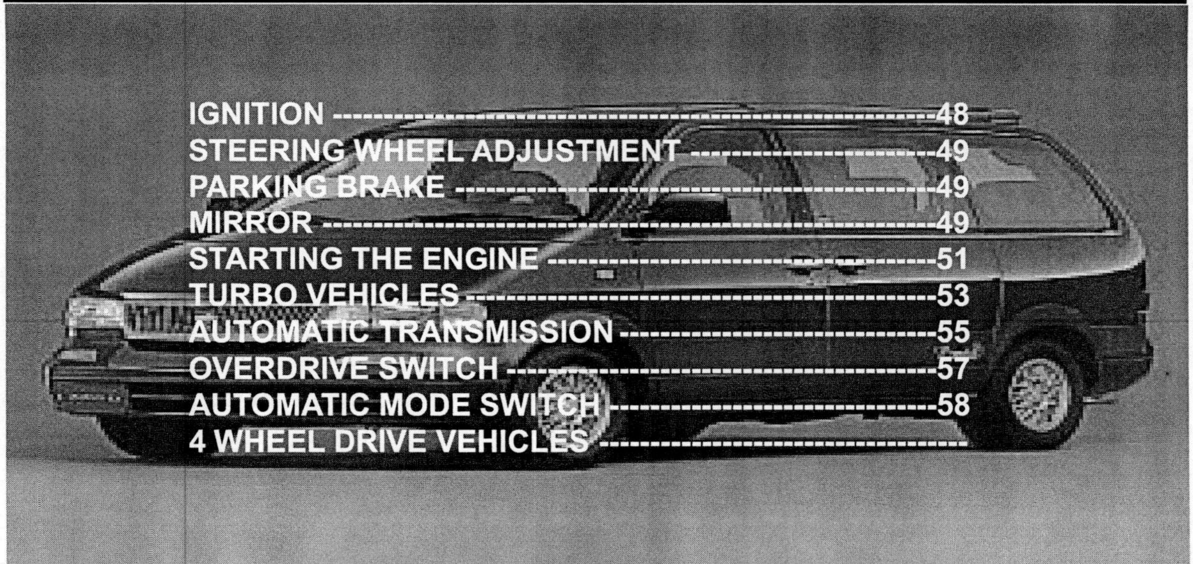



## NISSAN LARGO

# IGNITION

| Key position | Function |
|---|---|
| LOCK (0) | The key can be inserted and removed. The steering wheel locks when the key is removed. |
| OFF (1) | The push button can be pressed in this position. |
| ACC (2) | In this position, the engine will not run but accessories are operational (audio system, cigarette lighter, wipers). |
| ON (3) | The key is in this position when the engine is running. In diesel vehicles, the glow plugs will be heated. |
| START (4) | This position is only for starting the engine. After the engine has started, release the key and it will flip back to the ON position. |

Advice:

The select lever must be in "P" position to remove the key.

## REMOVING THE KEY

Place the select lever in "P" position, turn the key to the LOCK position and pull out the key.

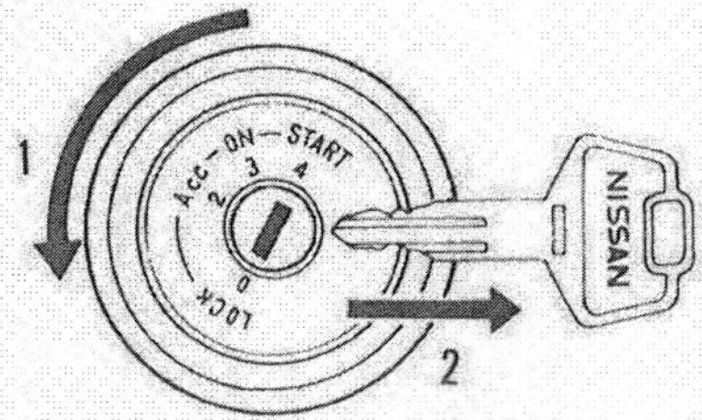


Note:

When it is difficult to move the key from the LOCK position, turn the steering wheel lightly to the left and the right.

Advice:

When the engine is turned off with the key still in the ignition and the driver's door is opened a buzzer will sound. This is to remind the driver that the key is still in the ignition.

## STEERING WHEEL ADJUSTMENT

Push the lever down and move the steering wheel up or down. When the steering wheel is in a suitable position, pull the lever up to lock the steering wheel in place.

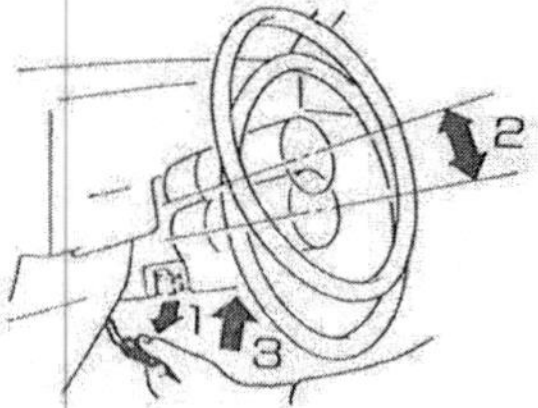


Caution:
Always adjust the steering wheel before driving. It is dangerous to adjust while driving.

## PARKING BRAKE

Always press the parking brake completely when parking. To release the parking brake, pull the brake release lever that located left side of the steering wheel.

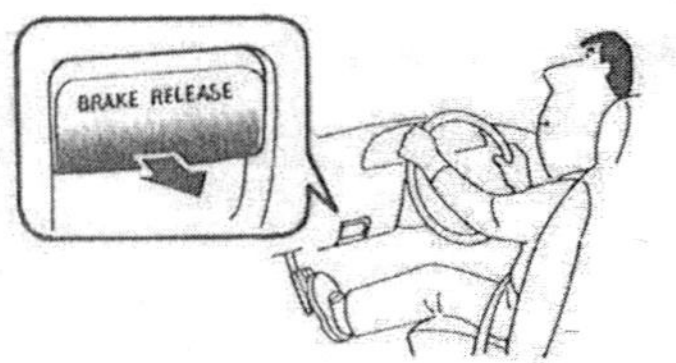


Caution:
Do not drive with the parking brake applied as this cause the brakes to overheat and wear quickly, and reduce the effectiveness of the brakes.

## REAR VIEW MIRROR

### Angle adjustment

Move the body of the mirror to adjust the mirror view angle so that you can see clearly behind you.

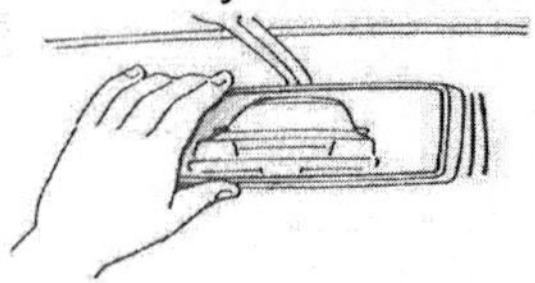

### Anti-dazzle rear view mirror

At night, pull the lever towards you to reduce the brightness from the headlighs of the following vehicles. For normal driving conditions, the mirror should be pushed back in the standard position.

# ELECTRIC DOOR MIRROR

## Angle adjustment

The ignition must be in ACC position.

Select the left or right side mirror and use the angle adjustment switch to adjust the mirror up, down, left or right.

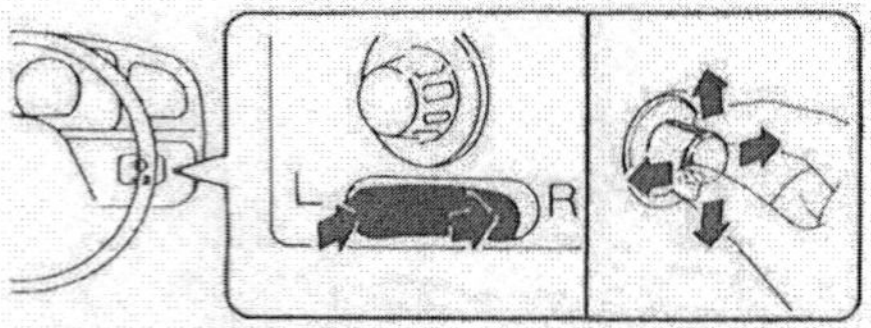


Caution:

- Do not adjust the door mirrors while driving.
- Be careful that hands do not get caught while adjusting the door mirrors.
- Do not drive with the mirrors retracted as you will be unable to check the rear of the vehicle

# MIRROR RETRACTION

- Retract it by pushing towards the body of the vehicle.
- When putting the mirror back to its position, push it until you hear a "click".

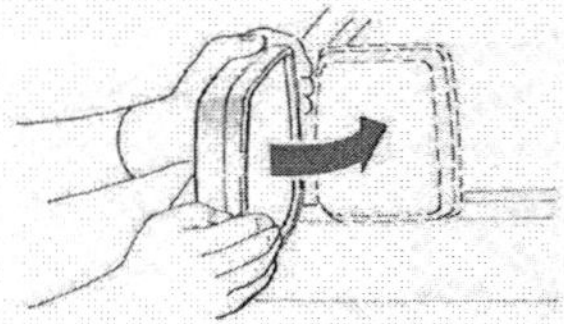

Advice:

The image in the mirror appears further away than it actually is, so exercise caution. The mirror project further than the vehicle body, so take care not to knock them.

# RETRACTABLE MIRRORS

Push the bottom of the mirror-retracting switch to retract the mirrors. Push the top of the switch to open the mirrors.

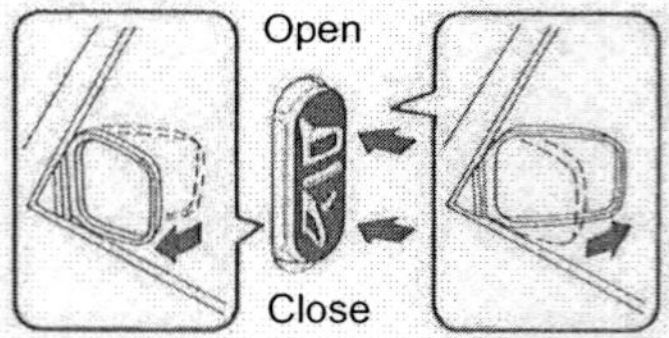

## DOOR MIRRORS WITH HEATERS

The ignition must be in ACC position.
The door heater mirrors are used do defrost or defeat the mirrors. Push the rear defogger switch. The indicator display light on the meter panel will flash. To turn the heater off, push the switch again.

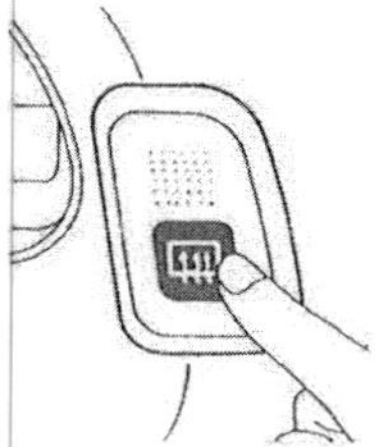

Advice:

The heaters consume a lot of power, so do not use them for an extended

## REAR UNDER MIRROR

This is used to check immediate rear side of the vehicle.

### Angle adjustment

Hold edge of the mirror in both hands and move it to the left or right.

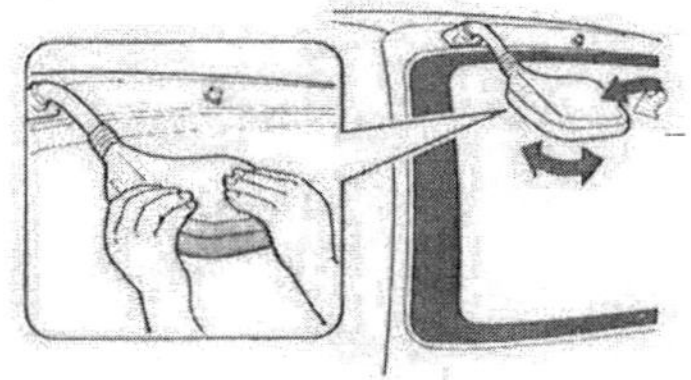

# STARTING THE ENGINE

## BEFORE STARTING THE ENGINE

Sit correctly in a comfortable position. Adjust the seat and steering wheel position, and check that the parking bake is applied and the select lever is in "P" position.

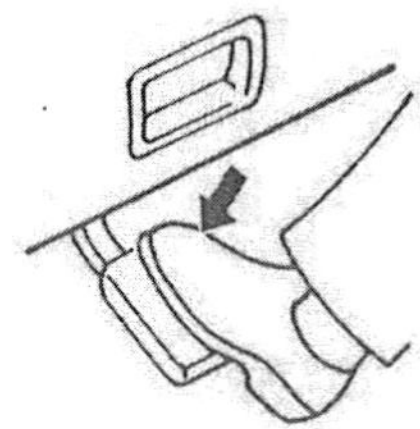

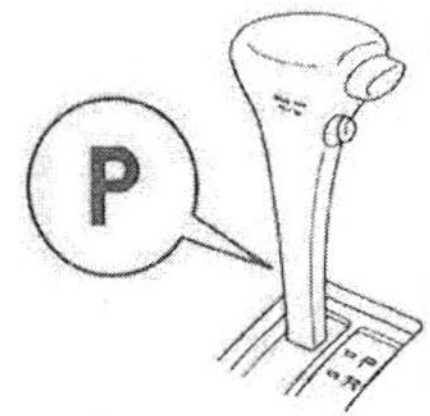

Advice:
Vehicles will start with the shift lever in "N" position, but for safety purpose it is advised to start the vehicle with the shift lever in "P" position.

## STARTING THE ENGINE

### Starting gasoline engines

1. Without pressing the accelerator pedal, turn the key to START and the engine will turn over.
2. Wait a short while for the engine to warm up. The engine rev will automatically drop when the engine has warmed up.

### Starting diesel engines

1. Turn the ignition to the ON position. This will start warming up the glow plugs and the engine preheating light will come on.

2. Make sure the engine preheating light has gone off. This means the glow plugs have finished heating.
3. Do not press the accelerator.
4. Turn the key to START and start the engine.
5. Warm up the vehicle. The engine rev will automatically drop when the engine has warmed up.

Warning:
- Do not leave the engine running in closed spaces where there is insufficient ventilation, as this could cause gas poisoning.

Advice:
- Do not keep idling or rev the engine unnecessarily after the engine has started as this may damage the engine.
- When the water temperature meter needle begins to move, the engine has warmed up sufficiently.

**For gasoline engines**
- Do not keep the ignition in the START position for more than 10 seconds, as this will drain the battery

**If engine doesn't start in 10 seconds**
Turn the key back to the LOCK position to give the battery time to recover (more than 10 seconds). Push the accelerator approximately one-fifth of the way down.

Note:

The length of time the engine preheating light stays on differs according to the water temperature. If the water temperature is high, it will only light up for a short time.

**If the engine doesn't start in 30 seconds**

Turn the key back to the LOCK position to give the battery time to recover (more than 10 seconds). Push the accelerator approximately one-fifth of the way down.

**For diesel engines**

- Do not keep the ignition in the START position for more than 10 seconds.

**If the engine preheating light doesn't come on**

The engine preheating light will not come on if the engine is warm or outside air temperature is high. If the engine preheating light does not come on, turn the key to the START position

**If the engine doesn't start in 30 seconds**

Turn the key to "0" LOCK position to give the battery time to recover ( more than 20 seconds ) and try again.

## USING A TURBO CHARGED VEHICLE (DIESEL VEHICLES)

Turbochargers are precisely-built devices which extract large horsepower from an engine by supplying it with a large volume of air. In order to avoid damaging the turbocharger while utilizing it to its full capacity, pay attention to the following points.

**Driving immediately after starting the engine**

When the engine is cold, do not rev it or drive the vehicle at high speed.

**Turning off the engine**

After travelling at high speed or on hills, turn the engine off after idling

| Driving Situation | | Idling Time |
|---|---|---|
| City of general driving | | Unnecessary |
| High speeds | About 80 km/hr. | Approx. 30 seconds |
| | About 100km/hr. | Appox. 1 minutes |
| Prolonged driving on steep roads | | Approx. 2 minutes |

Advice:
The cooling fan will operate automatically if the engine is still hot after turning off the engine.
The cooling fan will stop automatically when the engine cools down.

## Changing the engine oil and oil filter

Take care to use the specified oil and change at the specified times

| Engine oil change | Every 5,000km or 6 months |
|---|---|
| Oil filter change | Every 10,000km or 1 year |

Advice:
Failing to use the specified oil and changing as specified can cause damage, including seizure of the turbocharger's bearings and the development of abnormal noise.
The most suitable engine oil is Nissan's genuine motor oil "Diesel Save" 10W-30, CD class.

# AUTOMATIC TRANSMISSION

## SELECT LEVER POSITION

| Select Lever Position | Function |
|---|---|
| **Parking** P | For parking and starting the engine. In this position the key can be taken out. |
| **Reverse** R | For reversing. A buzzer will sound inside the vehicle as a signal to the driver. |
| **Neutral** N | No power is transmitted from the engine when the lever is in this position. The vehicle may be started in the gear, but for safety reasons, please start in "P". |
| **Drive** D | |
| **Overdrive switch** | ON — Action: The transmission will change automatically between 1st and 4 th (overdrive) — Meter display: O/D OFF |
| | OFF — Action: The transmission will change automatically between 1st and 3rd (overdrive) — Meter display: O/D OFF (lit) |
| **Second** 2 | For travelling on hills. Use when an engine brake is required. The gears will change automatically 1st or 2nd according to the vehicle speed. |
| **First (Low)** 1 | For travelling on hills. Use when heavy engine braking is required. The gear will not change from 1st. |

# OPERATING THE SHIFT LEVER

Always depress the brake pedal before moving the shift lever.

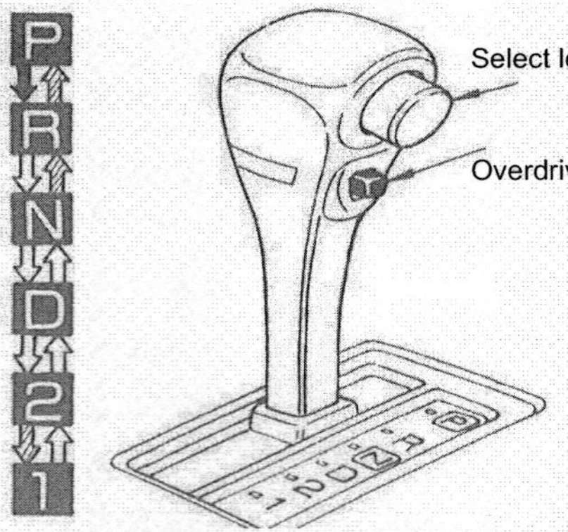


| Lever Operation | Button Operation |
|---|---|
|  | With the brake pedal held down, push the button and operate the lever |
|  | Move the lever without pushing the button |
|  | Push the button and operate the lever |

Advice:

When you park, put the shift lever into P.

Note:

- For vehicles with corner & back sonar, a buzzer will sound when the corner & back sonar is perceived any obstruction when the shift lever is any position other than P.
- Engine Braking

  This is the braking force on the engine when the braking accelerator is not applied. It is most effective in low gears.

Caution:

- Make a habit of moving the shift lever without pressing the shift button when moving in the direction of the white arrow.
- When moving the shift lever between "D" and "R", always place your foot firmly on the brake and stop the vehicle completely.
- After reversing, make sure to place the shift lever into "N" immediately.
- Before placing the shift lever into "P", make sure to stop the vehicle completely.

The following operations can damage the transmission, so avoid them:

- Putting the lever into "P" before the vehicle is stopped completely.
- Putting the lever into "R" when the vehicle is travelling forward
- Putting the lever into "D", "2" or "1" when the vehicle is travelling backward.

Advice:

- When shifting the gear selection lever out of "P", in some cases if the brake is pressed down with the button pushed in, you will be unable to move the lever. Step on the brake before pushing in the button.
- When the key is in ACC position, you will be able to move the lever without pressing the brake pedal.

**MAXIMUM SPEEDS**

To avoid over revving the engine, do not exceed the speeds shown on the chart below.

(Unit:km/h)

| Shift lever position | Gasoline vehicles | | Diesel vehicles |
|---|---|---|---|
| | 2WD | 4WD | |
| 2 | 85 | 80 | 60 |
| 1 | 45 | 40 | 30 |

## OVERDRIVE SWITCH

The overdrive switch can be used when the shift lever is in "D". It is for switching the car between 4th gear (3rd + overdrive) and 3rd gear. In normal driving conditions, have the overdrive switched ON. When driving on hills or in the following situations, turn the overdrive OFF.

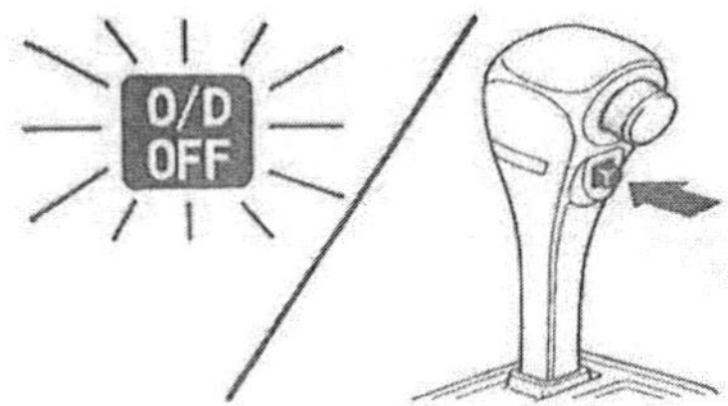

| Road Condition | Switch Position | Function | Meter display |
|---|---|---|---|
| Driving on the normal road | ON | Over dive driving is possible | O/D OFF |
| Driving on the sloping road | OFF | The light engine braking is applied. When travelling up a hill requiring many gear changes. | O/D OFF |

Advice:
When the automatic transmission oil temperature is low, the transmission will not change gear into overdrive.

## AUTOMATIC MODE SWITCH

Press the switch to select the appropriate mode for the driving conditions. There are three driving modes; Auto mode, Power mode and Snow mode.

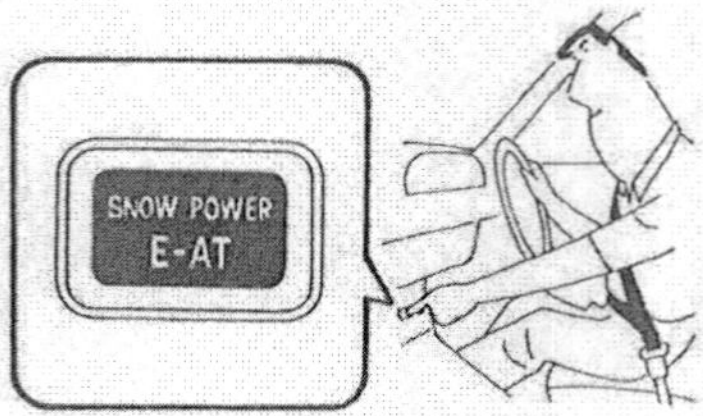

| | A/T mode switch | Performance | Meter display |
|---|---|---|---|
| **AUTO MODE**<br><br>For normal driving conditions |  | Vehicle performs with an emphasis on economy and good mileage. When the accelerator is pushed down fully and or quickly it will automatically switch to the power pattern | 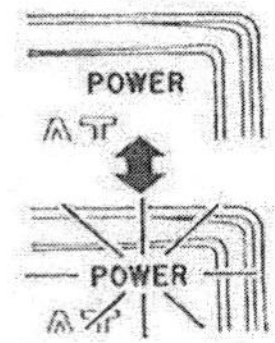 |
| **POWER MODE**<br><br>For powerful driving |  | The power mode is suitable for rapid acceleration and hill climbing as it has high pick up after gear changes | 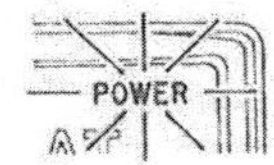 |
| **SNOW MODE**<br><br>For snowy road driving conditions |  | Use on slippery surfaces such as gravel or snow. If the gear selection lever is put into "D", the vehicles drive capacity becomes suited to a slippery surface and starting off, driving and stopping will be easier. |  |

Advice:

- When there is a possible fault with an automatic electronic control system, the "POWER" light will flash in the meter panel for approximately 8 seconds when the ignition is placed in the ON position.
- See your Nissan dealer if the "POWER" light flashes.
- If there is not error in the system, the "POWER" light will flash in the meter panel for approximately 2 seconds when the ignition is placed in the ON position.

Note:

Combination of the snow mode and select lever is to change the shift transmission shown below.

| D | Start in 2nd and gears change between 3rd and O/D |
|---|---|
| 2 | Gear is fixed in the 2nd |
| 1 | Gear is fixed in the 1st |

## OPERATING 4 WHEEL DRIVE (4 WD) VEHICLES

The 4WD system transfers the engines power to all 4 wheels enabling safe driving in rough terrain ( snow covered, deep snow, sandy and other punishing roads) and steep roads. To ensure you get the most of the great endurance capabilities unique to 4WD vehicles, please read the following points and enjoy safe and comfortable driving.

## TYRES AND CHAIN FITTING

- Make sure all four tyres are the same size, brand and tread. The front and rear tyres are different for vehicles fitted with bias tyres ( not radial tyres).
- Rotate the position of the tyres ( approx. every 5,000km ) and regularly check the air pressure, to increase the life of the tyres and to ensure even wear.
- Check the tyre pressure regularly.
- If there is a deference in wear or the air pressure is significantly different between tyres, the vehicle my not perform properly. This may cause a serious accident, especially if the wear difference between tyres is wear or if different size tyres are fitted.

- Fit chains on the rear wheels

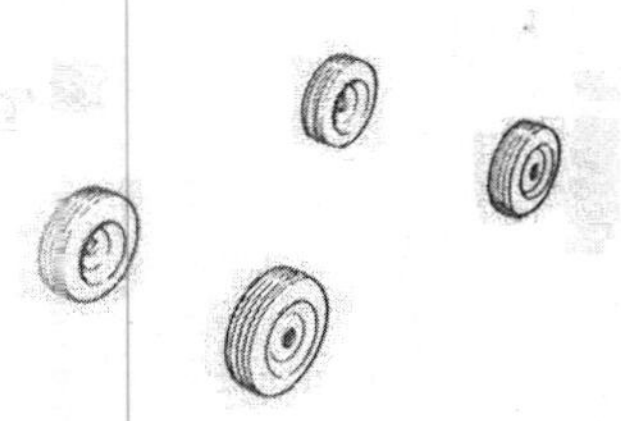

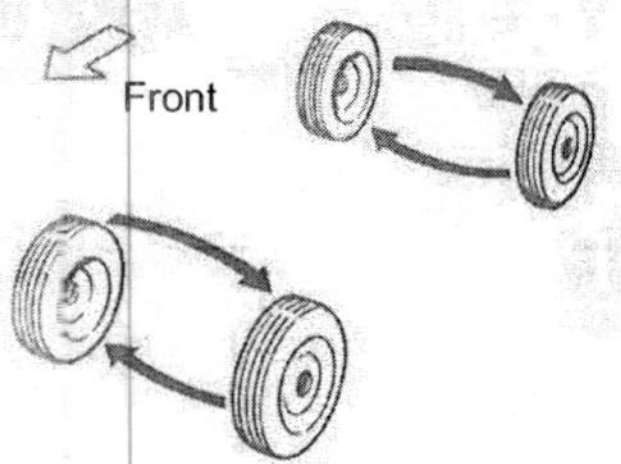


Advice:

- Largo vehicles are always 4WD there is no need to change over.
- Fit chains on the wheels when driving on the snowy road.
- When driving with chains keep under 30km/h.

Caution:

- Do not fit snow tyres on just the front or rear wheels.
- See your Nissan dealer when replacing the tyres.
- If towing is required, make sure that all 4 wheels must be either on / off ground
- When changing the tyres make sure all four tyres are the same size, brand and tread

# DRIVING AN AUTOMATIC VEHICLE

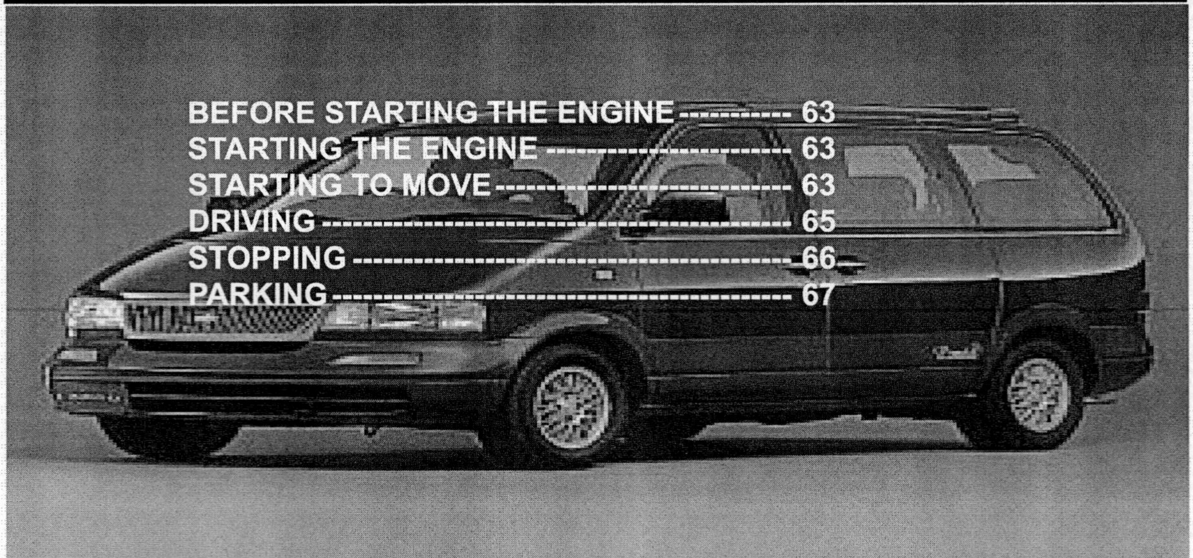



## NISSAN LARGO

# DRIVING AN AUTOMATIC VEHICLE

## BEFORE STARTING THE ENGINE

- Sit correctly in a comfortable position.
- Check that the parking brake is applied.
- Check that the shift lever is in "P"
- Check the position of the brake pedal and accelerator pedal with your right foot.

Warning:

- Step on the accelerator and brake pedals alternatively with your right foot until you have a firm idea of their respective positions.

## STARTING THE ENGINE

1. Hold the brake pedal down firmly with your right foot.
2. Check that the shift lever is in "P" and start the engine.

Advice:

- Automatic vehicles will start with the shift lever in "N", but for safety purposes it is advised to start the vehicle with the shift lever in "P".

- A click will sound when pressing or depressing the brake pedal.

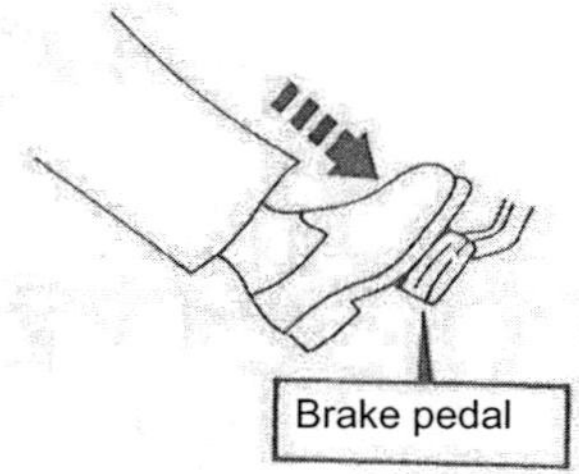


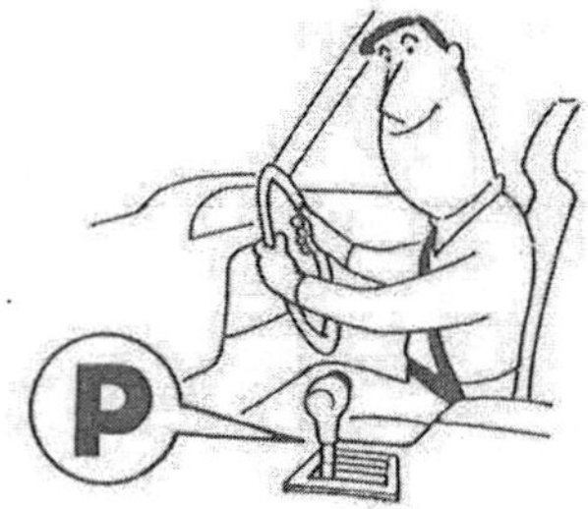


## STARTING TO MOVE

1. Hold the brake pedal down firmly with your right foot.
2. Check that the shift lever is in "D" if travelling forward, and in "R" if travelling backward.

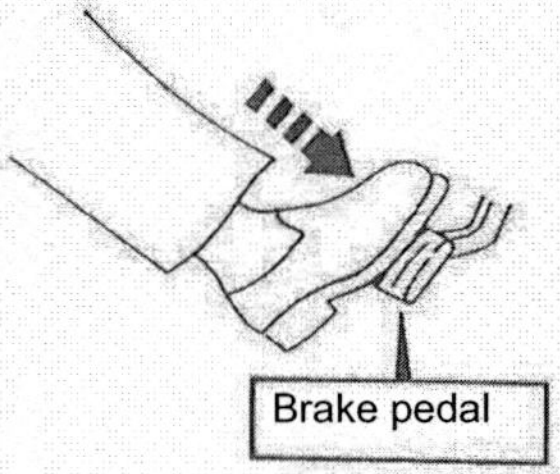


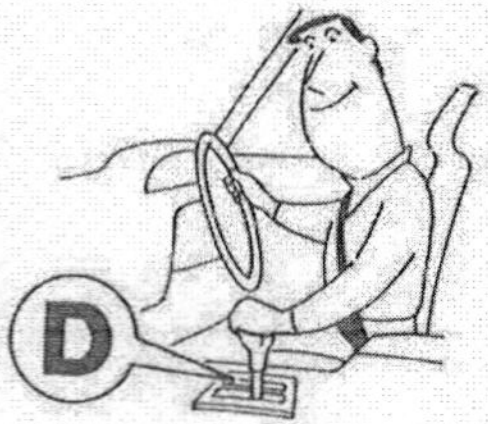


Caution:

**CREEP MOTION**

- When the shift lever is in any other position than "P" or "N", the vehicle may creep forward even when the accelerators not depressed. The creep motion can be used to your advantage when in congested traffic or in narrow spaces as the vehicle can be controlled just by applying the brake

Advice:

- You must have your foot on the brake pedal to move the select lever out of "P".

3. Release the parking brake
4. Gradually ease up on the brake pedal and slowly step on the accelerator.

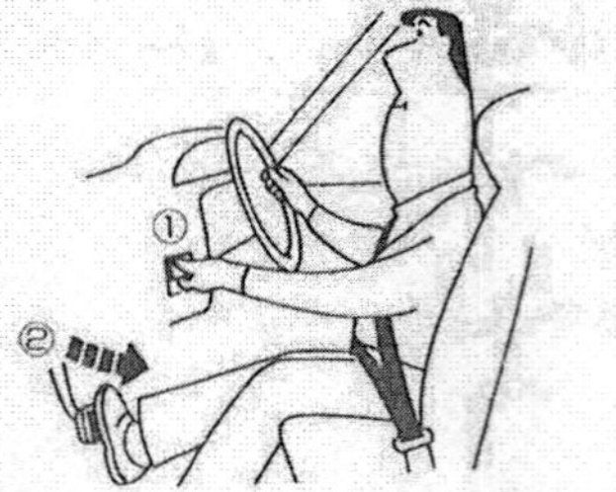


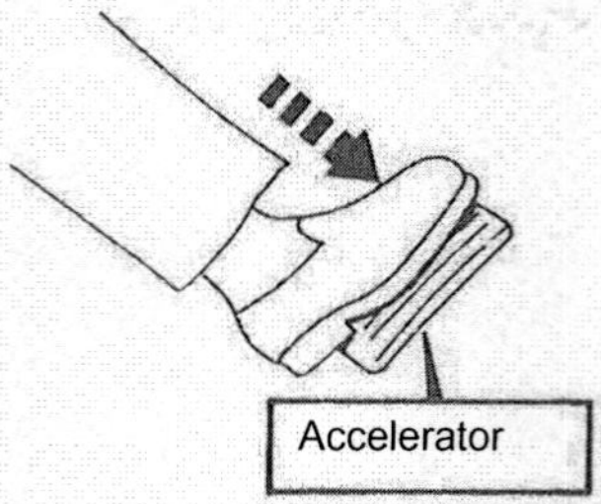

Warning:

- Never move the shift lever while the accelerator is depressed. The vehicle may jump forward and cause a serious accident

## TAKING OFF ON A STEEP SLOPE

1. Check the position of the shift lever visually.
2. With the parking brake on, gradually ease up on the foot brake and move your right foot to the accelerator.

Advice:

- Do not maintain a stationary position depressing the accelerator on an upward sloping hill as this will damage the transmission

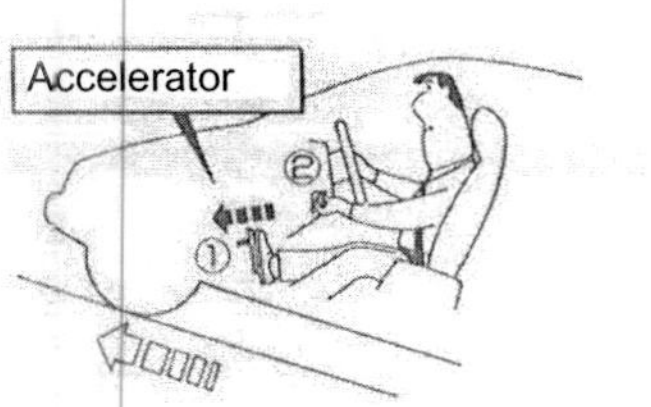


# DRIVING

### Normal driving conditions

- Drive with the shift lever in "D". Increase and decrease speed by operating the accelerator and brake pedals only.

### Sudden acceleration

- Depress the accelerator fully. This will cause the kick down function to activate and the vehicle to accelerate quickly.

### Driving up hills

- Drive with the shift lever in "D". Turning the AT mode switch to the power mode according to the slope of the hill will make driving smoother.

### Driving down hills

- According to the slope of the hill, depress the brake pedal to reduce the vehicle speed. Then use the engine brake by placing the shift in 2 or 1.

Caution:

- Do not use engine braking suddenly on slippery road surfaces, as there is a danger that the tires will slip.

## KICK DOWN

- When the accelerator is pressed down fully, this will cause the transmission to kick down to a lower gear giving the vehicle instant power.
- If the gear is changed to a lower gear ( kick down ), the engine revolutions will increase suddenly.

## ENGINE BRAKE

- Engine braking refers to the brake effect which accrues when the accelerator is released while travelling. Engine braking works best in lower gears.
- Do not use engine braking suddenly on slippery road surfaces, as there is a danger that the tires will slip
- Never place the shift lever in "N" while driving. The engine brake will cease to function, and may cause an unexpected accident and damage the transmission.

Warning:

- When driving in "D", the engine braking effect is weak. As a result, in some cases the vehicle may gain too much speed. In these situations, the burden on the foot brake may cause the brakes to heat up, reducing their effectiveness. Always use the foot brake in conjunction with engine braking while travelling down hills.

## STOPPING

- With the shift lever in "D" apply the parking brake as necessary.
- When stationary for a long time, place the shift lever into "N".

Advice:

- When stationary on a steep upward slope, the force pulling the vehicle backwards will exceed the force of the creeping motion pushing the vehicle forward, and the vehicle will move backwards down the slope. Press the foot brake firmly and apply the parking brake.
- Depressing the accelerator to maintain a stationary position on an upward sloping hill will damage the transmission.

## PARKING

- Stop the vehicle completely, press the brake pedal and apply the parking brake
- When leaving the vehicle, always stop the engine.

Caution:

- Always put the select lever into "P" when parking. In the event that you forget to put the selection lever into "P", the vehicle will move as a result of creeping.
- Check that the position of the select lever visually when starting the engine again.
- Always sit correctly in a comfortable position even when moving the vehicle a short distance.
- It is particularly important to ensure the brake pedal can be reached when the body is twisted around for reversing.
- Make a habit of shifting the transmission from "R" into "N" immediately after reversing, as it is easy to forget that the vehicle is in "R".

# DOORS, WINDOWS, BONNET & FUEL LID

## NISSAN LARGO

FRONT DOOR

## Locking / unlocking doors with the key

Insert the key and turn clockwise to lock, and anticlockwise to unlock.

## Locking the doors without the key

Press down the lock knob inside the door, and shut the door while holding up the door handle.

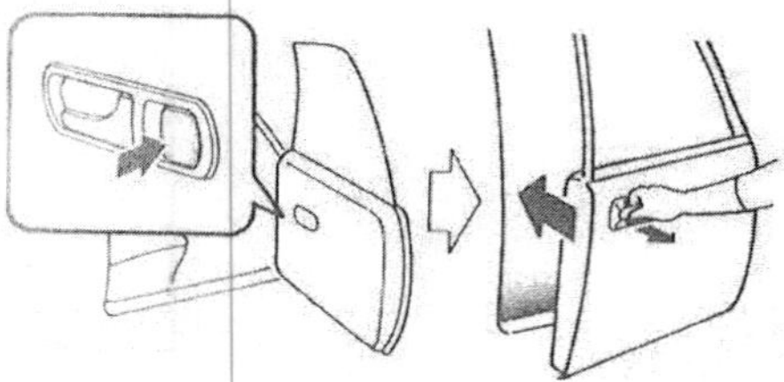

## Locking / unlocking the doors from inside the vehicle

Press the lock knob down to lock, and pull up to unlock.

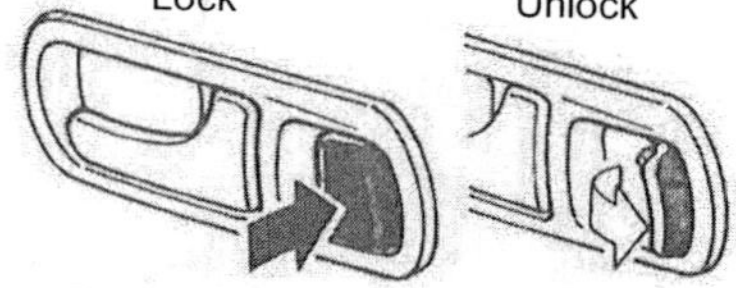


Warning:

- When closing the windows, take care not to jam other people's hands or heads in the window. Take extra care when there are children in the vehicle.

Caution:

- When opening the doors, check that it is clear in front and behind you.If the door is opened suddenly, it may be struck by a following vehicle. Take particular care when opening doors in strong winds.
- Ensure all doors are closed properly as an accident may occur if a door swings open while travelling.
- You must not open/ close the doors while driving. Apply the child safety locks when travelling with children.

Advice:

- Always stop the engine and lock the vehicle when leaving to prevent theft or accidents.
- Always check you have the key with you when locking the door to avoid locking the keys in the vehicle

## SLIDE DOOR

### Locking / unlocking the doors with key

Insert the key and turn clockwise to lock, and anticlockwise to unlock.

### Locking / unlocking the doors from outside the vehicle

Press down front part of the lock knob inside the door and shut the door.

Caution:

- Always hold the door handle to open / close the slide door to avoid get your hands caught in the door.
- When opening the slide door on the down hill slopes, make sure the slide door is opened fully to be locked

## Locking / unlocking the doors from inside the vehicle

Press down the front part of the lock knob to lock and press down the back part of the lock knob to unlock.

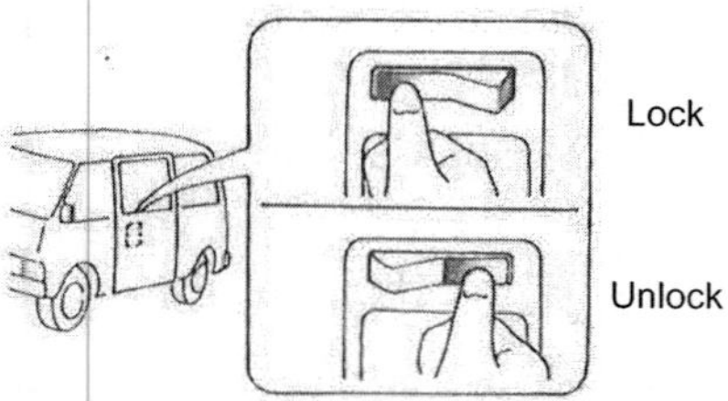


## SLIDE DOOR EASY CLOSER

The slide door will automatically close fully, when it is not closed properly.

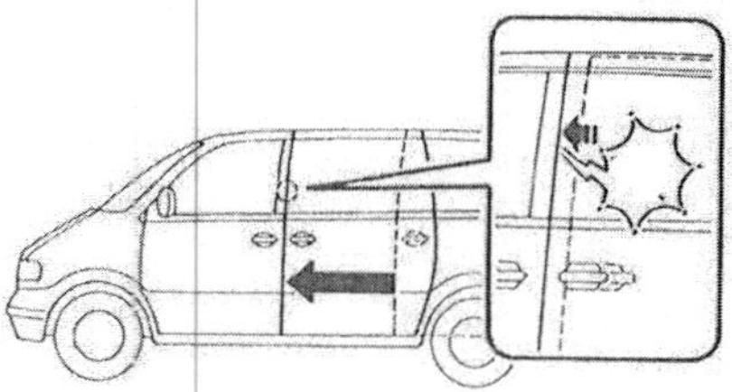

Caution:

- As the slide door automatically closes when half closed, beware not to get your hands caught in the door. Do not allow children to operate the doors.

Advice:

- When the slide door is not opened, have the vehicle checked by a Nissan dealer.

## AUTOMATIC SLIDE DOOR

- Press down the "OPEN" side of the switch to open the slide door automatically and press down the "CLOSE" side of the switch to close the slide door automatically when the ignition is ON and the select lever is in "P" position.
- For safety reason, the slide door is automatically stopped before it is fully closed (approx. 30cm ).
- A buzzer will sound just before opening the slide door (approx. 2 seconds) and while operating the slide door.

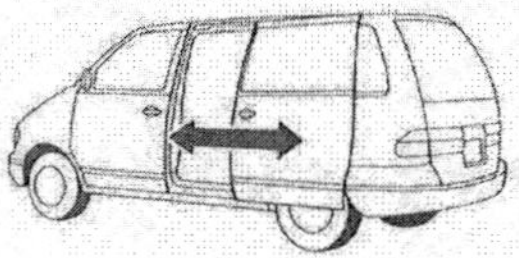

Caution:

- When operating the automatic slide door, check that it is clear in front and behind you. If the door is opened suddenly, it may be struck by a following vehicle. Take particular care when opening doors in strong winds.
- Do not use the automatic slide door on the down / up hill slopes as the slide door may not operate normally.

Advice:

- When the switch is no longer pressed, the operation will stop so when stop pressing the switch make sure that the slide door is closed fully.
- The slide door is able to open / close manually.
- When the door is locked, you can open the slide door automatically.
- Ensure that there is no foreign matter from getting into the clearance gap of the step as this may cause failure.

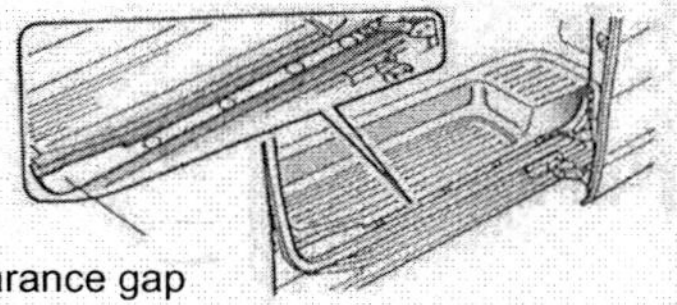


- The slide door will automatically close fully, when it is not closed properly.

## REAR DOOR

### Locking / unlocking the rear door with key

Insert the key and turn clockwise to lock, and anticlockwise to unlock. To open the rear door, pull the lever.

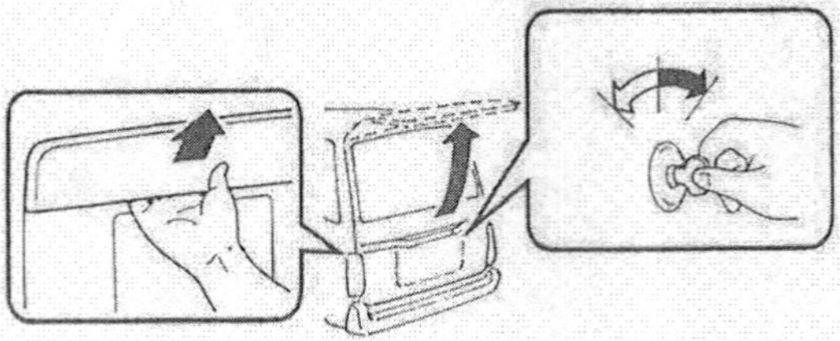

Caution:

- Always open the rear door fully- wind or other elements may cause it to slam closed if it is left half-open.
- When opening the rear door, check that it is clear in front and behind you. If the door is opened suddenly, it may be struck by a following vehicle. Take particular care when opening doors in strong winds.
- Ensure the rear door is locked when closed, as it will pose a danger should it open while travelling.
- Do not get on and off the stay that supports the rear door as this may cause failure.
- Do not ride on the luggage room.

## CENTRAL LOCKING

Turn the key in the drivers door clockwise to lock all the doors and anti-clockwise to unlock all the doors.

Push down the lock knob inside the drivers to lock all the doors and pull up to unlock all the doors.

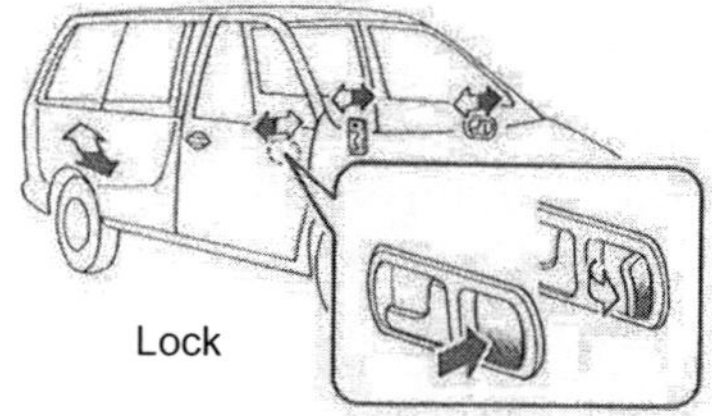


Push down the armrest part of the switch to lock / unlock all the doors.

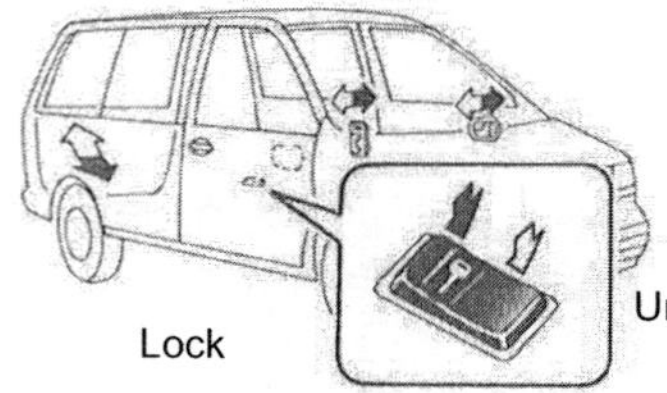

## CHILD SAFETY LOCK

If the lever on the slide door is put into "LOCK" and the doors are closed, the doors will be unable to be opened from the inside. Use the child safety lock to prevent the doors opening unexpectedly through the child playing or getting up to mischief.

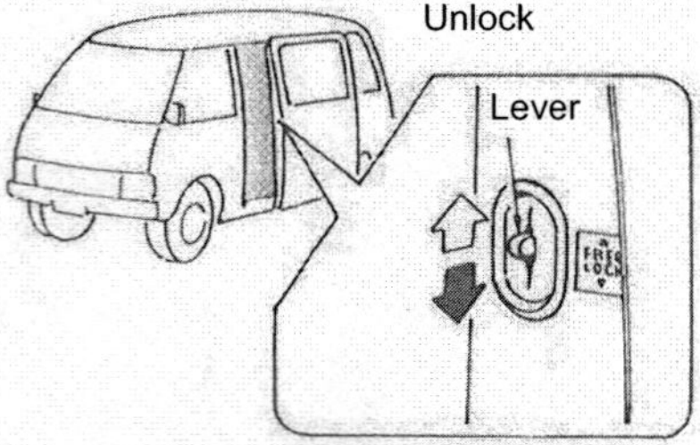


To open the door, first unlock the door using the lock knob on the door and then open from the outside.

# WINDOW

## POWER WINDOW

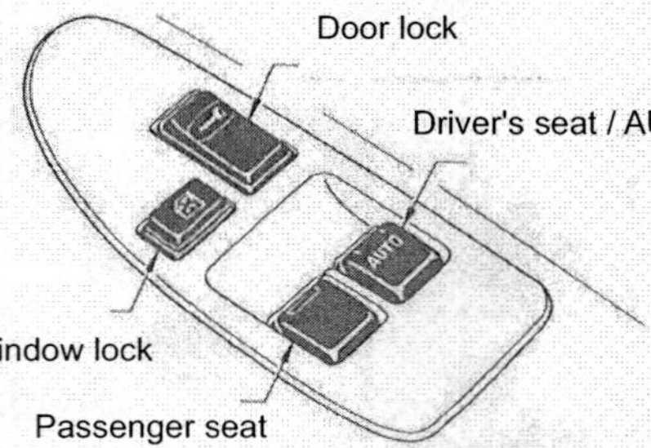


### Drivers seat power window switch

The ignition must be in the ON.

Press down each switch to open. Lift up the switch as shown in the diagram to close. Release finger to stop the window.

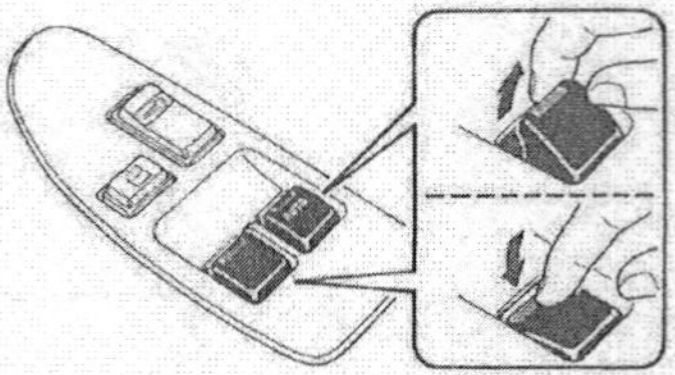

When using the AUTO switch, the driver's seat window open / close automatically even if releasing finger to stop the window.

Lift up the switch firmly and release finger to close the window fully. Press down the switch firmly to open the window fully. To stop halfway press the opposite side of the AUTO switch.

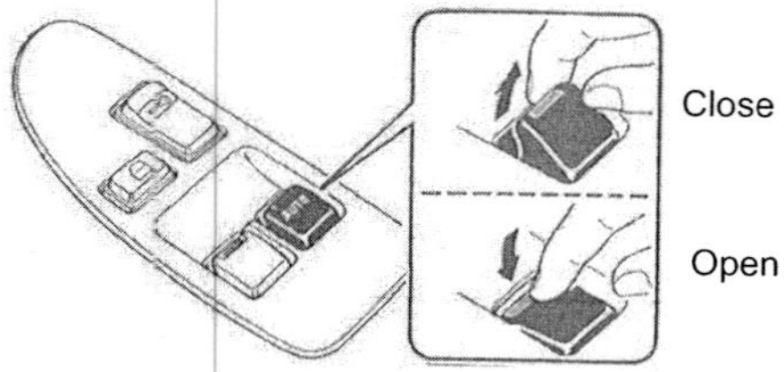


Warning:

- Do not allow children to operate the power window
- When closing the windows, take care not to jam other people's hands or heads in the window. Take extra care when there are children in the vehicle.

Advice:

- To avoid flattening the car battery only operate windows while engine is running.

## Passenger's seat power window switch

The ignition must be in the ON.

Press down each switch to open. Lift up the switch as shown in the diagram to close. Release finger to stop the window.

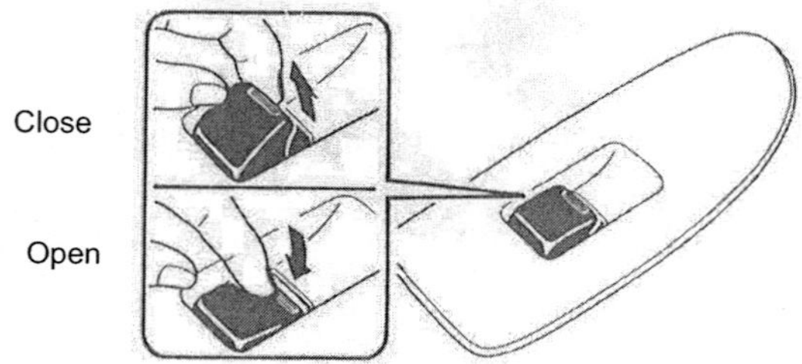


## POWER WINDOW LOCK SWITCH

When the window lock switch is ON ( pushed down) only the driver's window can be opened or closed. Press the switch again to unlock it and allow all windows to be operational.

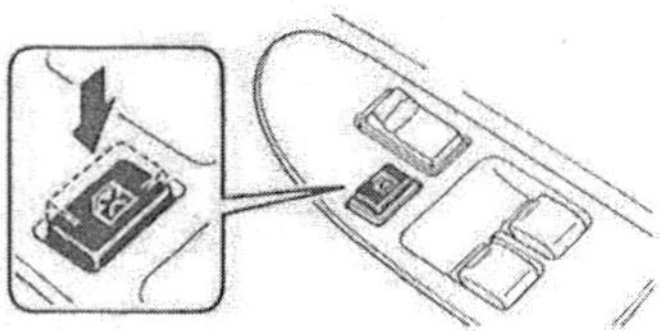

Warning:
Always apply the window lock when children are travelling in the vehicle. When children play with the electric windows they may jam their neck or hands in the window.

## SLIDE TYPE WINDOW

Press and push the knob in the direction of the arrow as shown in the diagram to open the window. To close the window, pull the knob and restore it.

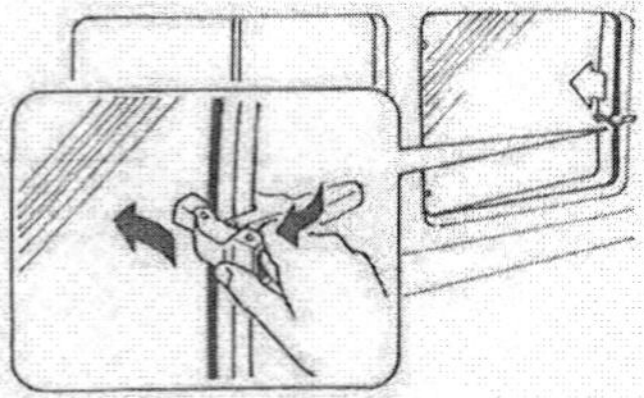

Caution:

- When closing the windows, take care not to jam other people's hands or heads in the window. Take extra care when there are children in the vehicle.

Advice:

- The 2nd and 3rd windows in the slide door and the right side of the vehicle will open.

## SUN ROOF

### Opening / closing the sunshade

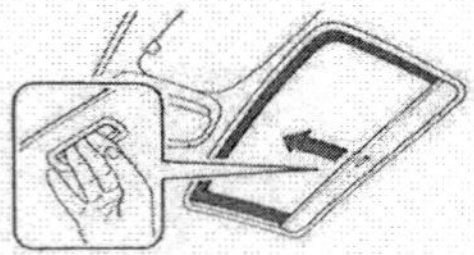

Front

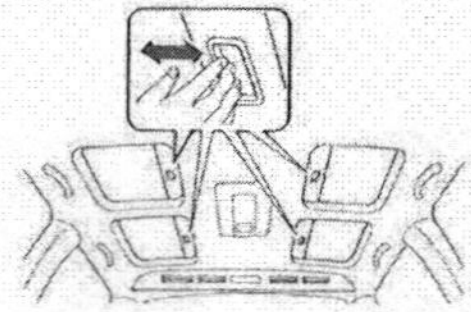

Rear

### Operating the sunroof switch to the tilt-up position (the front of the sunroof)

The ignition must be in the ON.
Place the switch to the "OPEN" position to operathe the sunroof to the tilt-up position. Place the switch to the "CLOSE" position to close the sunroof.

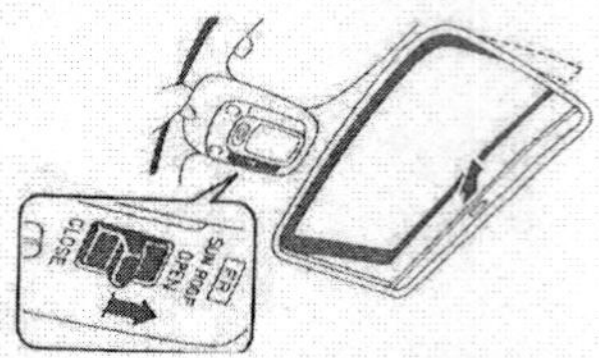

Note:
The tilt-up sunroof can be opened / closed by hand for ventilation. ( only the front roof ).

Warning:
- Do not put heard, hands or objects out the sunroof while travelling as they may strike objects outside the vehicle and this could lead to serious injury. Furthermore, sudden braking could also cause injury. When opening and closing the sunfoof take care not to catch hands or fingers.
- Do not drive with the luggage or passengers sitting on the sunroof. It may cause serious injuries in a sudden braking situation.

## ENGINE HOOD

### To open

1. Move the seat forward and pull the lever to make passenger's seat move forward and fold down.

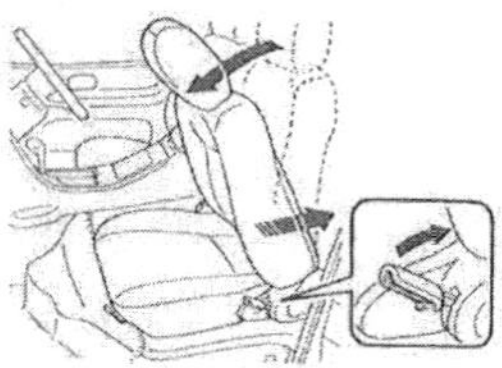

2. Unstick the hook and loop fastener of the floor carpet located of the front side of the seat and remove the locks ( 2 locks ).

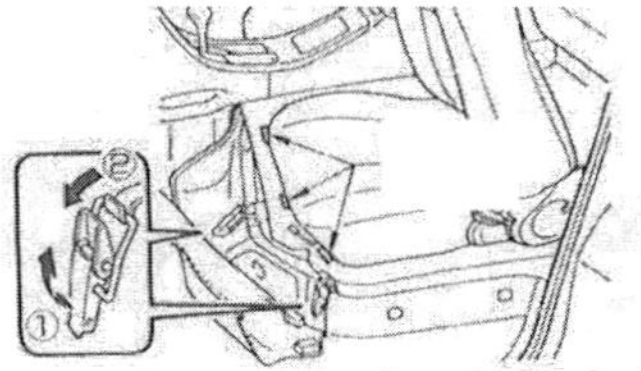

hook and loop fastener

3. Lift up the engine cover ( seat cushion part ).

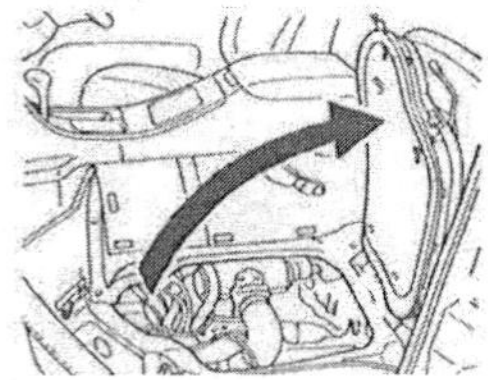

### To close

Follow the steps for opening the engine cover in reverse order.

Caution:

- Do not open the engine cover with the luggage or passengers sitting on the engine cover. It may cause serious injuries.
- Do not put hands, clothing or tools into the engine bay while the engine is running. This could result in unexpected injuries.
- Do not touch the hot parts of the engine just after it has been turned off, as it may cause burns.
- Check that the locks are completely locked before you start driving. If it is not closed properly, it may fly up and obstruct your vision.

## FUEL FILLER LID

### Opening / closing the fuel lid

Pull the lever to open the fuel lid and push the lever down

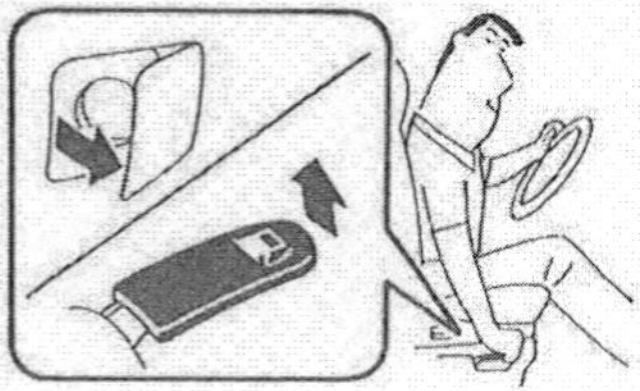

### Opening / closing the fuel cap

Turn the cap to open/close the fuel cap. Turn the cap clockwise until you hear more than two "clicks".

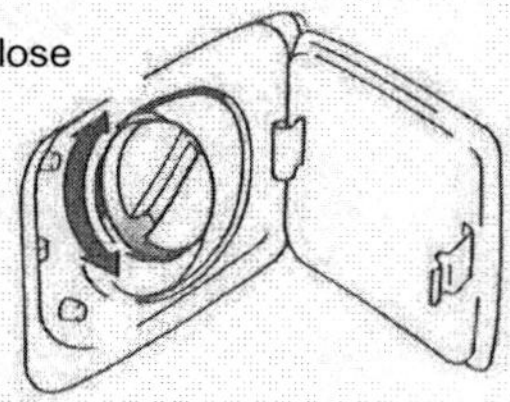


Caution:

- Always stop the engine before refuelling.
- Do not smoke or strike matches around the area of the fuel tank while refuelling the vehicle.
- Open the cap slowly to arrow the pressure inside the tank to escape before opening.
- Ensure the cap is sealed properly when replacing the fuel cap. If it is not, the fuel will leak when driving and may cause a fire.

Note:

- The fuel tank capacity is approx. 65 liters for the 2WD vehicles and approx. 60 liters for the 4WD vehicles.

## BONNET

### To open

1. Pull the bonnet release lever.

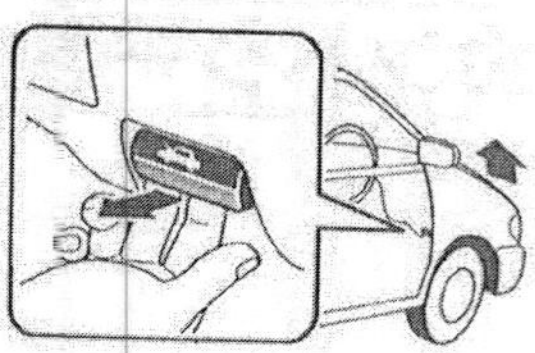

2. Place your hand under the front of the bonnet and find the lock lever. Pull this lever to open the bonnet.

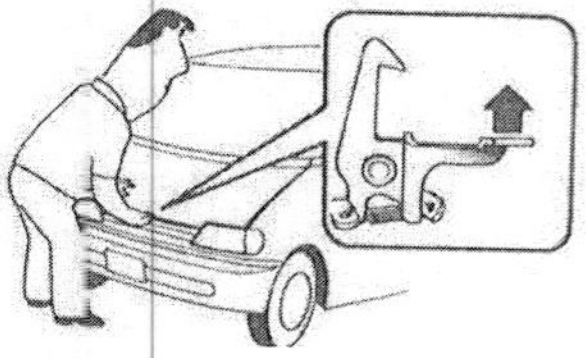

3. Insert the bonnet stay into the stay hole to secure the bonnet.

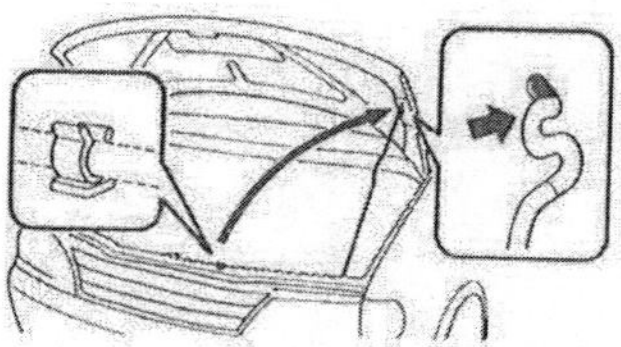

### To close

Push down the front edge firmly to lock.

Caution:

- Take care opening the bonnet in windy conditions as the bonnet may be flung back by the wind.
- Check that the bonnet is completely closed before you start driving. If it is not closed properly, it may fly up and obstruct your vision.

# SEATS & SEAT BELTS

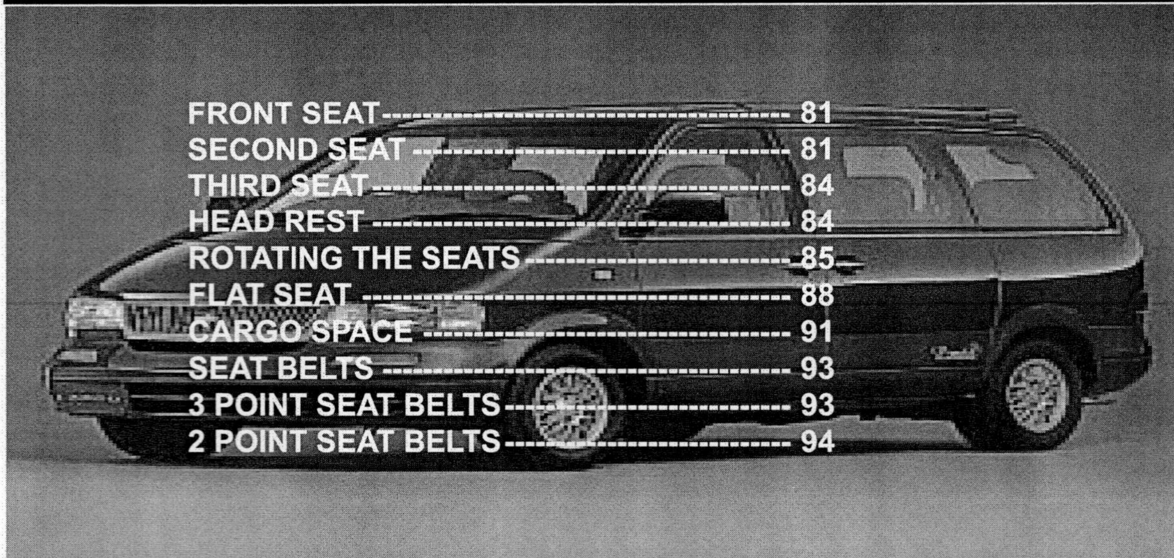



## NISSAN LARGO

## FRONT SEATS

### Forward / backward adjustment

Pull the lever and move the seat forward / backward

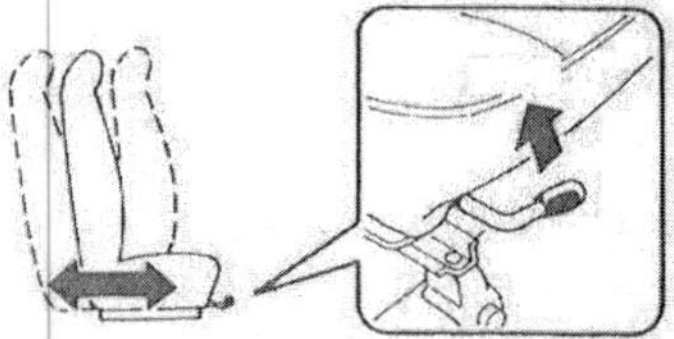

### Reclining adjustment

Pull the lever and lift your body off the seat back .

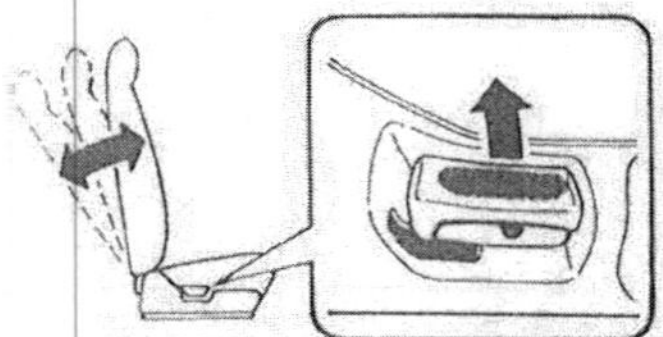

<u>Caution:</u>

- Always adjust the seat before driving. It is dangerous to make adjustments while driving.
- When adjusting the seats, take care not to jam your fingers or hands.
- Do not place cushion between yourself and the back rest. This may reduce correct driving posture and result in an accident.
- After adjusting the seat, check that it is securely fixed.
- Adjust the seats to the position when the pedal and steering wheel can be reached comfortably.
- Do not recline the seats beyond what is necessary, as the seat belt may not function properly.

## SECOND SEATS

### Forward / backward adjustment

Pull the lever and move the seat forward / backward

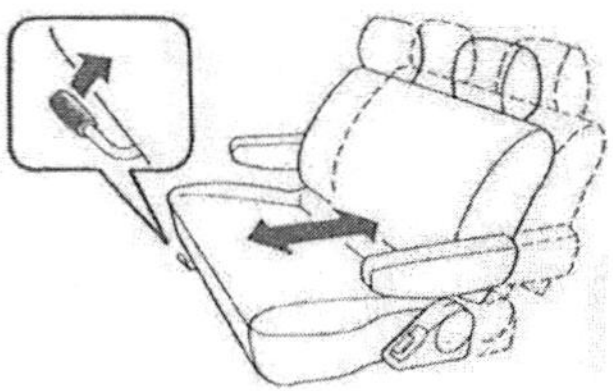

## Reclining adjustment

Pull the lever and lift your body off the seat back

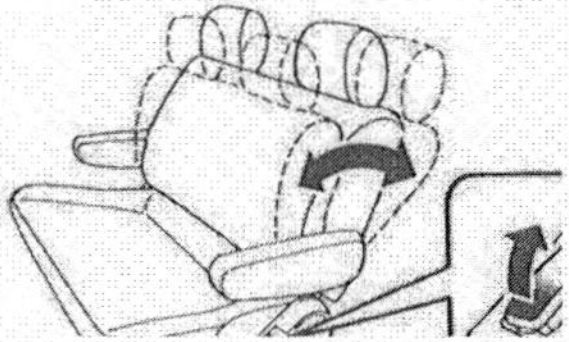

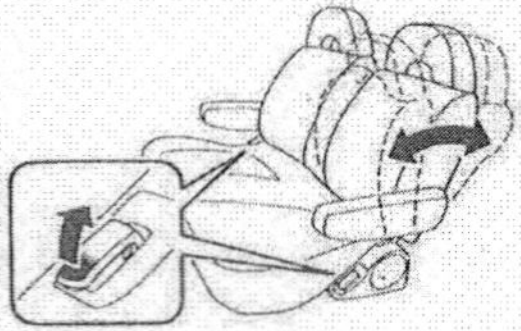

Note:

- For 8-seat vehicles, the 2 person bench seat and 1 person bench seat are able to move separately.

Advice:

- Do not install the child seat on the 1 person bench seat of 8-seat vehicles. This may jam children's fingers or hands when opening and closing the slide door, and also it may obstruct getting on and off the third seat

## Centre arm rest( 7-seat vehicles )

The arm rest can be used by pulling it towards you.

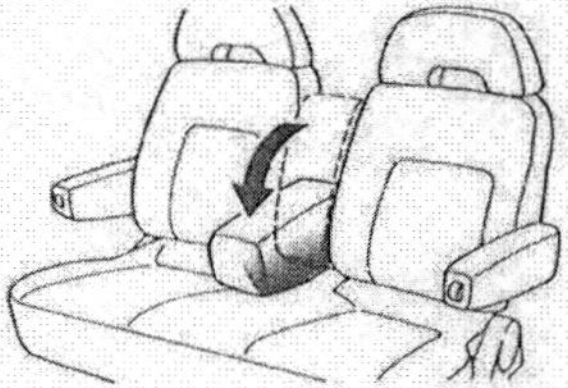

## Side arm rests ( 7-seat vehicles )

Fold down the arm rests located on either side of the seat back to use.

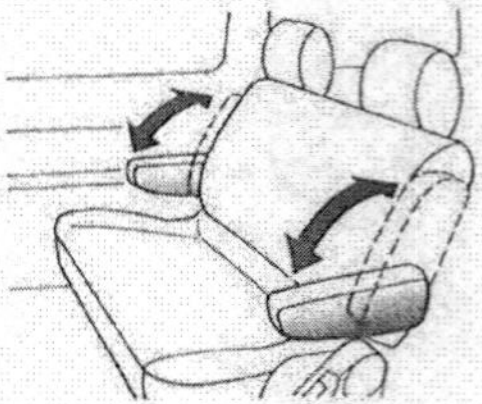

## Adjustable side arm rest ( 7-seat vehicles )

Pull the knob located the front edge arm rest to adjust the angle of the side arm rest.

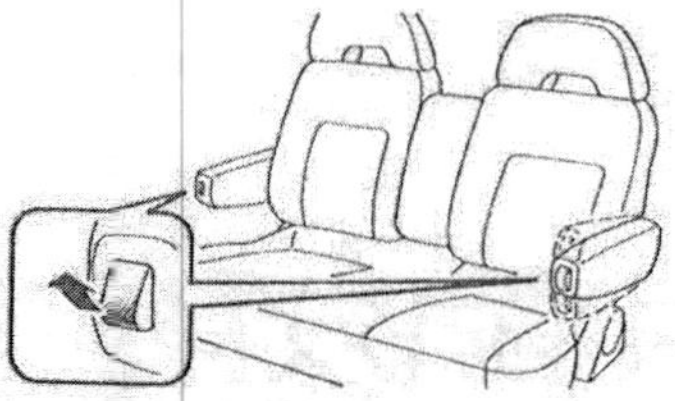

## Walk in System ( 7-seat vehicles )

Turning the second seat gives you access to the third seats.

1. Either pulling up the reclining adjustment lever or pulling the walk-in lever located on the left back of the seat and move the seat forward.

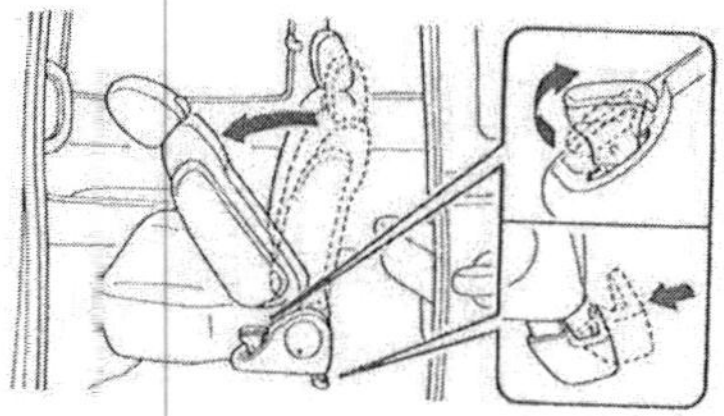

2. Turn the seat to the right.

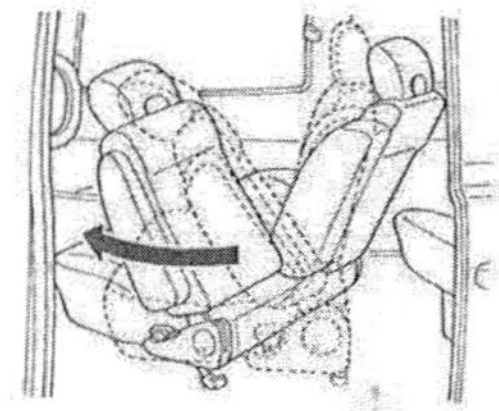

Advice:

- When wearing the seat belt, restore the arm rest first to make it easier to put the seat belt on.
- Adjust the angle of the arm rest according to the angle of the recline.
- Ensure that the seat is securely fixed after returning the back rest to its original position.

## Walk in System ( 8-seat vehicles )

Moving and folding down the 1 person bench seat of the second seats gives you access to the third seats. Either pulling up the reclining adjustment lever or pulling the walk-in lever located on the right back of the seat

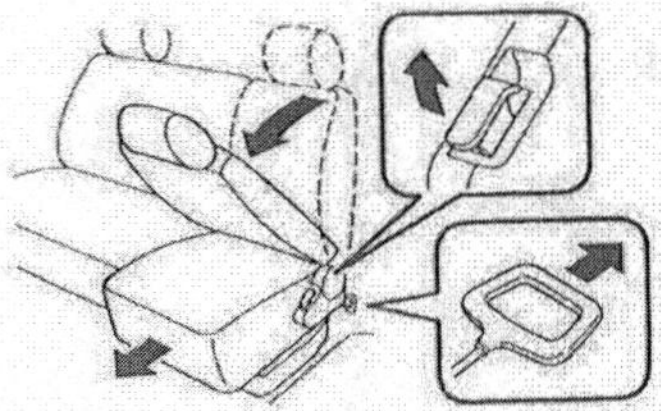

## THIRD SEAT

### Reclining

Pull the lever and lift your body off the seat back.

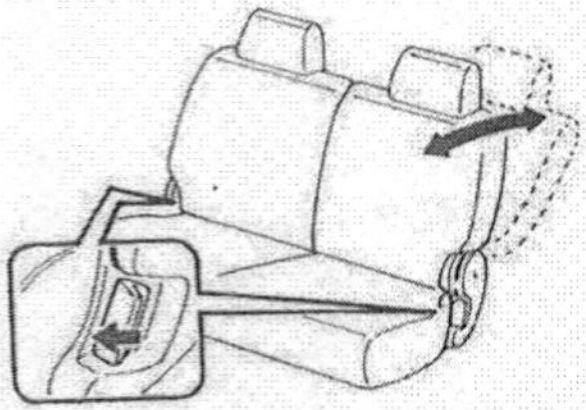

## HEADREST

### Headrest adjustment

Adjust the headrest so that the centre is positioned around the ear.

- To rise the headrest simply lift to the desired height.
- To lower, while pushing the button, lower as desired.

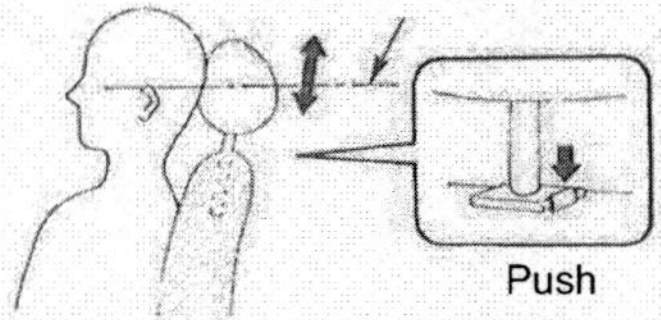


### Removing / attaching the headrest

To remove the headrest, press the button and lift the headrest off.

To attach the headrest, press the button and push the headrest down.

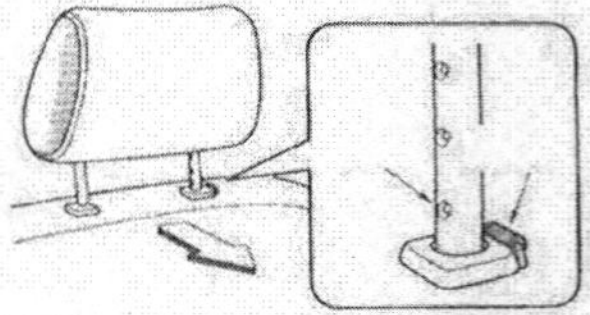

Warning:

- Never drive without the headrest. It could cause a serious injury in an accident situation.

Caution:

- When attaching the headrest, ensure it is facing in the correct direction.
- After attaching the headrest, check that it is secured by pulling upwards.

## ROTATING THE SEATS ( 7-seat VEHICLES )

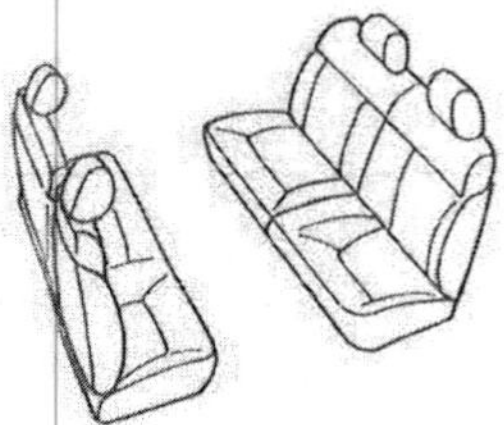

1. Pull the lever to move the seat to the front

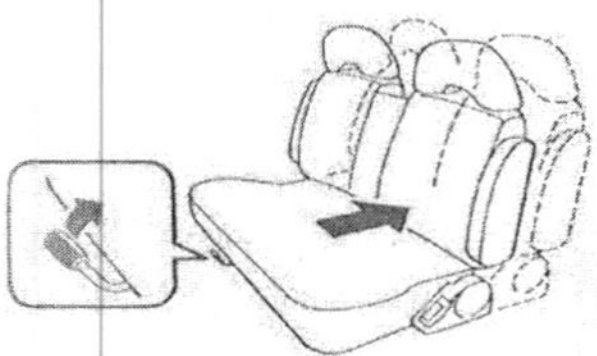

2. Pull up the arm rest and pull the reclining adjustment lever to move the back rest forward

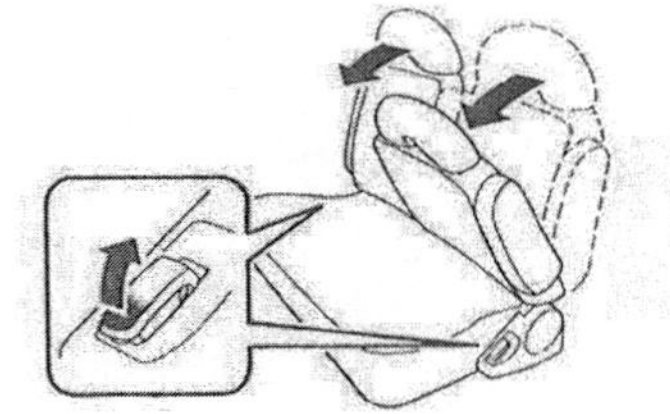

3. Pull up the turning lever and rotate the seat 180 degrees.

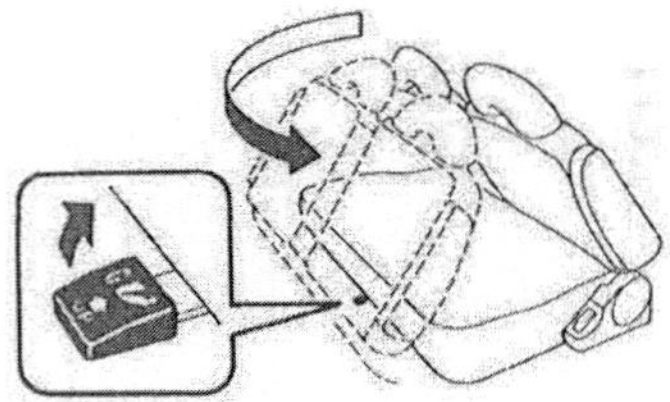

4. Retract the back rests.

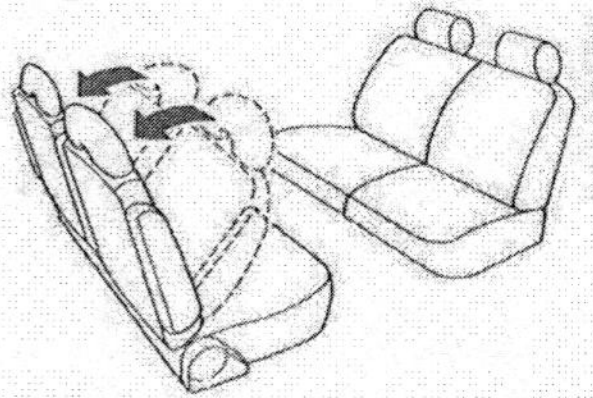

Caution:

- Do not rotate the seats while driving.
- Do not place hands or feet underneath the seats when rotating.
- Do not allow children to operate the rotating seats.

Advice:

- When the back rest is over recline. The rotating seat may not working.
- Do not drive with the luggage or passengers sitting on the seat facing the outer side as this may cause serious injuriesi n an accident situation.

Note:

- When doing step 3, turn the seat anticlockwise while pulling up the rotating lever when the seat has turned 90 degrees it will lock position.

To return the seat to its original position, follow the steps for rotating the seat in reverse order.

## ROTATING THE SEATS ( 8-seat VEHICLES )

1. Move the 2 person bench seat forward until it is locked and fold the back rest fully toward the front side of the vehicle.

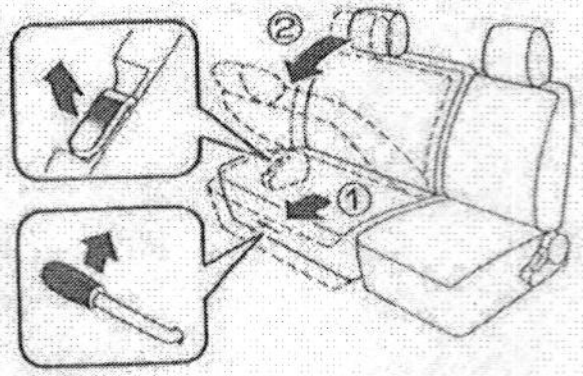

2. Retract the back rest of the 1 person bench seat. After that, raise the back rest up until it is locked.

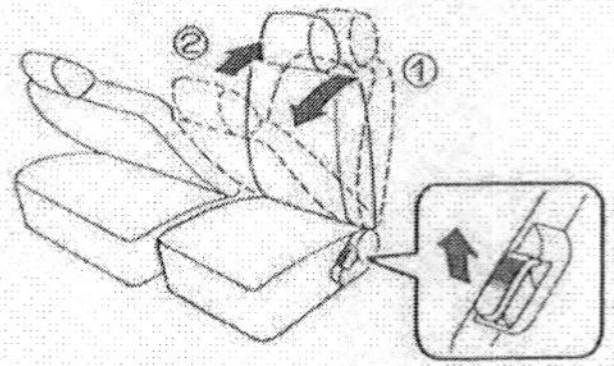

3. Move the 1 person bench seat futher forward.

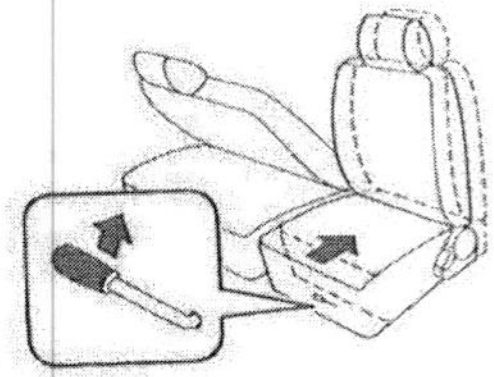

4. Pull the turning lever of the 1 person bench seat and turn the seat 90 degrees to the right

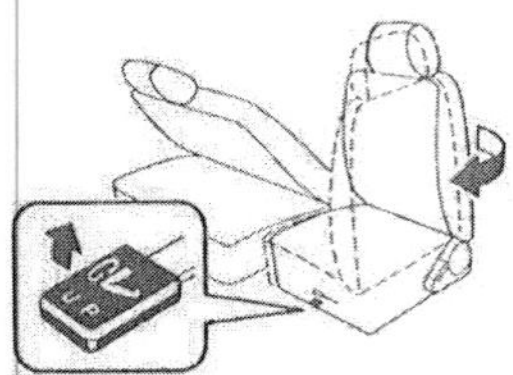

5. Pull the turning lever of the 2 person bench seat and turn the seat 180 degrees to the left and retract the back rest.

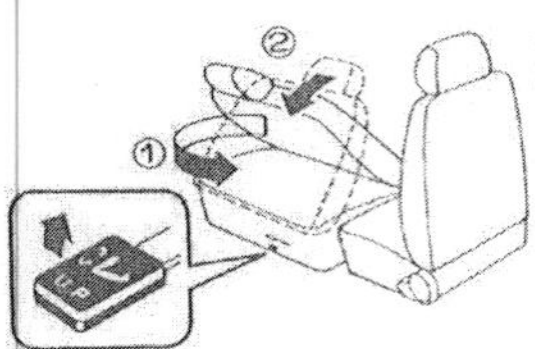

6. Turn the 1 person bench seat 90 degrees to the right and retract the back rest.

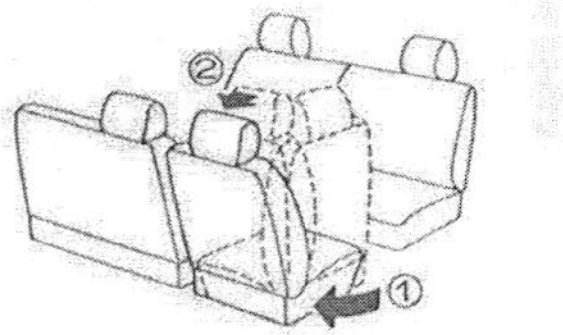

To return the seat to its original position, follow the steps for rotating the seat in reverse order.

Caution:

- Do not turn the seat during driving as this may cause serious injuries in a sudden braking situation. Always turn the seat when the vehicle is stop and make sure that the slide door is open.
- Do not place hands under the seat when turning around the seat. They may get injured.
- Do not turn the seat with passengers sitting on the back seat.
- Do not allow children to turn the seat.

- Do not use the seat in positions other than forward or backward facing. The seat will not be locked into other positions than forward or backward facing. In any other positions, the seat may move suddenly during driving and cause an accident and serious injuries.

Advice:

- When the back rest is over recline. The rotating seat may not working.

## FLAT SEAT

### Between the front seat and second seat

1. Restore the arm rest ( 7-seat vehicles ), move the seat fully forward and pull the reclining lever to recline the seat fully.

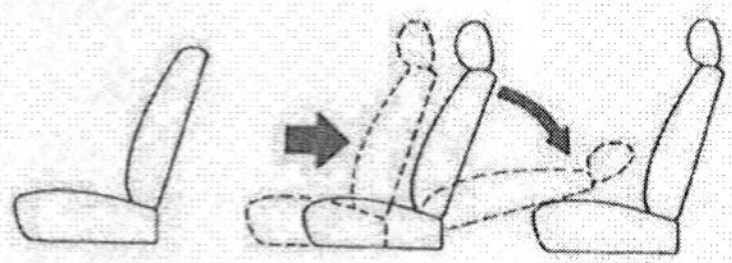

2. Remove the front seat headrests, pull the reclining lever and recline the seat fully. Shift the seats backward.

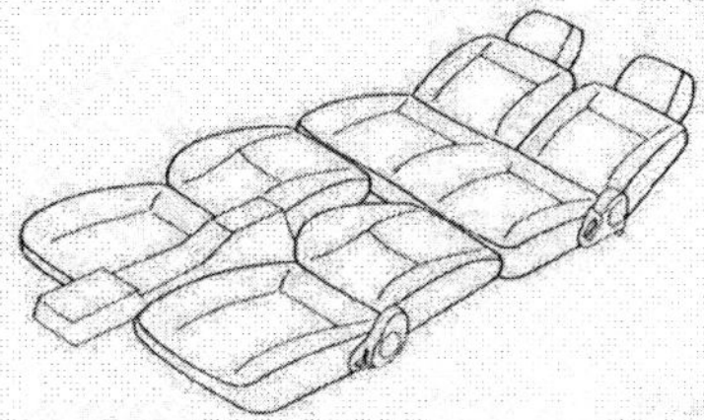

Reverse the procedure to return the seats to the normal position.

Caution:

- Do not run over the top of the flat seats.
- When moving across the flat seats, make sure to step on the centre of the seat slowly.
- Do not drive with the luggage or passengers sitting on the flat seats. It may cause serious injuries in a sudden braking situation.

Advice:

- After removing the headrests, store them under the seat before making the flat seats.

## Between the second seat and third seat

1. Remove the third seat headrests and pull the reclining lever to recline the seat fully.

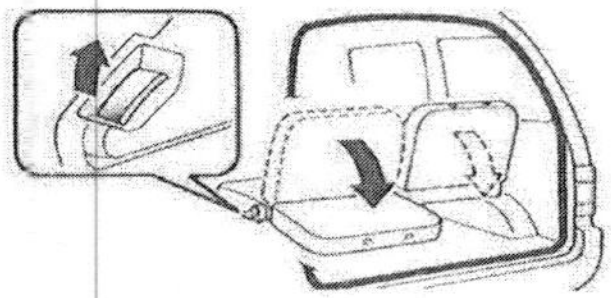

2. Remove the front seat headrests and move the seat forward.

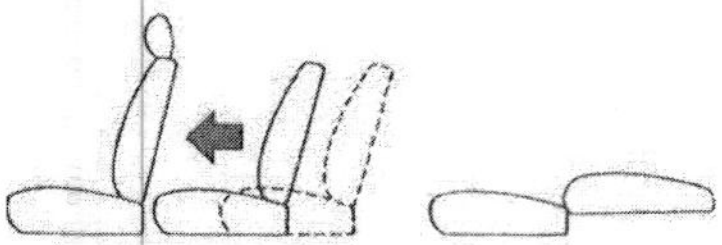

3. Pull the reclining lever to recline the second seat. ( For 1 person bench seat of 8-seat vehicle, move the seat backward )

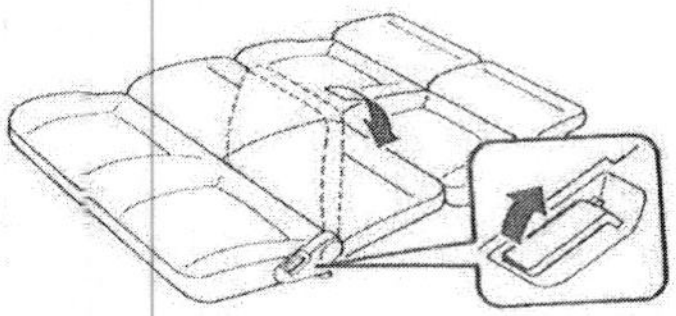

Reverse the procedure to return the seats to the normal position.

Caution:

- When raising the back rest, support the back rest while operating the reclining lever. Failure to do so may cause the back rest to raise suddenly and cause injuries.

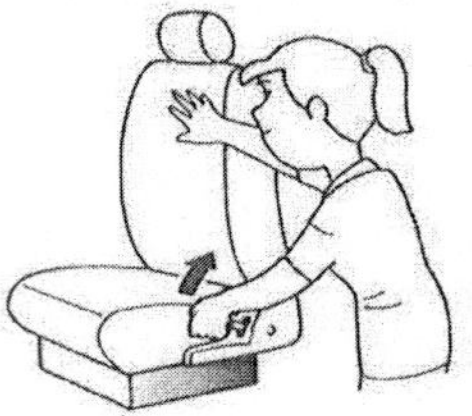

Advice:

- Rock the seat gently to check that the seat is locked securely into place after making the seat into the flat seat or restoring the seat.

## Between the front seat and third seat

1. Remove the third seat headrests and pull the reclining lever to recline the seat.

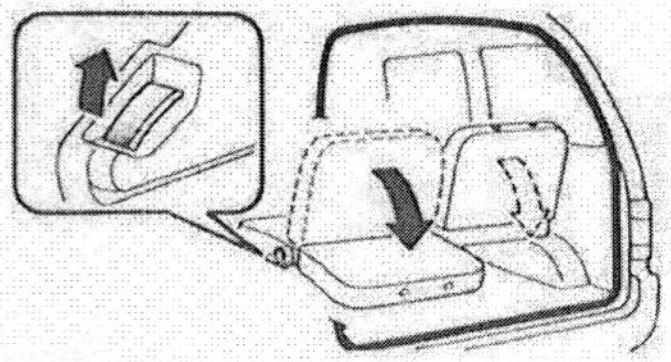

2. Restore the second seat arm rest ( 7-seat vehicles ), remove the headrests, move the seat fully forward and pull the reclining lever to recline the seat.

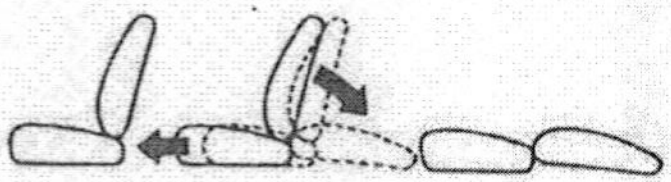

3. Remove the front seat headrests, move the seat fully forward and pull the lever to recline the seat.

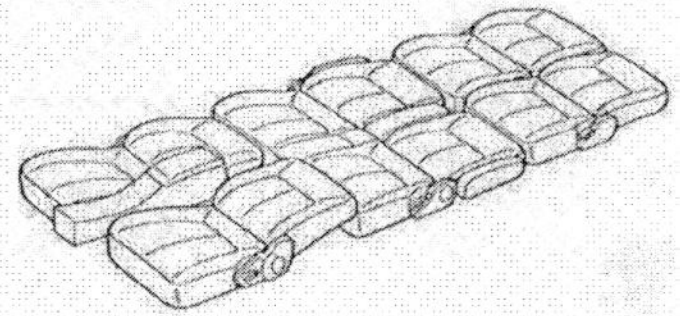

Reverse the procedure to return the seats to the normal position.

Caution:

- Do not run over the top of the flat seats.
- When moving across the flat seats, make sure to step on the centre of the seat slowly.
- Do not drive with the luggage or passengers sitting on the flat seats. It may cause serious injuries in a sudden braking situation.

Advice:

- After removing the headrests, store them under the seat before making the flat seats.
- The passenger seat back rest and second seat cushion are not able to in a horizontal position

Caution:

- When raising the back rest, support the back rest while operating the reclining lever. Failure to do so may cause the back rest to raise suddenly and cause injuries.

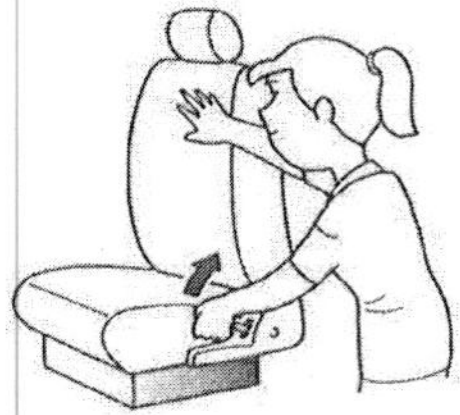

## HOUSE THE THIRD SEAT

This mode gives more space inside the vehicle by housing the third seat.

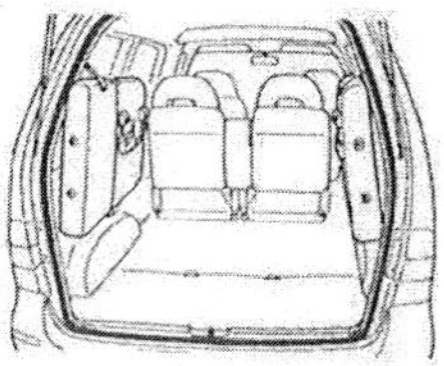

Warning:

- Do not house the seat during driving as this may cause serious injuries in a sudden braking situation.

### To house the third seat

1. Remove the headrest, pull the lever located on the backside of the seat from the rear door to recline the seat fully.

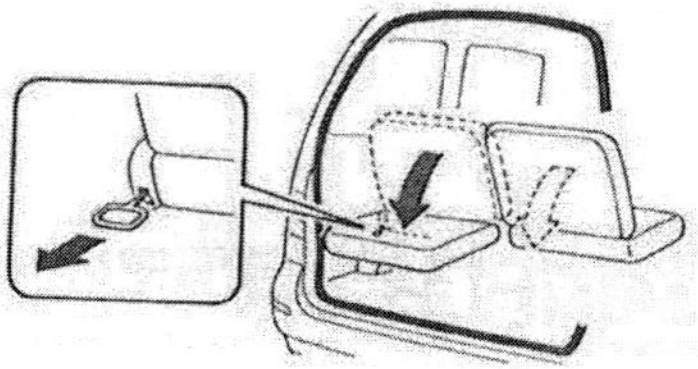

2. Pull the seat unlock lever to unlock and fold the seat to the window side.

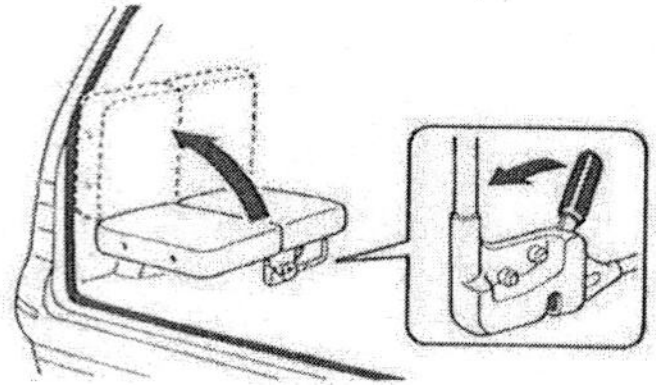

3. Connect the tag belt located on the backside of the back rest onto the hook on the seat belt.

4. Fold the seat foot to the seat cushion side.

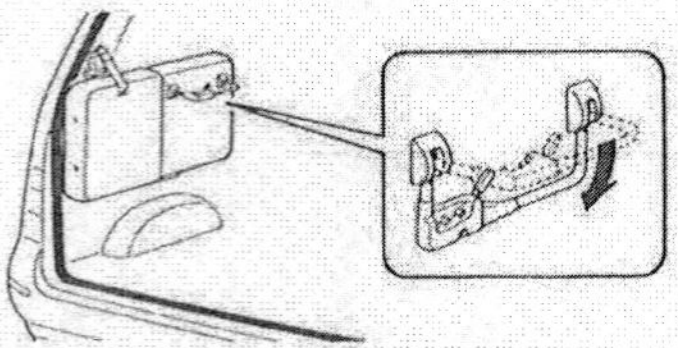

Reverse the procedure to return the seats to the normal position.

Note:

Put the headrest that has been removed in the space between the side of the vehicle and seat cushion.

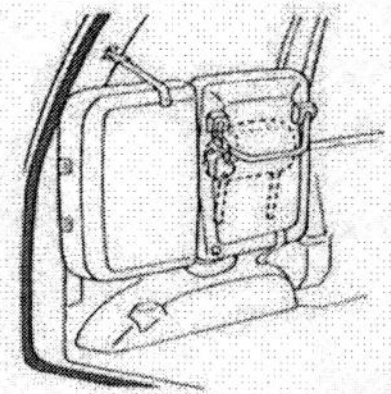

- You can house the only one side of the seat.
- Connect the tag belt onto the hook when it is not in use.

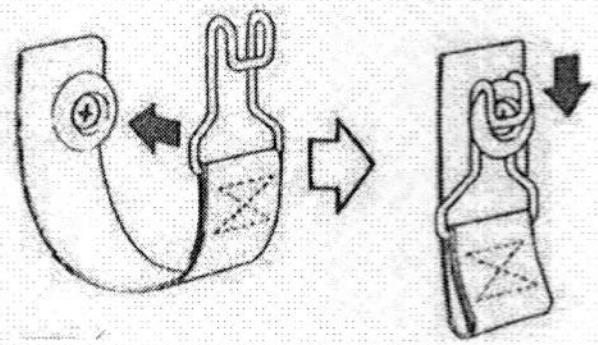

Advice:

- Make sure to return the seat foot to its original position when returning the seat to normal position.

# SEAT BELT

Warning:

- Make sure all passengers are wearing their seat belts correctly before driving.
- The seat belt is designed for one person only. Do not try to belt two passengers in with one seat belt.
- Have the seat belt positioned firmly as low as possible across the hips.
- Never have the seat belt across your neck or under your arm. Always place the seat belt over your shoulder.
- Pregnant women or people with chest or stomach related problems should seek doctors advice before using seat belts.
- If the seat belts become frayed or worn or do not function properly contact your Nissan dealer to have them replaced.
- Ensure the seat belt is not twisted, as this decreases the width of the seat belt considerably and could cause pain or injury to the passenger in an accident situation.
- Use a junior seat for children who are to small for 3 point seat belt ( children aged 4 years to 12 years ). Nissan recommends using a child seat for children aged 4 months - 4 years.

## 3 POINT SEAT BELT

### FASTENING / UN FASTENING THE SEAT BELTS

To fasten the seat belts, hold the tongue and pull the belt. Insert the tongue into the buckle until you hear "click".To unfasten the seat belts, press the button and remove the tongue and slowly rewind the seat belt.

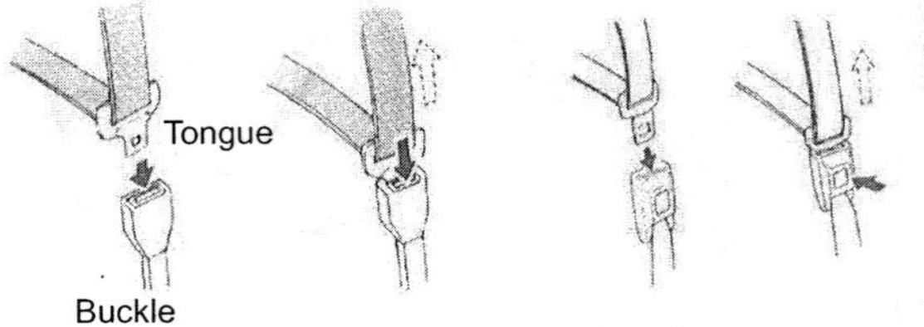


**Front seat**
**8-seat vehicle**
**Left side of the second seat**

**Second seat**
**Third seat**

## ADJUSTABLE SHOULDER ANCHOR

**( Front seats )**

The height of the shoulder belt anchor can be adjusted to four positions. While pushing on the knob, move the anchor up or down until the belt is positioned on the shoulder. Always check that the seat belt anchor is locked securely in place after adjusting.

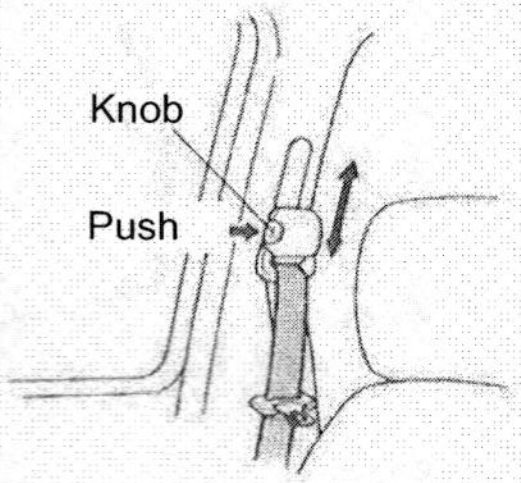


Advice:

- The 3 point seat belt is locked automatically when it is pulled out vigorously or if there is a sudden reduction in speed. Always pull the seat belt out slowly.

### Seat belt tension reducer

The ignition must be in ON.

The seat belt tension reducer system reduces the feeling of pressure against drivers and passengers when wearing the seat belt.

- For 7-seat vehicles, make sure when wearing the second seat belt, insert the centre tab into the buckle marked centre and insert the left and right tabs into the left and right buckles.
- For 8-seat vehicles, only centre seat has the sign of "CENTRE" on the tab and buckle.

Warning:

- Make sure to adjust the seat belt firmly on your shoulder and the anchor is locked securely. If it is not secured properly, the belt comes off from the shoulder and a serious injury may be a result.

## 2 POINT SEAT BELT

**( For centre seat of second seat 8-seat vehicles . For centre seat of third seats )** .

Adjust the length of the belt to the necessary length. Making sure there are no twists in the seat belt, insert the tongue into the buckle securely.

To remove the seat belt, press the buckle button.

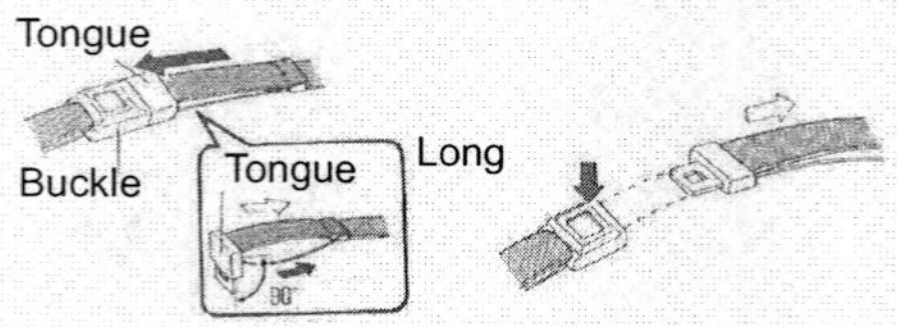

Warning:
Adjust the length so that the belt comes across the hip tightly. Do not keep it loose or wear it across your abdomen. If the belt is not worn correctly, the seat belt may not function in an accident situation and may result in a serious injury.
Advice:

- Be careful that the seat belt does not go under the seat.

## Rotable seats

Use the 2 point seat belt when rotating the seats. To wear / remove the 2 point seat, follow the procedure in previous page.

## 7-seat vehicles

The tongue is located at the right rear side of the drivers' seat and left side of the passengers' seat. To get out the tongue, unstick the hook and loop fastener and pull the carpet off.

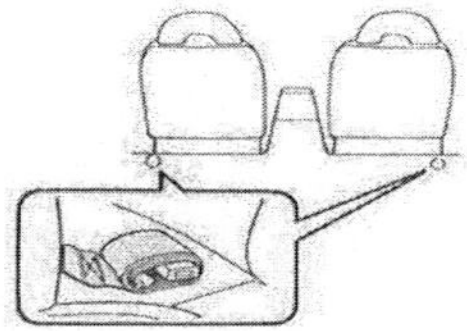

When the seats facing forward, use the 3 point seat belt ("1" "2"•"3" "4"). When rotating the seats use the 2 point seat belt ("2" "5"•"3" "6") as shown in the diagram below.

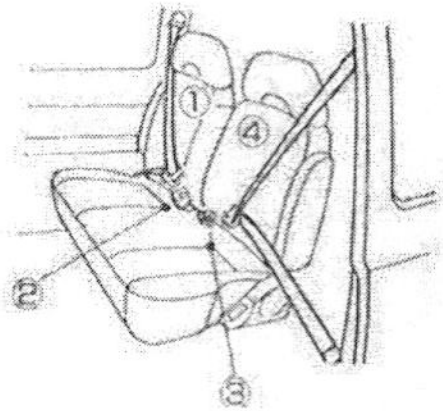

Seats facing forward

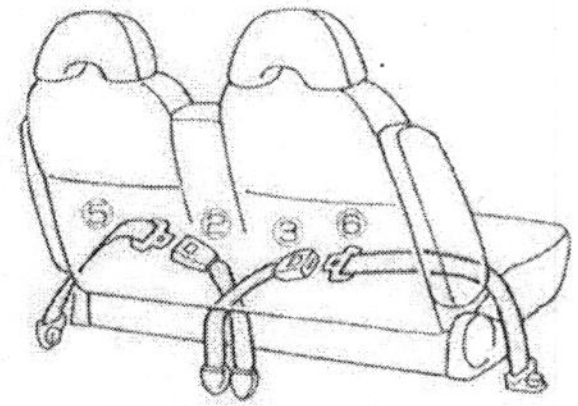

At rotating seats

## 8-seat vehicles

The tongue of the outer seat is located right rear side of the drivers' seat. To get out the tongue, unstick the hook and loop fastener and pull the carpet off. The tongue of the centre seat is located the floor between 1 person bench seat and 2 person bench seat.

**Outer seat**

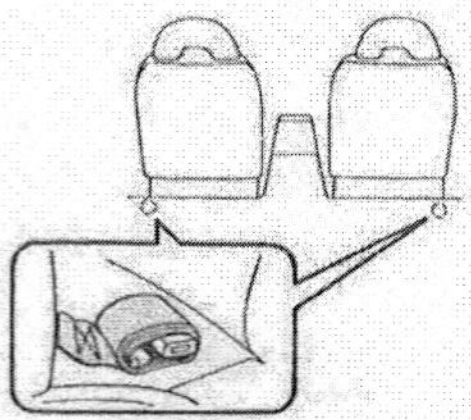

**Centre seat**

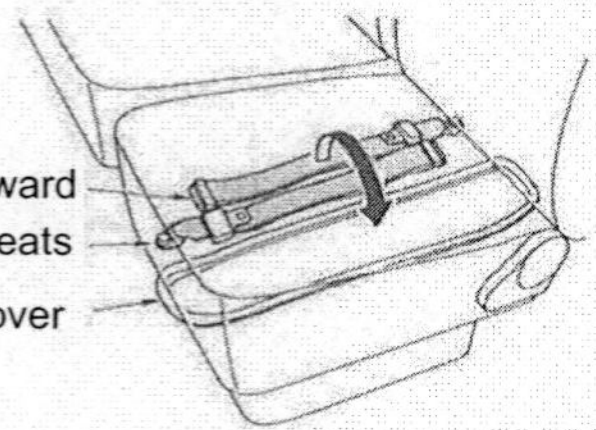


For the outer seat, when the seats facing forward, use the 3 point seat belt ("1" "2"•"5" "6"), for centre seat, use the 2 point seat belt ("3" "4"). When rotating the seats use the 2 point seat belt ("3" "8"•"2" "9"•"7" "10") as shown in the diagram below.

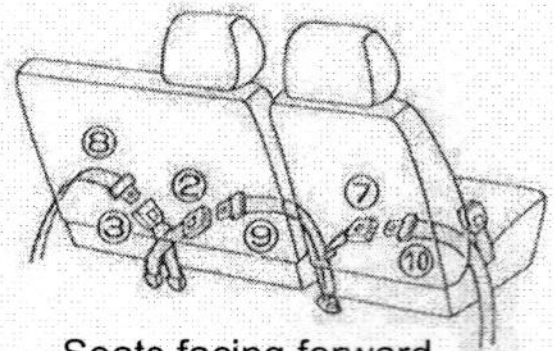

Seats facing forward

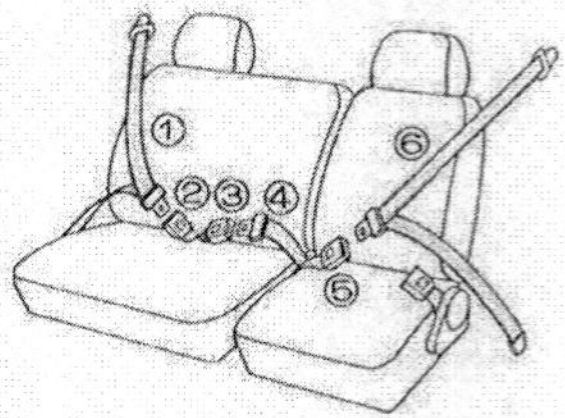

At rotating seats

# INTERNAL APPARATUS

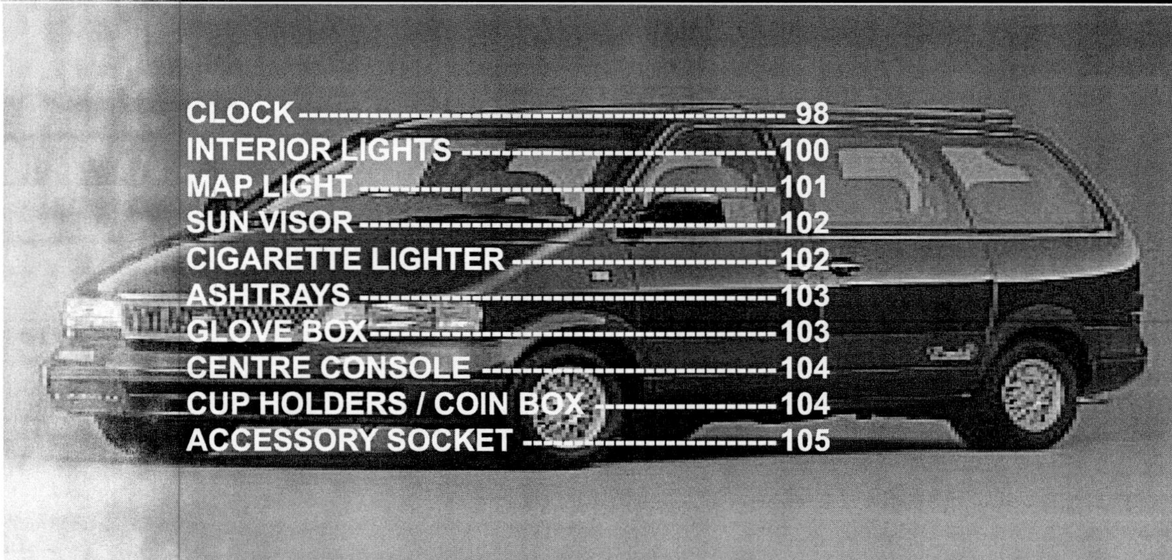



# NISSAN LARGO

# CLOCK

## AM / FM radio

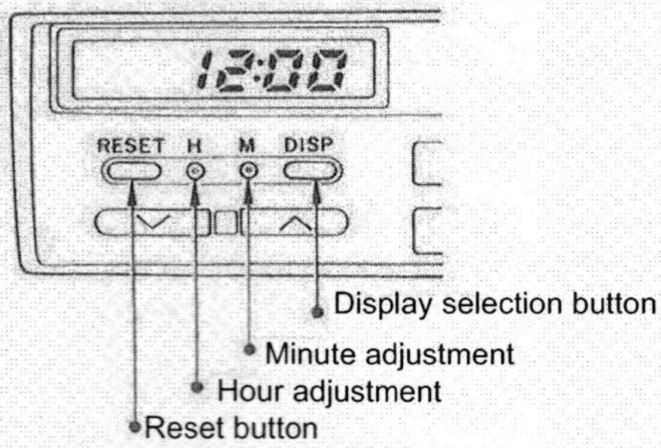


## AM / FM radio with cassette type

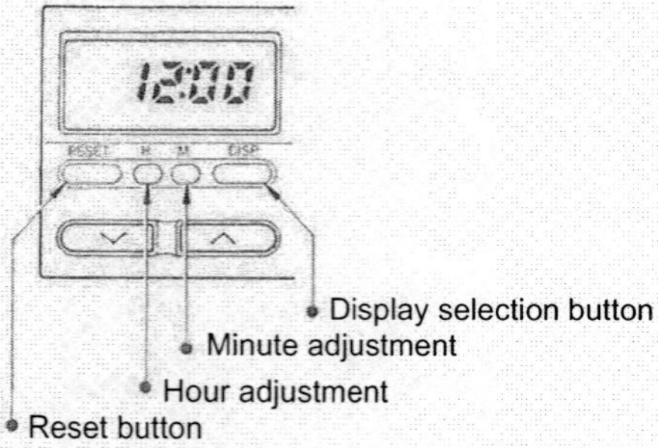


Note:

- The clock can be used when the ignition is in ACC or ON position.

Advice:

- If the battery is disconnected, the clock will need to be reset.

## Largo Super Sound System

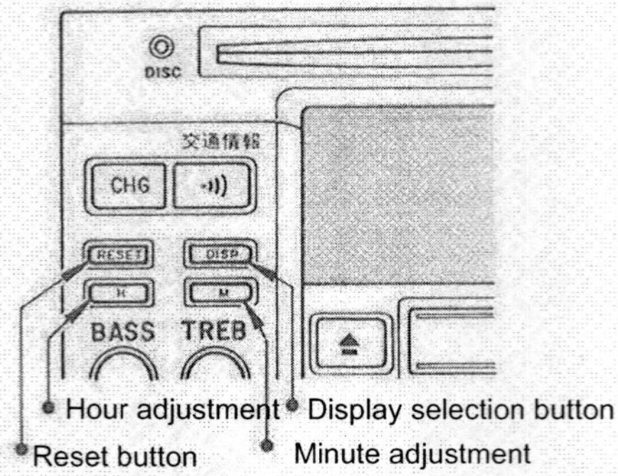

**Audio less vehicles**

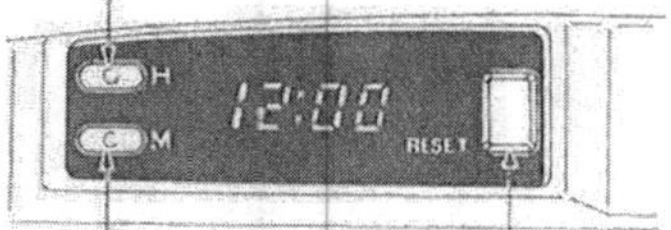


## Setting the time

Pushing the H switch will cause the hour time display to fast foward.

## Synchronising the clock with the time signal

Push the "RESET" button in time with signal.

.

Example:

**Vehicles with radio**

If the "RESET" button is pushed between 9:55 and 10:05, the time displayed will be 10:00.

**Audioless vehicles**

If the "RESET" button is pushed between 10:01and 10:29, the time displayed will be 10:00

If the "RESET" button is pushed between 10:30 and 10:59, the time displayed will be 11:00.

Advice:

The clock will not display when the battery is disconnected. After reconnecting the battery, set the clock to correct time. The clock cannot be set to a time announcement when not displaying a time between :55 and :05.

## Display selection button

When the display selection button is pushed, the display panel will show the status of the radio frequency for 5 seconds and return to the clock display.

# INTERIOR LIGHTS

**Vehicles without sun roof**
The interior light will come on or go out according to the switch positions shown below.

| Switch position | Function |
|---|---|
| ON | Light is on |
| • mark | When a door is opened the light will come on, and will go out when the door is closed |
| OFF | Light is out |

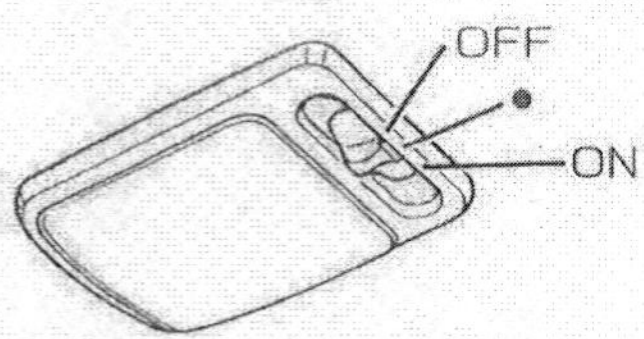


**Vehicles with sun roof**
The interior light will come on or go out according to the switch positions shown below.

| Switch position | Function |
|---|---|
| ON | Light is on |
| • mark | When a door is opened the light will come on, and will go out when the door is closed |
| OFF | Light is out |

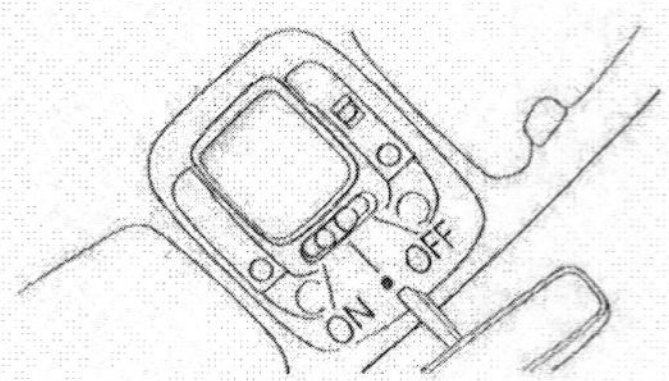

**Rear interior light**

The interior light will come on or go out according to the switch positions shown below.

Push the switch to turn OFF / ON the light

| Switch position | Function |
|---|---|
| ON | Light is on |
| DOOR | When a door is opened the light will come on, and will go out when the door is closed. when the switch is pushed again, the light will not come one when a door is opened. |

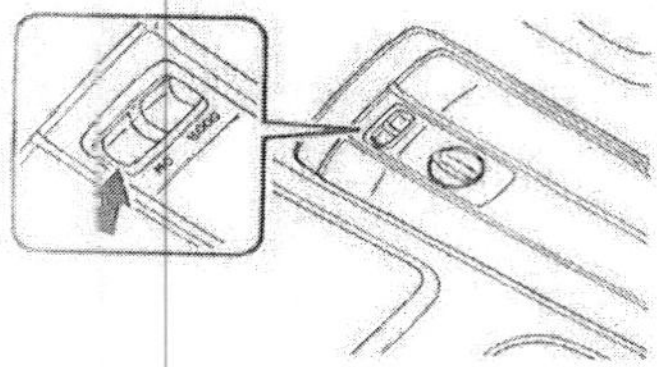

While the light is on, you can adjust 3 level brightness by turning the dial.

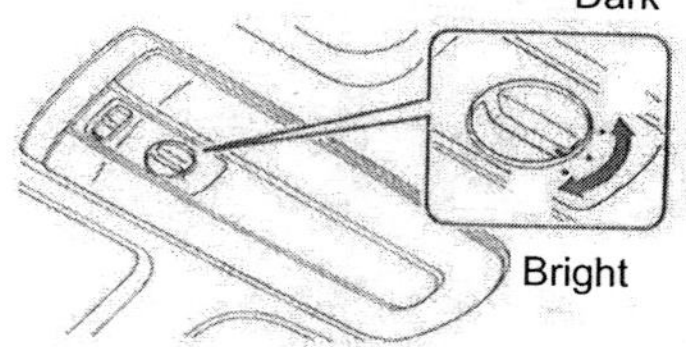


# MAP LIGHT

The light will come on when the switch is pressed in, and will go out when the switch is pushed back.

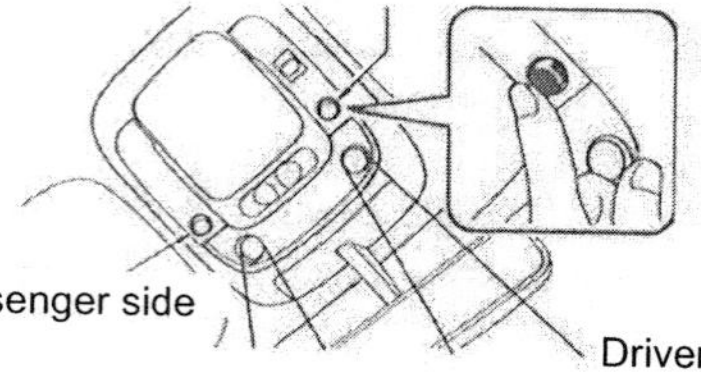

# SUN VISOR

Flip the sun visor down when travelling into bright, sunny condition.

The sun visor may also be twisted around to the side to stop direct sunlight coming in from the side.

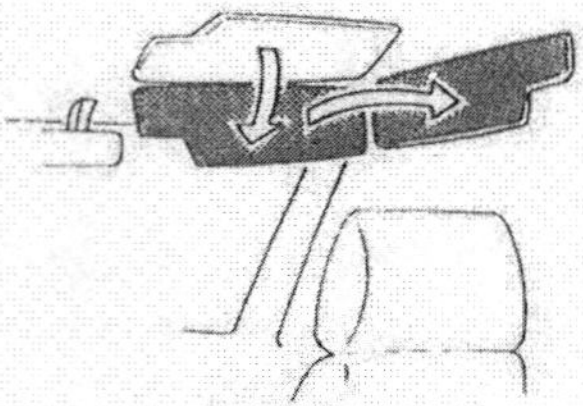

Note:

**Vanity mirror**

The vanity mirror is located on the reverse side of the driver's seat sun visor.

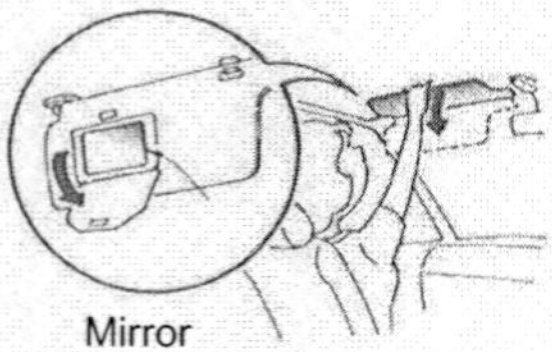


# CIGARETTE LIGHTER

The ignition must be in ACC or ON.

Push the cigarette light in and wait approximately 10 seconds. When the lighter is ready, it will automatically pop out to its original position. Pull it out to use.

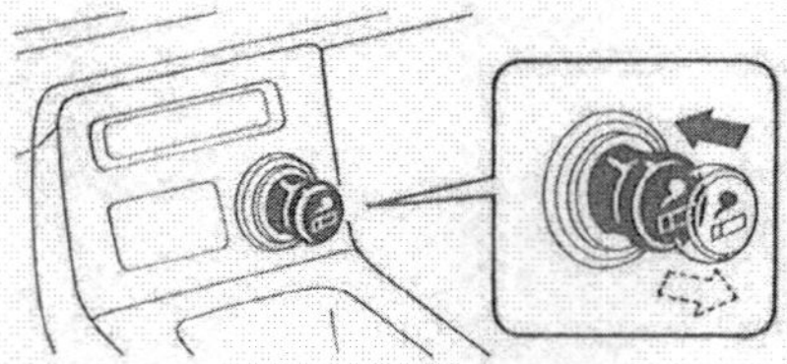

Caution:

- Do not touch the metal area of the cigarette lighter as you may get burnt.

Advice:

- Do not hold the cigarette lighter in, as this will cause it to overheat and will damage it.
- Do not use a lighter from another vehicle, or insert electrical products except genuine Nissan products, as this may cause it to burn out or a fire may result.
- If the lighter does not automatically pop out to the original position after 30 seconds, pull it out manually and have it checked by your Nissan dealer.

# ASH TRAYS

## FRONT ASH TRAY

The front ashtray is located next the select lever.

- Pull the lid towards you to open.
- To clean, pull it out while pushing the button down.
- To replace after cleaning, push it back into the slot.

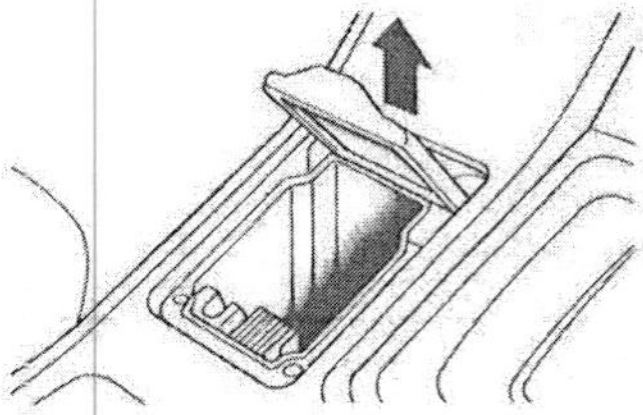

## REAR ASHTRAY

For the second seat, the rear ashtray is located backside of the centre console. For the third seat, it is located right side of the seat.

**Second seat**

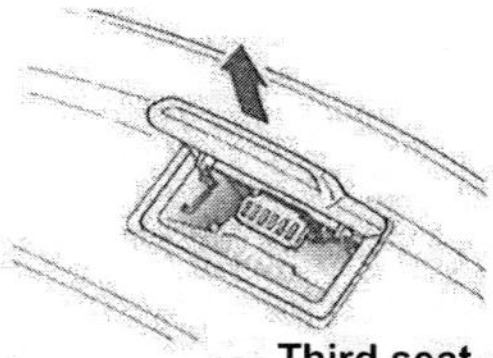

**Third seat**

Caution:

- Ensure any stubs or matches are completely out before putting them in the ashtray.
- Keep the ashtray properly closed when not in use.
- Do not overfill the ashtrays, nor put paper or other flammable objects in them. A fire may result.

# GLOVE BOX

## To open / Close

Pull the handle toward you to open. To close push back until it is locked.

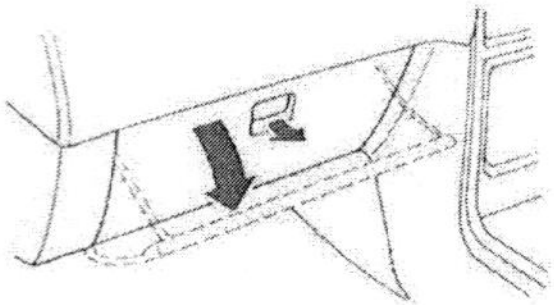

Caution:
Do not drive with the glove box open. The contents inside may be thrown around, and injuries may occur in heavy braking.

## CENTRE CONSOLE BOX

To open the box, simply lift the lid.

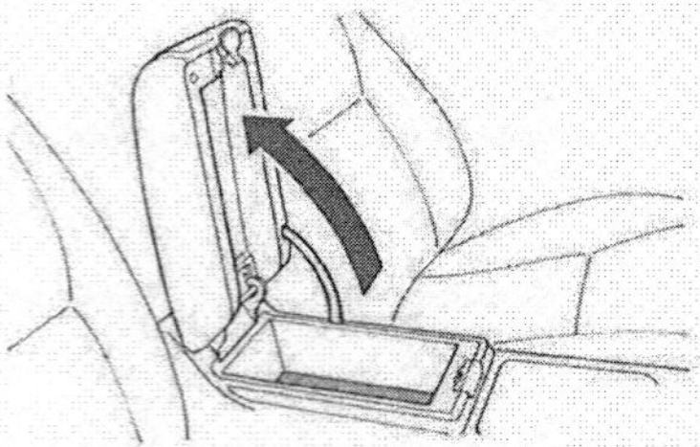

Caution:
Do not drive with the centre console box open. The contents inside may be thrown around, and injuries may occur when braking heavily.

## CUP HOLDER / COIN BOX

To use the cup holder and coin box, open the lid located on front centre console box.
To open, push the "PUSH" mark on the lid.

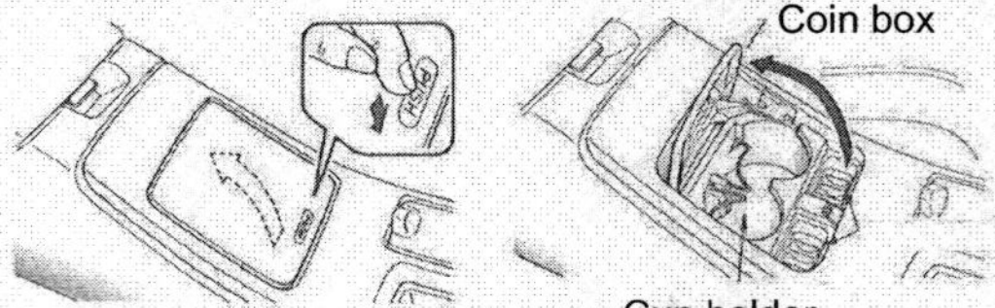


Another coin box is located on the left side of the steering wheel.

Caution:
- It is dangerous to take a beverage in and out of the cup holder while driving. Only use when the vehicle is stationary such as when waiting at traffic lights.

Advice:
- For diesel vehicles or vehicles with electric control suspension switch, there is only one coin box located.

# ACCESSORY SOCKET

- The accessory socket is located on the right side of the third seat.
- You can use electrical applications in the vehicle by plugging them to the socket.
- To use, open the cap
- The electrical application must be 12V with a maximum current of 10A.

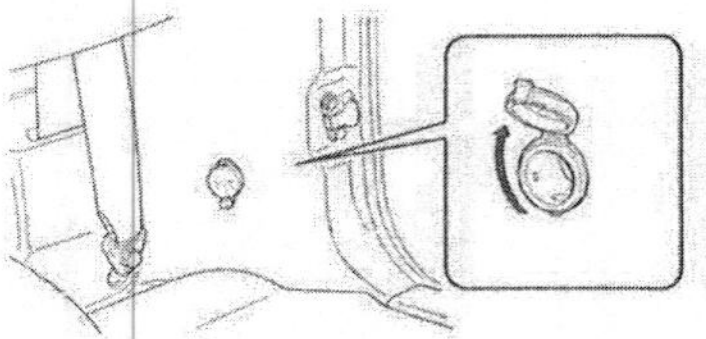

Advice:

- Electrical applications exceeding the recommended voltage or wattage may cause fuses to blow.
- Do not use the accessory socket for a long time when the engine is not running as this may drain the battery. Even if the engine is running, using the socket for a long time while idling may drain the battery.
- Do not spray water to the accessory socket as this may damage the accessory socket.
- Do not plug the cigarette lighter to the socket.

# AIR CONDITIONER & HEATER

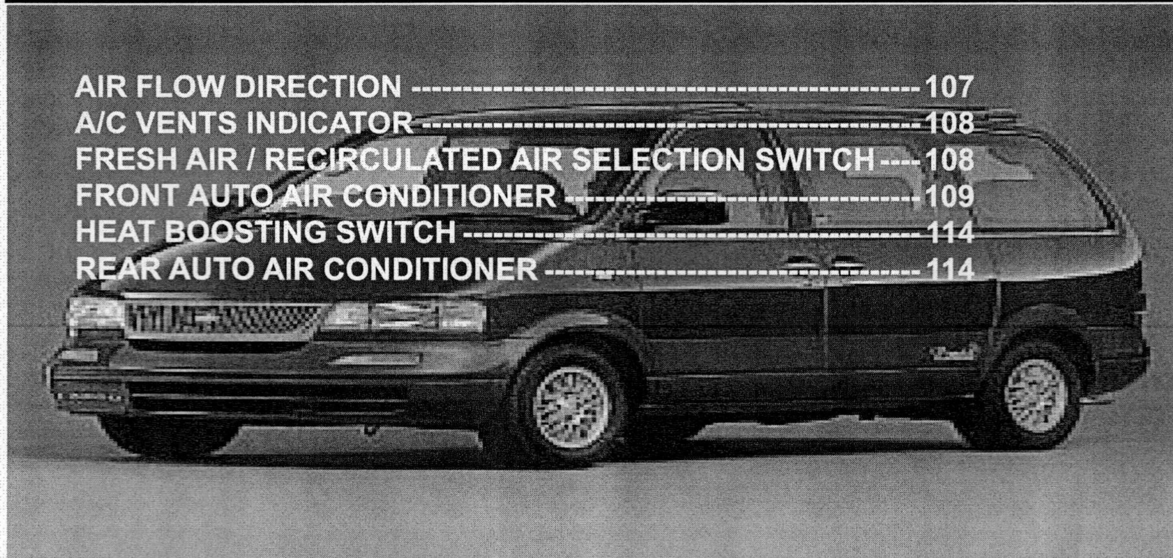



## NISSAN LARGO

# AIR FLOW DIRECTION

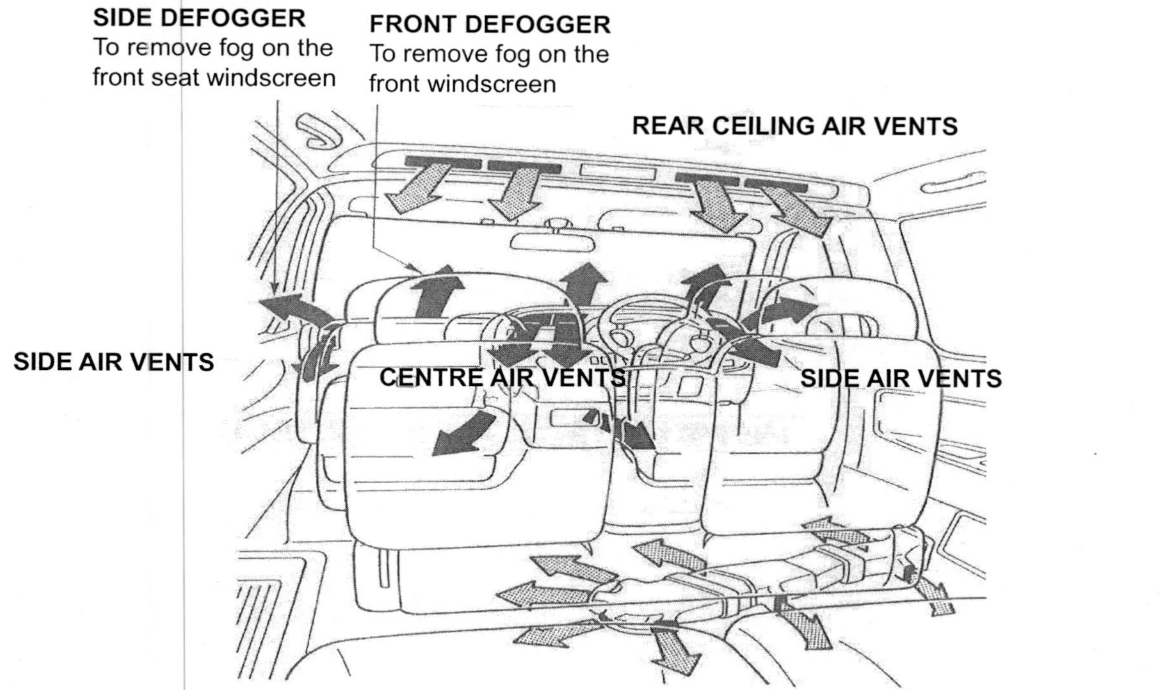


- **Adjust the air flow**
  Adjust the air flow of the centre vents, side air vents and rear ceiling air vents using the centre knob.

# A/C VENTS INDICATOR

| Air flow direction | Function |
| --- | --- |
| Air flow to the upper body area |  |
| Air flow to the upper body and lower leg area |  |
| Air flow to the lower leg area |  |
| Air flow to the lower leg area and windscreen |  |
| Air flow to the windscreens | 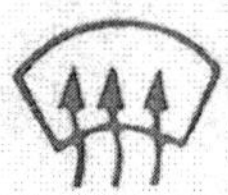 |

Caution:
The ignition must be ON to adjust the air conditioner, deffoger and heater
Advice:
The insolation sensor is located left edge front deffoger. Do not place any objects on the insolation sensor spray.

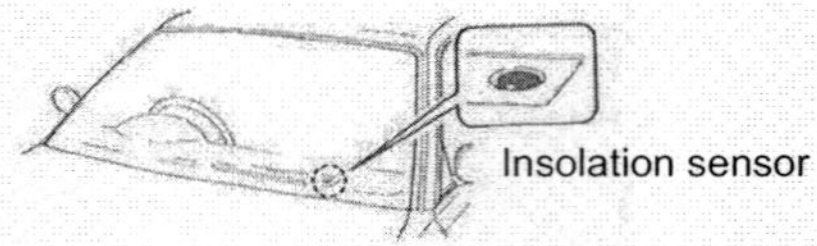


Note:
Always use a new refrigerant gas, HFC 134a (R134a)

## FRESH AIR RECIRCULATED AIR SELECTION SWITCH

Use this switch to select fresh air from outside the vehicle or to recirculate air already inside vehicle.

| Switch position | Function |
|---|---|
| 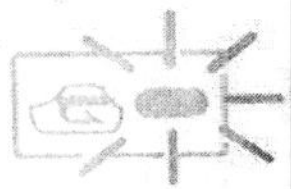 Light on | • Air will not enter vehicle from outside.<br>• When driving in tunnels or in traffic jams where the outside air is dirty, or when you wish to cool down the interior quickly. |
|  Light off | • Air will enter vehicle from outside.<br>• When the "AUTO" is flashing on the display, the system automatically changes between recycled air and fresh air. The switch indicator will come on when activating the recycling function. |

Warning:

Do not use the recycling function any more than necessary. In normal circumstances use fresh air. In a case where there are holes or cracks in the exhaust system caused by corrosion or damage, there is a danger of carbon monoxide poisoning occurring as a result of exhaust gases.

Advice:

If air recycling is used for a prolonged period, it will cause the windows to fog up. Do not use this function any more than necessary.

## FRONT AUTO AIR CONDITIONER

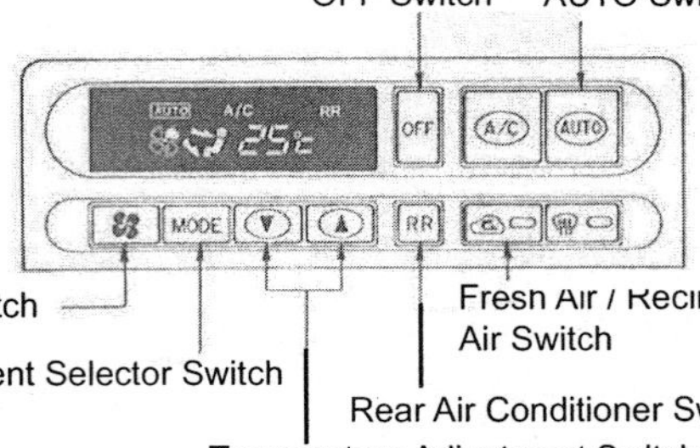


## USING THE FRONT AUTO AIR CONDITIONER FOR ALL SEASON

1. The ignition must be ON. Press the AUTO switch. The display light "AUTO A/C" will come on in the display.

2. Set the temperature adjustment switch to the desired temperature. The temperature can be adjusted between 18 to 32 degrees.

Press ▲ side to increase the temperature.
Press ▼ side to decrease the temperature.

**FAN SWITCH**

Press the fan switch to operate the fan.

**AIR VENT SELECTOR SWITCH**

Press the air vent selector switch to operate the air vent system.

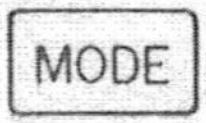


**FRESH AIR / RECIRCULATED AIR SWITCH**

Press the fresh air / recirculated air switch to select fresh air from outside the vehicle or to recirculate air already inside the vehicle. The display light "AUTO" will come on in the display.

| Switch | Change of functions every time press the switch |
| --- | --- |
| Fan Switch |  Low air flow~high air flow |
| Air Vent Selector Switch |  Upper body~upper body/lower leg~lower leg~lower leg/deffoger |

3. Press the OFF switch to stop operation.

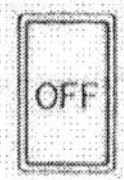


Advice:

**Rear air conditioner switch**

- The display light "RR" will come on when the rear air conditioner is operating.
- While the display light "RP" is illuminating, you can operate the rear air conditioner by the front control panel.
- The display light automatically changes to the front air conditioner display when the switch is not pressed in 10 seconds.

- When set the temperature to 18 degrees using the temperature adjustment switch and press the (▼) switch for more than 3 seconds to change to Full Cool mode. The display light "FC" will come on in the display.

- When setting the temperature 32 degrees by the temperature adjustment switch and press the (▲) switch for 3 seconds will change to the Full Hot mode. The display light "FH" will come on in the display.

Note:

- The air conditioner and dehumidifier will not operate when the outside temperature approaches 0 degrees.

Advice:

- Switch to recirculated air mode when the outside air is polluted or when you wish to cool or warm the air quickly, however using it for an extended period of time may cause air pollution in the vehicle. If can also cause windows to become foggy. Use the recirculated air mode only when necessary.

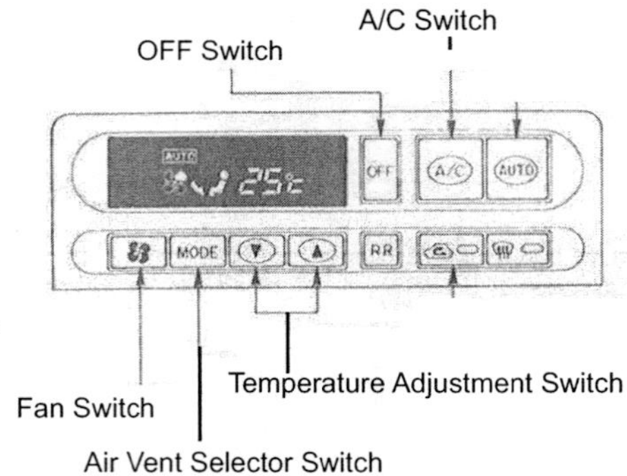


## AUTO HEATER

1. The ignition must be ON. Press the auto switch and press the A/C switch. The display light "AUTO" will come on.

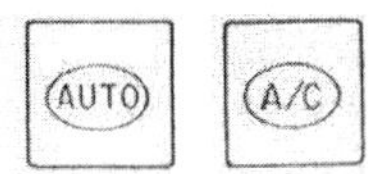

2. Set the temperature adjustment switch to the desired temperature. The temperature can be adjusted between 18 to 32 degrees.

Press ▲ side to increase the temperature.
Press ▼ side to decrease the temperature.

**FAN SWITCH**

Press the fan switch to operate the fan.

**AIR VENT SELECTOR SWITCH**

Press the air vent selector switch to operate the air vent system.

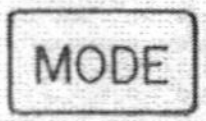


**FRESH AIR / RECIRCULATED AIR SWITCH**

Press the fresh air / recirculated air switch to select fresh air from outside the vehicle or to recirculate air already inside the vehicle. The display light "AUTO" will come on in the display.

| Switch | Change of functions every time press the switch |
|---|---|
| Fan Switch | 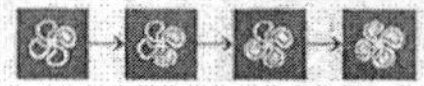 Low air flow~high air flow |
| Air Vent Selector Switch |  Upper body~upper body/lower leg~lower leg~lower leg/deffoger |

3. Press the OFF switch to stop operation.

Advice:

- When setting the temperature 18 degrees by the temperature adjustment switch and press the ▼ switch for 3 seconds will change to the Full Cool mode. The display light "FC" will come on in the display.

- When set the temperature to 32 degrees using the temperature adjustment switch and press the (▲) switch for more than 3 seconds to change to Full Hot mode. The display light "FH" will come on in the display.

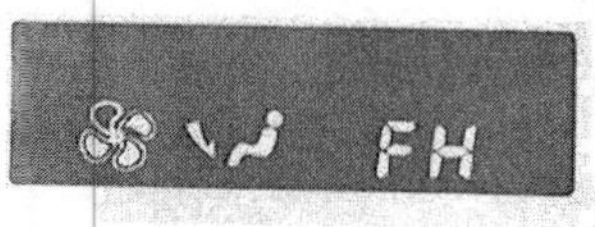


Note:

- The room temperature does not become colder than the

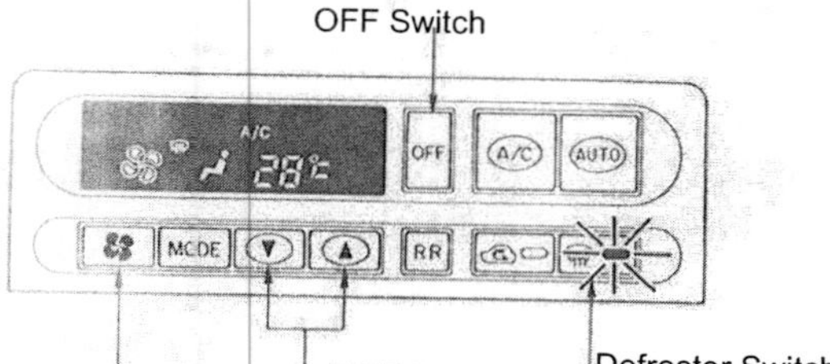


## TO REMOVE FOG ON THE WINDSCREEN

1. The ignition must be ON. Press the defroster switch. The display light " " will come on.

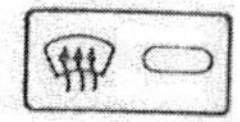

To remove the fogging quickly, set a room temperature over 28 degrees and select a large air volume.

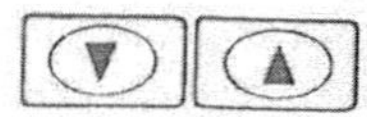

Temperature adjustment switch

Fan switch

3. Press the OFF switch to stop operation.

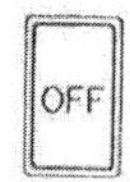


Caution:

When the air conditioner is set to a low temperature, the outside windows may fog up.
If air re circulation mode is used for an extended period of time, the window may fog up.

- When set the temperature to 32 degrees using the temperature adjustment switch and press the [A] switch for more than 3 seconds to change to Full Hot mode. The display light "FH" will come on in the display.

# HEAT-BOOSTING SWITCH (DIESEL VEHICLES)

This switch will increase the idling, which elevates the heating effect.
If the switch is pushed the heat-boosting system will operate. (The display light inside the switch will come on)

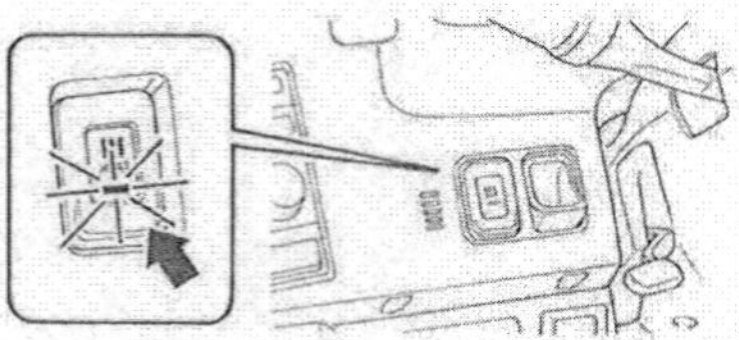

Advice:

**Heat-boosting system**

- This system is a system which boosts the effect of the heater by increasing the engine's revs when idling and lifts the temperature of the cooling fluid
- This system will operate when the gear selection lever is in "P" or "N"
- This system will cease operating automatically once the temperature of the cooling fluid rises or the accelerator is touched.
- This system will begin operating automatically once the accelerator returns to its original position and the engine revs drop.

# REAR AUTO AIR CONDITIONER

**Remote control**

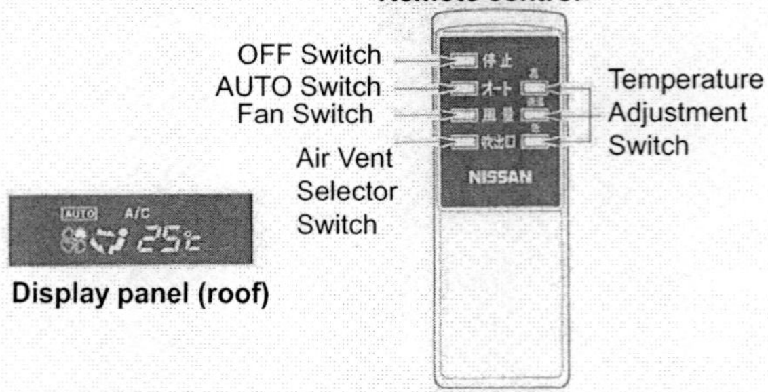


**Display panel (roof)**

Advice:

- Do not splash water on the remote control and do not keep it warm place as this may damage the remote control.
- Do not drop the remote control.
- When the remote control does not operate properly, the battery needs to be changed.
- When the front air conditioner is operating the auto heater, only the rear air conditioner and the heater can be operated.
- It is impossible to use only rear air conditioner for air conditioner.

## USING THE REAR AUTO AIR CONDITIONER

- Engine must be running..
- Use the remote control to operate the rear auto air conditioner.
- Operate the front air conditioner before operating the rear auto air conditioner. If the front air conditioner is not operating, the rear auto air conditioner will not operate as an air conditioner or dehumidifier.

1. Press the auto switch. The display light "AUTO" will come on.
2. Set the temperature adjustment switch to desired temperature.

| | |
|---|---|
| LOW | Set on low temperature up to 18 degrees |
| SUITABLE TEMPERATURE | Set on 25 degrees |
| HIGH | Set on high temperature up to 32 degrees |

If you wish to set the fan, simply press the fan switch. If you wish to set air vent, simply press the air vent switch. The display light "AUTO" will come on.

Advice:

- When setting the temperature 18 degrees by the temperature adjustment switch and press the (▼) switch for 3 seconds will change to the Full Cool mode. The display light "FC" will come on in the display.

- When set the temperature to 32 degrees using the temperature adjustment switch and press the [▲] switch for more than 3 seconds to change to Full Hot mode. The display light "FH" will come on in the display.

| Switch | Change of functions every time press the switch |
|---|---|
| Fan Switch |  Low air flow~high air flow |
| Air Vent Selector Switch |  Upper body~upper body/lower leg~lower leg~lower leg/deffoger |

3. Press the OFF switch to stop operation.

## TO STORE THE Remote control

To store the remote control in the pocket located right side of the second seat when it is not used.

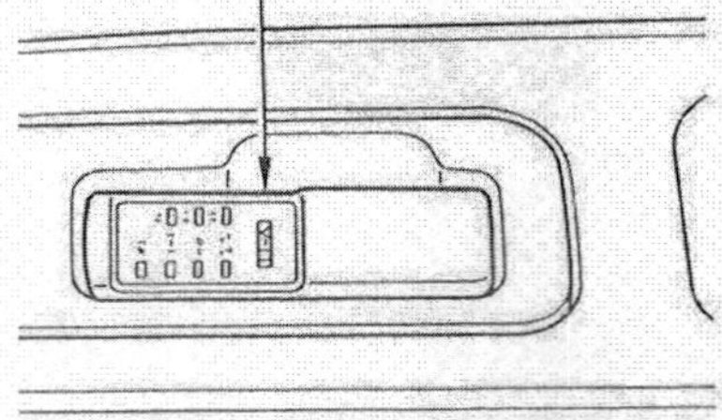


## BATTERY REPLACEMENT

Remove the cover on the back of the controller, and insert the batteries (+) and (-) poles pointing in the proper direction.

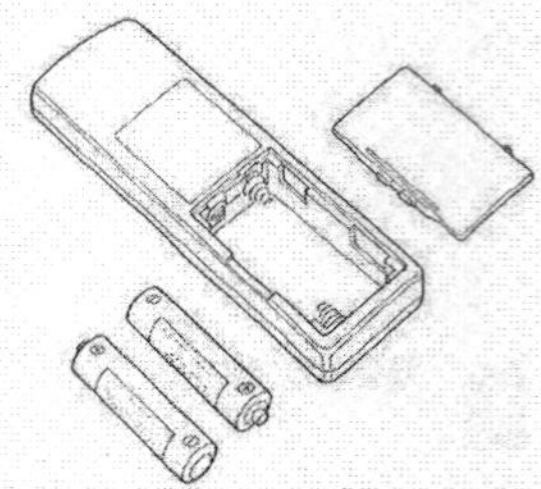

Advice:

- Use only A3 batteries.
- Remove the batteries if the remote control is not used for a month or longer.
- Do not attempt to recharge the supplied batteries.
- All batteries should be replaced at the same time, do not mix old battery .
- Do not dispose of the batteries in a fire as they may explode.

Advice:

- There is the filter in the sink hole located right bottom of the second seat. The filter needed to be replaced if the air flow decreases, contact with your Nissan dealer.

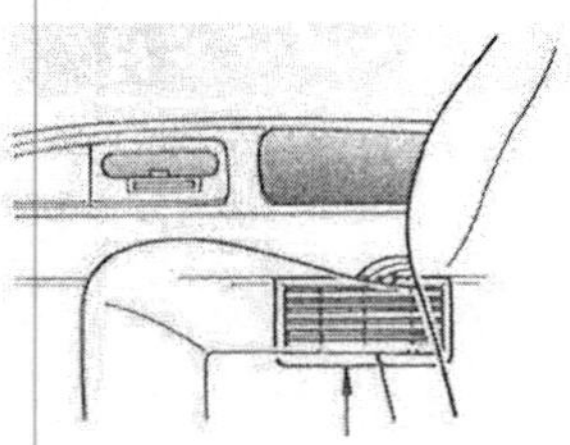

# AUDIO SYSTEM

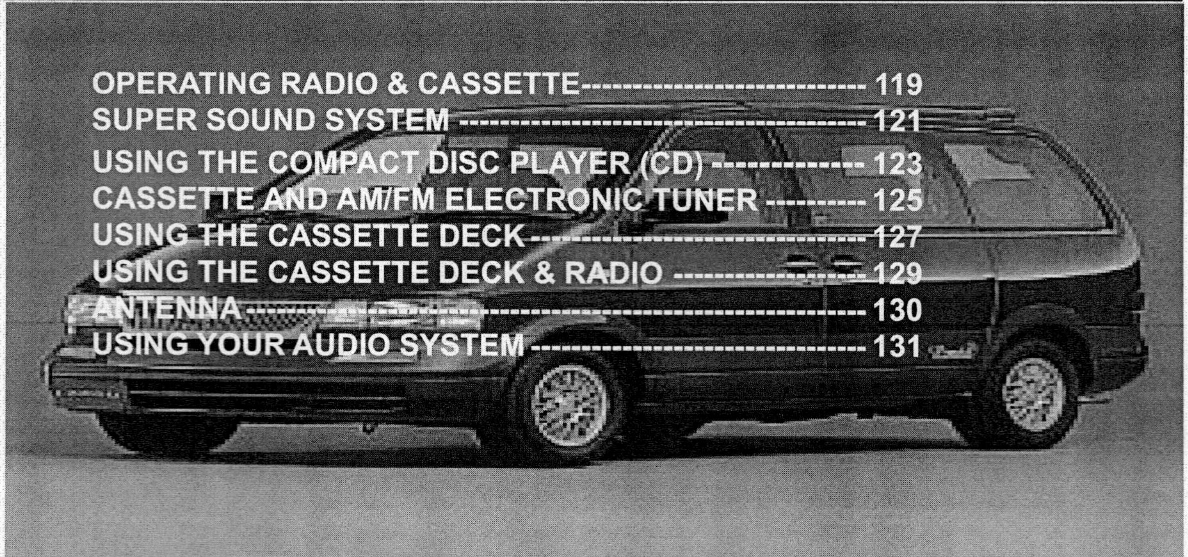



NISSAN LARGO

# OPERATING RADIO & CASSETTE

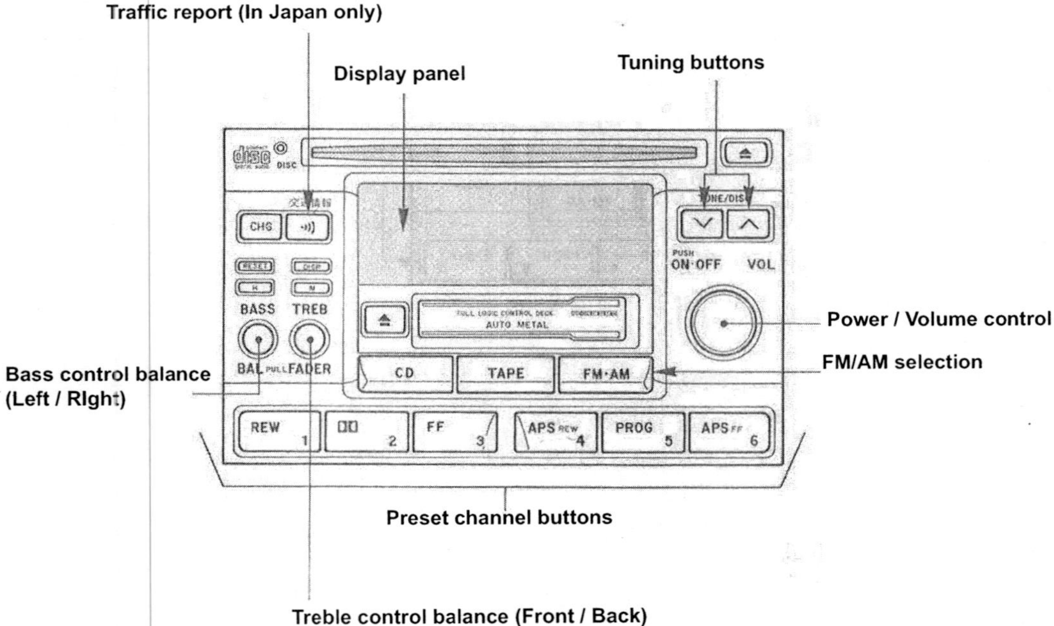

## ADJUSTING THE VOLUME • SOUND QUALITY AND BALANCE

Use when listening to the radio, cassettes, etc.

Adjust by turning the knobs.

**Adjusting volume:**

Down 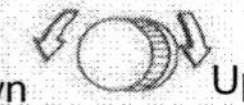 Up

Using the sound quality and balance knob:
If the knob is pushed once it will extend, and can be used to adjust the sound quality.
If it is pulled out further it can be used to adjust the balance.

**Adjusting sound quality: (treble / bass)**

BASS

Weak  Strong

TRE

Weak 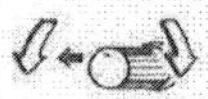 Strong

**Adjusting sound quality: (front / back, left / right)**

BAL

Left  Right

FADER

Front 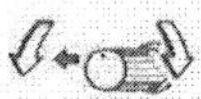 Back

## USING THE RADIO

1. The ignition must be ON. Extend the antenna fully, push the power button and push the FM/AM button.
2. Choose FM or AM broadcasts by pushing the FM/AM button.

Advice:

Use manual tuning when the radio transmission is weak and automatic tuning is not possible.

# SUPER SOUND SYSTEM

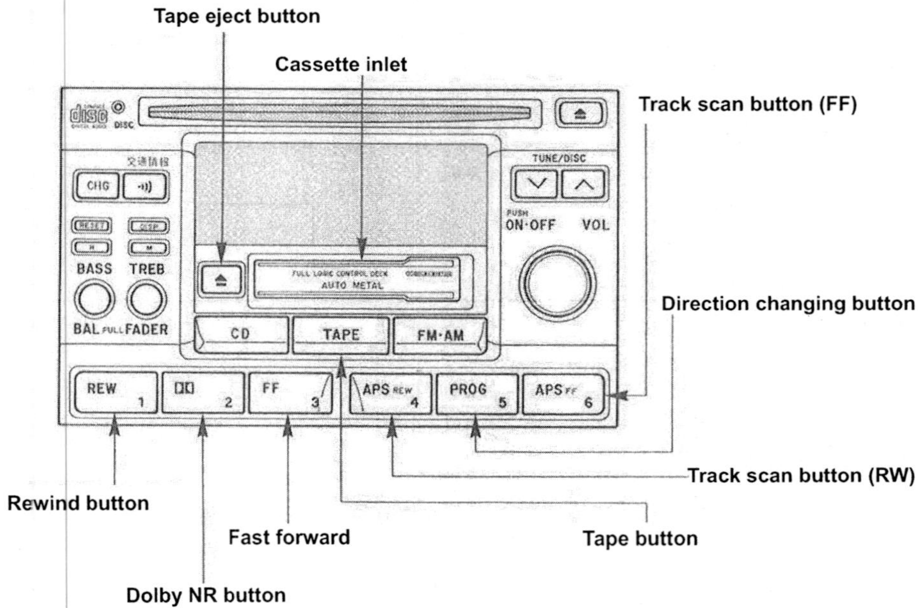

- **Tape Eject Button**
  Push the tape eject button to eject the cassette tape.
- **Track Scan Button (FF)**
  To skip ahead to the start of the next track, push the tracn scan button (FF).
- **Track Scan Button (RW)**
  To skip back to the start of the next track, push the track scan button (RW).
- **Direction Changing Button**
  To change the tape play direction. If the button is pressed while the tape is being fast-forwarded or rewinded, the tape will start playing.
- **Tape Button**
  Press the button to start playing a tape. Press the button while fast forwarding or rewinding, the tape will stop playing.
- **Fast Forward Button**
  Press this button to fast forward. Press this button again or the tape button to stop fast forwarding.
- **Rewind Button**
  Press this button to rewind the tape. Press this button again or the tape button to stop rewinding.
- **Dolby NR Button**
  Press this button when playing tapes recorded in Dolby NR button

Note:
Dolby Noise Reduction is manufactured under license from Dolby Laboratories Licensing Corporation. Dolby and the Double D system symbol ▯▯ are trademarks of Dolby Laboratories Licensing Corporation.

## PRESETTING A STATION (FM / AM)

1. Turn the radio to the station you wish to preset.
2. Push one of the preset buttons (1~6) until a beep is heard.

Advice:
Each button can be preset to both an AM and FM station.

Note:
If the car battery is disconnected, stations stored in the preset memory will be erased, and it will be necessary to repeat the presetting procedure.

## TO LISTEN TO CASSETTES

The ignition must be ON. Insert a tape into the tape inlet and it will begin playing

## TO TURN THE AUDIO SYSTEM ON/OFF

Press the power button to turn the audio system on and off

# USING THE COMPACT DISC PLAYER (CD)

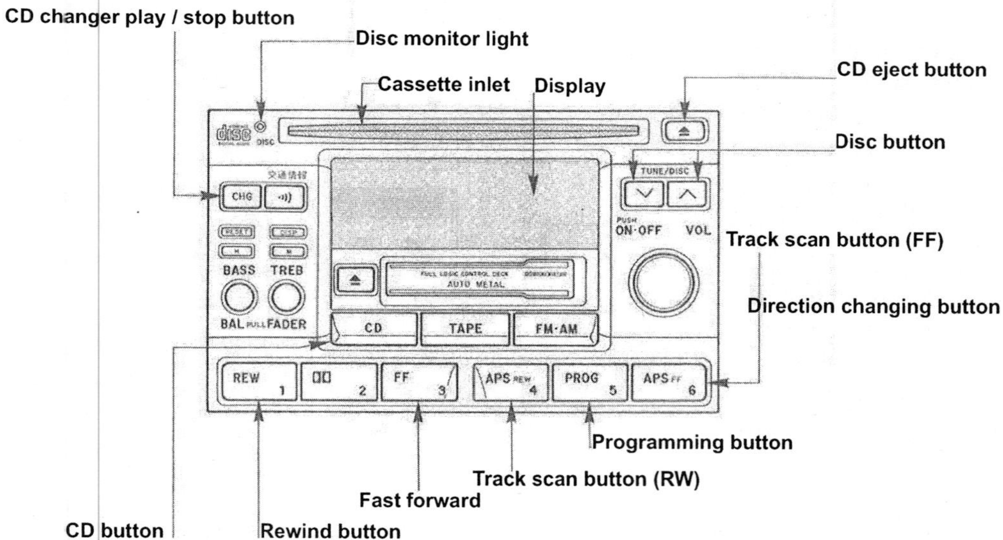

- **CD Eject Button**
  Push the CD eject button to eject the CD.
- **Track Scan Button (FF)**
  To skip ahead to the start of the next track, push the track scan button (FF).
- **Track Scan Button (RW)**
  To skip back to the start of the next track, push the track scan button (RW).
- **Programming Button**
  Press this button to change the order in which songs are played. The display will change each time the programming button is pressed, and the songs will be played as follows:

  ALL → 1 → RANDOM

- **CD Button**
  Press the button to start playing a CD. Press the button while fast forwarding or rewinding, the CD will stop playing.
- **Fast Forward Button**
  Press this button to fast forward. Press this button again or the CD button to stop fast forwarding.
- **Rewind Button**
  Press this button to rewind the tape. Press this button again or the CD button to stop rewinding.

## TO LISTEN TO A CD

The ignition must be ON. Insert a CD into the CD inlet with the label facing up and it will begin to play.

Advice:

8-inche (single) CDs can also be used, without an adaptor. Adaptors may cause damage to the player, so avoid using them.

## USING THE PROGRAMMING BUTTON

The display will change each time the programming button is pressed, and the songs will be played as follows:

ALL → 1 → RANDOM

| | |
|---|---|
| ALL | : All the songs will be played in or der, repeatedly. |
| 1 | : The dame song will be played re peatedly. |
| RANDOM | : The order in which the songs are played will change automatically |

Light out : All songs will be played in order, and the CD will stop

Note:
When listening to a CD in RANDOM mode, the same song may be played in succession.

# CASSETTE AND AM/FM ELECTRONIC TUNER

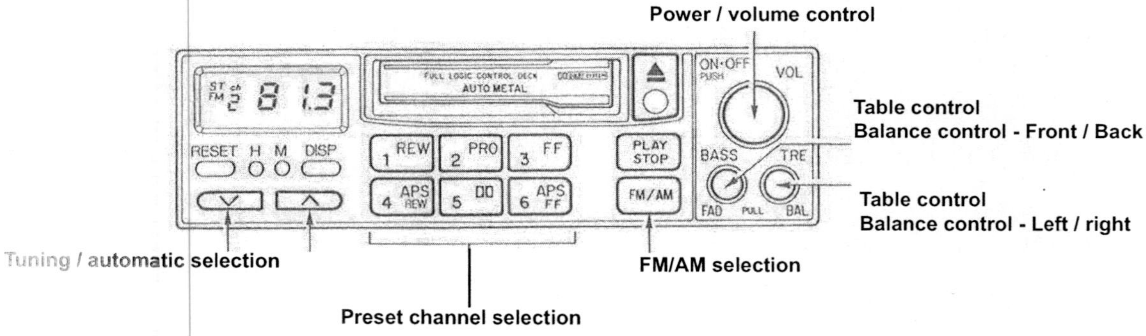

## ADJUSTING THE VOLUME • SOUND QUALITY AND BALANCE

Use when listening to the radio, cassettes, etc.

Adjust by turning the knobs.

**Adjusting volume:**

Down 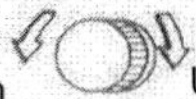 Up

Using the sound quality and balance knob:
If the knob is pushed once it will extend, and can be used to adjust the sound quality.
If it is pulled out further it can be used to adjust the balance.

**Adjusting sound quality: (treble / bass)**

BASS

Weak  Strong

TRE

Weak 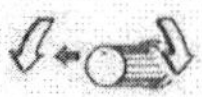 Strong

**Adjusting sound quality: (front / back, left / right)**

BAL

Left  Right

FADER

Front 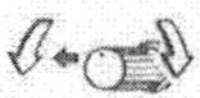 Back

## USING THE RADIO

1. The ignition must be ON. Extend the antenna fully, push the power button and push the FM/AM button.
2. Choose FM or AM broadcasts by pushing the FM/AM button.

Advice:
Use manual turning when the radio transmission is weak and automatic tuning is not possible.

## PRESETTING A STATION (FM / AM)

1. Turn the radio to the station you wish to preset.
2. Push one of the preset buttons (1~6) until a beep is heard.

Advice:
Each button can be preset to both an AM and FM station.

Note:
If the car battery is disconnected, stations stored in the preset memory will be erased, and it will be necessary to repeat the presetting procedure.

# USING THE CASSETTE DECK

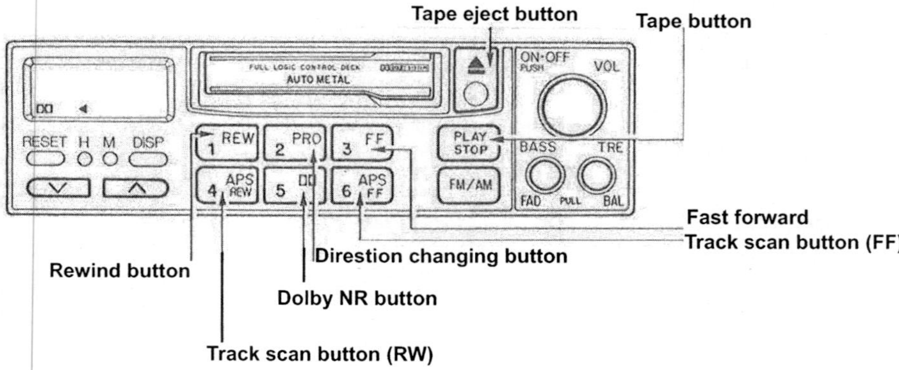


- **Tape Eject Button**
  Push the tape eject button to eject the cassette tape.
- **Track Scan Button (FF)**
  To skip ahead to the start of the next track, push the track scan button (FF).
- **Track Scan Button (RW)**
  To skip back to the start of the next track, push the track scan button (RW).
- **Direction Changing Button**
  To change the tape play direction. If the button is pressed while the tape is being fast-forwarded or rewinded, the tape will start playing.

- **Tape Button**
  Press the button to start playing a tape. Press the button while fast forwarding or rewinding, the tape will stop playing.
- **Fast Forward Button**
  Press this button to fast forward. Press this button again or the tape button to stop fast forwarding.
- **Rewind Button**
  Press this button to rewind the tape. Press this button again or the tape button to stop rewinding.
- **Dolby NR Button**
  Press this button when playing tapes recorded in Dolby NR.

Note:

Dolby Noise Reduction is manufactured under license from Dolby Laboratories Licensing Corporation. Dolby and the Double D system symbol ꟿ are trademarks of Dolby Laboratories Licensing Corporation.

## TO LISTEN TO CASSETTES

The ignition must be ON. Insert a tape into the tape inlet and it will begin playing

## TO STOP THE TAPE

When you wish to stop the tape, push the Play / Stop button or the power button. If the same button is pushed again, the tape will begin playing again.

## TO TURN THE AUDIO SYSTEM ON/OFF

Press the power button to turn the audio system on and off

# USING THE CASSETTE DECK & RADIO

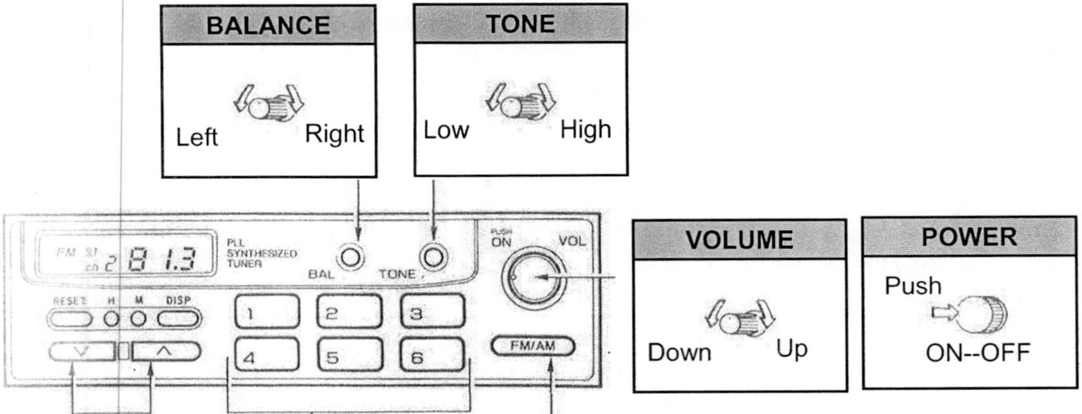


**Manual / auto tuning**
Press for less than 1 sec to tune manually.
Press for more than 1 sec to start auto-tuning. It will make a 'beep' sound and automatically go to the next station.

**Preset button**
Press button to select a preset station.

**FM / AM selection**

## USING THE RADIO

1. The ignition must be ON. Extend the antenna fully, push the power button and push the FM/AM button.
2. Choose FM or AM broadcasts by pushing the FM/AM button.

Advice:

Use manual turning when the radio transmission is weak and automatic tuning is not possible.

## PRESETTING A STATION (FM / AM)

1. Turn the radio to the station you wish to preset.
2. Push one of the preset buttons (1~6) until a "ch" light comes on.

Advice:

Each button can be preset to both an AM and FM station.

Note:

If the car battery is disconnected, stations stored in the preset memory will be erased, and it will be necessary to repeat the presetting procedure.

# ANTENNA

Extend the antenna fully when listening to the radio.

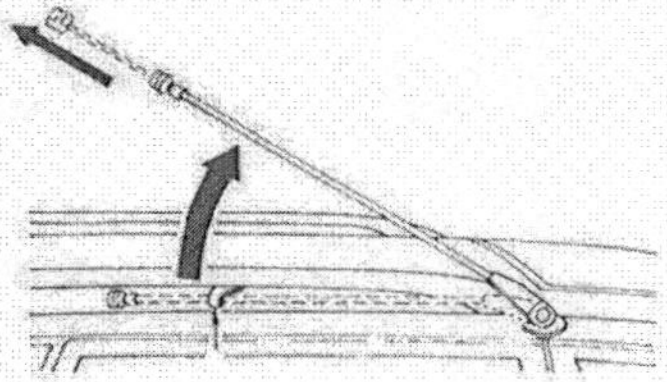

Advice:

- Make sure no one will be hit before extending the antenna. Retract the antenna when you leave the car
- Fix the antenna with the clip when using a car wash.
- Be careful not to hit the antenna when reversing the vehicle.

# USING YOUR AUDIO SYSTEM

## In the interests of safe driving:

While driving, keep the volume at a level which allows you to hear sounds outside the vehicle.

## Using compact discs (CD):

- In cold or rainy conditions, the CD player may not operate properly due to moisture buildup inside. Remove the disc and ventilate the CD player to remove the moisture before using again.
- If the temperature inside the vehicle is too hot, the CD player may not operate normally.
- If the vehicle vibrates strongly when travelling, the sound may jump. The CD player may also eject the CD to protect it.

## Using cassettes:

- A cleaning tape should be used to remove dirt from the cassette deck heads once a month.
- Do not use cassette tapes exceeding 90 minutes in length. The tape is too thin and may jam the cassette deck.
- Do not insert tapes into the cassette deck that have loose labels as they may get jammed inside the cassette deck.
- Wind the tape to remove any looseness before inserting it in the cassette deck to prevent the tape becoming tangled inside the cassette deck.

Advice:

JPNZ recommends that you keep tapes in cases, out of direct sunlight and away from dust or magnetic devices.

## DIY TROUBLE SHOOTING FOR YOUR CD PLAYER

**What to do when....**

| SYMPTOM | POSSIBLE CAUSE | HOW TO FIX |
|---|---|---|
| CD won't go in | Already CD in player | Press eject button and replace with new CD |
| | Not switched on | Turn ignition to ACC or ON |
| CD ejects by itself | CD is upside down | Insert with label facing up |
| | CD is very dirty | Clean the CD |
| | Temperature in the car is over 50 °C. | Lower the car temperature before using the CD player |
| | Condensation build up | Leave for a while before using |
| Won't start playing | CD has been stopped | Press the Play / Stop button |
| | CD is upside down | Insert with label facing up |
| CD skips even though there's no vibrations | Can be caused by the condition of the CD | Try changing the CD |

See your Nissan dealer if the problem is not fixed after carrying out the above suggestions or if the stereo is broken down in some other way.

# SPECIAL EQUIPMENT / SAFETY EQUIPMENT



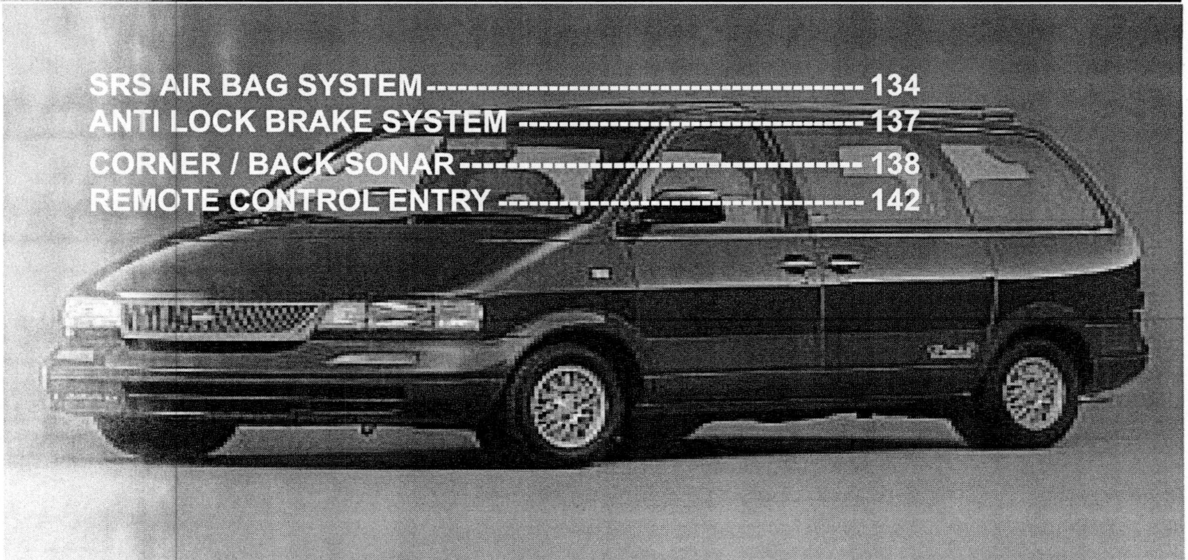

## NISSAN LARGO

# THE SRS AIR BAG SYSTEM

The SRS air bag is operational when the ignition is switched to ON. The air bag will operate when the vehicle suffers a major impact in a head-on collision. Used in conjunction with seat belts, this system increase safety.

Warning:

- The SRS air bag is a measure designed to supplement the seatbelts. It is not a substitute for seatbelts, and the air bag alone can not stop a person being thrown from the vehicle in an accident.
- Always wear a seatbelt. If the seatbelts are not worn correctly, the air bags will not work effectively, which could lead to serious injury.

Note:

- SRS is short for Supplemental Restraint System.

## Situations in which the air bags will not operate:

- When the vehicle collides with a solid immovable object, such as a concrete wall, at 20 km/h or less
- When the vehicle is hit from the side by another vehicle.
- Once the system has been activated, it can not be used again.

Caution:

- Do not change the steering wheel, or paste stickers or similar objects on the steering wheel's canter panel-the SRS air bag will not function correctly.
- Repairs in the vicinity of the steering wheel, instalment panel or enter console, or the installation of stereo or similar equipment may affect the SRS air bag, so consult a Nissan dealer first.
- Do not use a electric circuit tester for circuit diagnosis on the air bag system.
- The air bag will be hot after it has inflated, so do not touch it within 30 minutes of it activating.
- When the air bag inflates, an activating sound and white smoke will appear, but this is not a fire.
- The air bags can not be reused. Once they have been used, have them replaced by your Nissan dealer.
- Only a Nissan dealer should dismantle the SRS air bags.

## AIR BAG SYSTEM OPERATION

The air bag stored in the steering wheel inflates instantly.

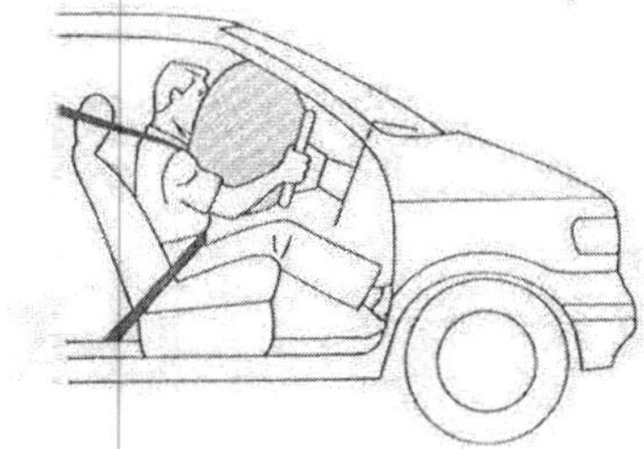

## AIR BAG WARNING LIGHT

The warning light is located inside the meter. When the ignition is switched to ON, it will come on for about 7 seconds, and then go out. If there is a malfunction in the SRS air bag, when the ignition is on the light will stay on or blink.

## SRS AIR BAGS WARNINGS:

- Do not place your hands, head or chest near the section of the steering wheel in which the air bag is stored, as this could lead to serious injury if the air bag activates.

## SITUATIONS IN WHICH THE SRS AIR BAG WILL OR WILL NOT ACTIVATE

- **Will activate:**
  In the following situations, if the impact is significant, the air bag system will activate:

**A head-on collision with a stationary or moving vehicle**

A head-on collision with a solid wall

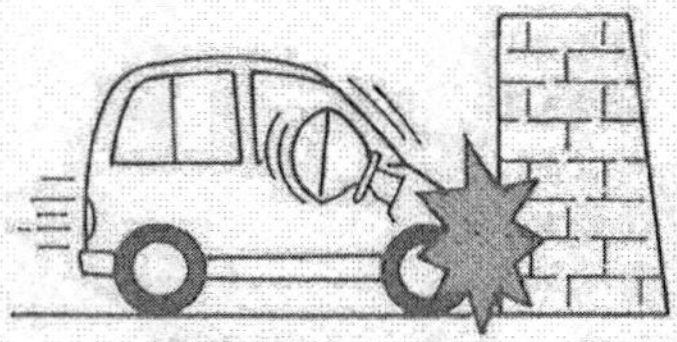

A collision in which the vehicle is driven under the rear deck of a truck

- **May not activate:**
  In the following situations, depending on the size of the impact, the air bag system may not always activate:

A head-on collision with power pole or similar

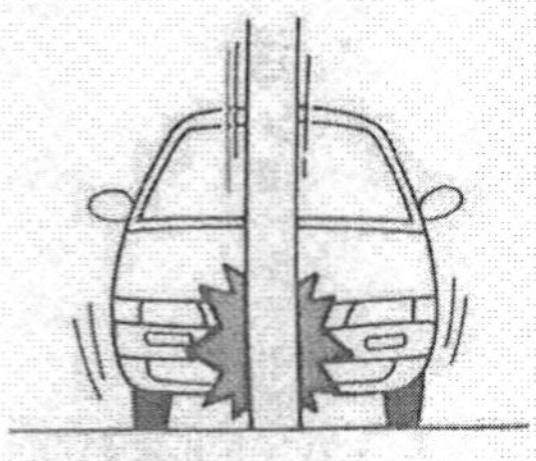

The vehicle falls into a large hole, ditch or similar

A frontal, diagonal collision

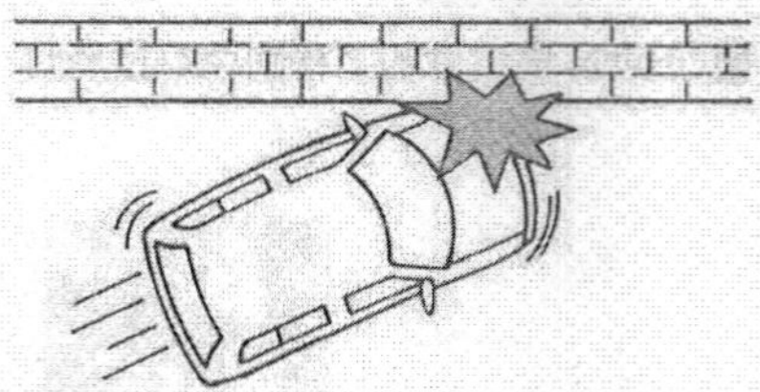

- **Will not activate:**
  The air bag system will not activate in the following situations:

**The vehicle is struck from the rear**

**The vehicle is struck from the side**

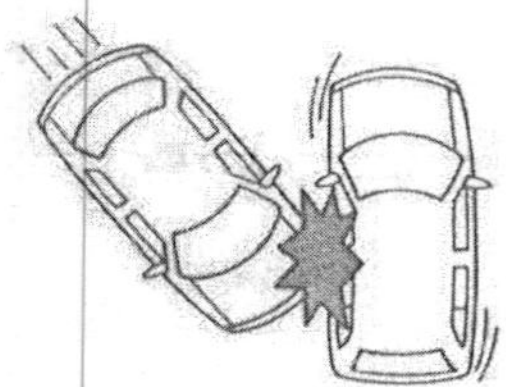

**The vehicle is rolled or flipped**

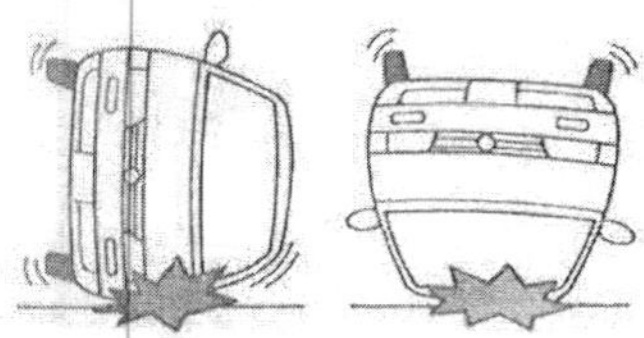

# ABS (ANTI-LOCK BRAKE SYSTEM)

When braking sharply on slippery roads and on snowy roads, the tyres may lock and skid. In this situation, ABS is a system that electronically controls the brake hydraulics and prevents this type of tyre locking, improving the stability of the vehicle and making it easier to avoid obstacles when steering.

No special operation is needed, but be careful about following things:

- There may be motor sounds form the engine bay when starting the engine or shortly after starting the engine. This is normal.
- When the ABS activates, you may hear a sound and feel vibrations in the brake pedal, the steering wheel and the vehicle body. This is not a fault.

- On uneven, gravel or snowy roads, the braking distance may be longer than vehicles without ABS. Reduce speed and maintain an adequate following distance.
- ABS is first and foremost a system that helps the driver's braking on all road surface. It does not provide an excuse for dangerous or careless driving. Take particular care when driving on slippery surfaces.

## ABS WARNING LIGHT

The ABS warning light will turn on when the ignition is turned ON, and then turn off when the engine is started.
If the light does not come on when the ignition is turned ON, or turns on while driving, there may be a fault with the ABS system. Contact your Nissan dealer to have it checked immediately.

## CORNER & BACK SONAR

The corner and back sonar informs the distance between an obstacle and the vehicle to the driver with a buzzer. This function is useful when parking the vehicle in a garage or parallel parking.

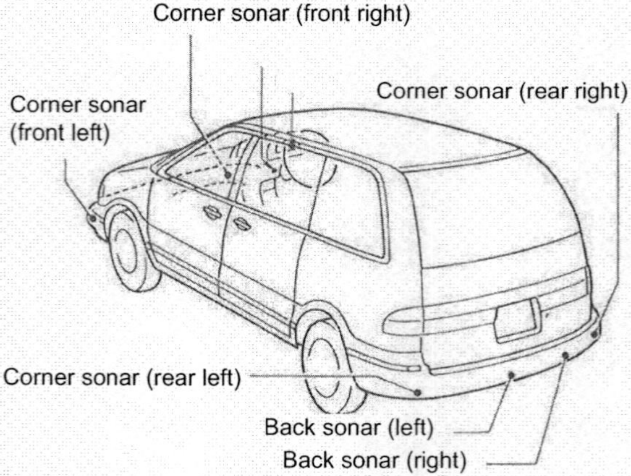

## HOW TO USE THE CORNER SONAR

The ignition must be in the ON position. Press the sonar switch. A short buzzer will sound and the operation light will be displayed.

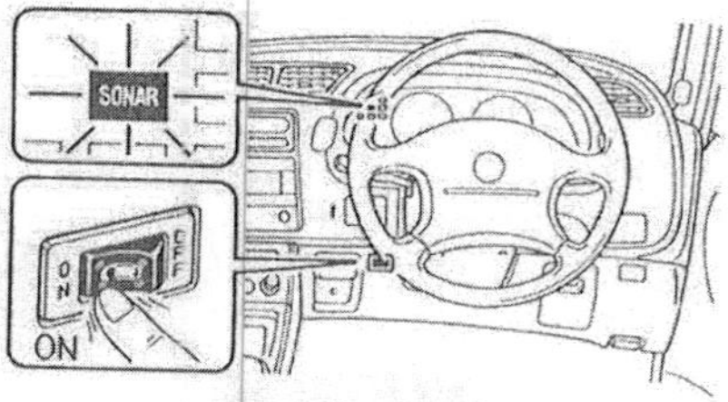


Corner sonar will operate when the vehicle speed is approximately less than 10km/h.

## HOW TO USE THE BACK SONAR

The ignition must be in the ON position. When the shift lever is placed into the "R" position, a short buzzer will sound and the back sonar will operate.

Caution:

- Detection range of the sonar is limited to the coloured area as shown in the diagram below. Make sure to check around the vehicle while reversing.

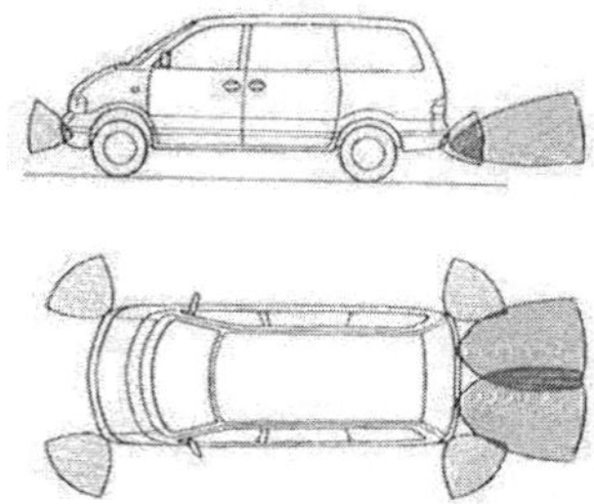

- Do not place any accessories in the detection area.
- If a long buzzer sounds when the switch is pressed or the shift lever is placed in the "R" position, there is possibly a fault with the sonar device. Contact your Nissan dealer to have the device checked as soon as possible.

Advice:

In the following cases the sonar device may not operate correctly:

- When ice, snow, mud etc. is adhered to the sensor.
- When the sensor is covered by hands.
- Extremely cold or hot condition.
- When objects that generates ultrasonic wave such as horn sound, motorbike engine etc. has come close to the vehicle.
- When raining hard, rain has sprayed on the sesor.
- When the vehicle power supply voltage has decreased.

## SONAR BUZZER

The buzzer sound is different depending on the distance between the vehicle and the obstacles.

### Corner sonar

| The distance between the vehicle and the obstacle | Buzzer sound |
|---|---|
| 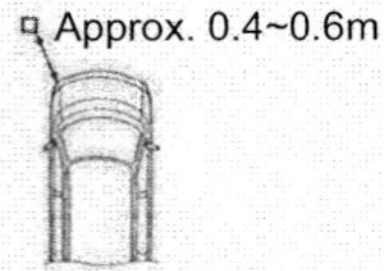  | Pip, pip, pip (short & fast) |
| 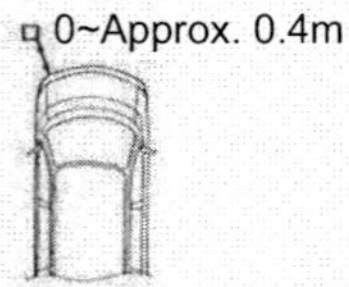  | Peeeep (continuous) |

A buzzer will sound from below the steering wheel when obstacles are detected.

| The distance between the vehicle and the obstacle | Buzzer sound |
|---|---|
| Approx. 0.8~1.5m 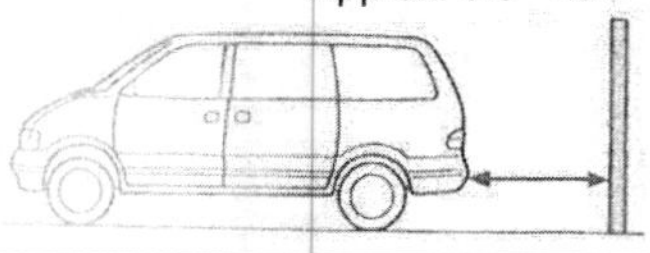 | Pee, pee (slow) |
| Approx. 0.4~0.8m 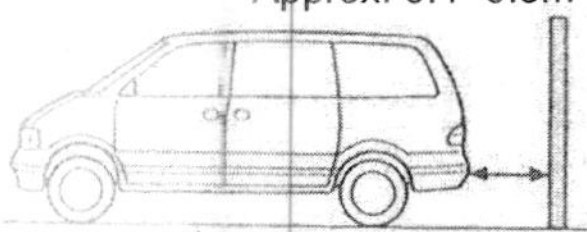 | Pip, pip, pip (short & fast) |
| 0~Approx. 0.4 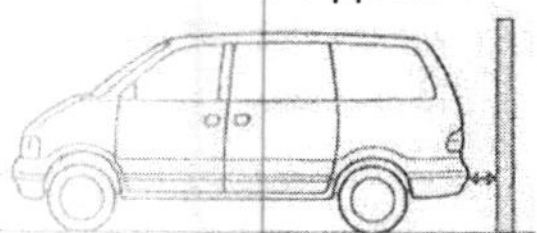 | Peeeep (continuous) |

The buzzer sill sound from the second seat when an obstacle is detected from behind vehicle.

Advice:

The device may not detect the following obstacles:

- Thin objects such as wire and rope etc.
- Objects that absorb sound waves such as cotton, sponge, snow etc.
- Low obstacles.
- The device does not detect objects below the bumper.
- The corner only detects obstacles on the corner of the vehicle.
- Do not use this device to measure the distance between your vehicle and the vehicle in front.
- A buzzer will sound continuously when there is a fault with the sensor. Have the device checked by Nissan dealer.

# REMOTE CONTROL ENTRY

It is possible to lock and unlock all doors form approximately 1 meter away from the vehicle using a remote control.

Advice:

- Always make sure the doors have been locked after using the remote for locking.
- The remote control has a water repellent surface, but to protect the electric parts, do not spill water on the remote control. If any water does get on the remote control, wipe it up straight away.
- It is possible to obtain up to 4 remote controls for your vehicle. See your Nissan dealer for details.

## LOCKING / UNLOCKING THE ALL DOORS

Press the door lock button to lock all doors.
Press the door unlock button to unlock all doors.

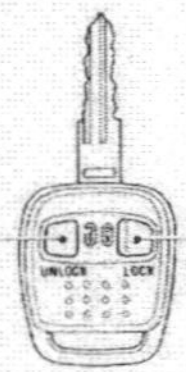


Note:

In the following circumstances the remote control will not operate.

- When the key is still in the ignition.
- When the door is not completely shut.
- When the distance between the vehicle and the remote control is too great.
- When the remote control battery is running out.

# CHANGING THE BATTERY

When the remote device will not operate as a result of the battery running out, change the battery according to following the procedure.

1. Use a driver to open the lid.

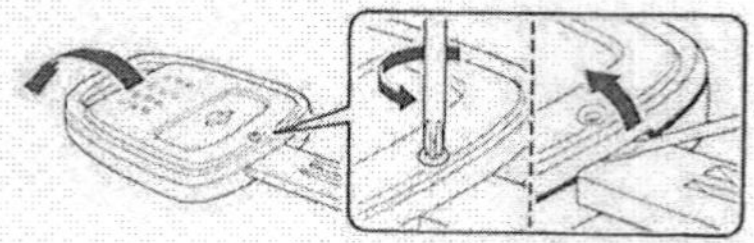

2. Take out the battery, and place a new battery in the compartment, with the battery's positive (+) side facing the lid. (use a CR1620 lithium battery)

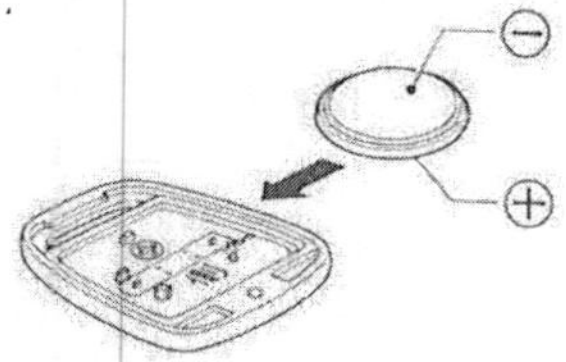

3. Follow the step for opening the lid in reverse order to close the lid securely.

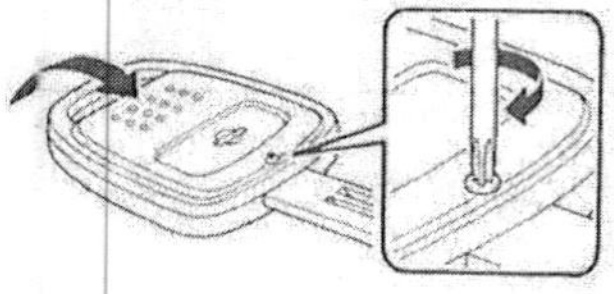

Advice:

- Do not touch the inside of the device, as it may damage it.
- When replacing the battery, take care that there is no dirt or oil on it.

## IF YOU LOSE YOUR REMOTE CONTROL

If you lose your remote control, contact Nissan as soon as possible.

Follow the procedures below to unable the remote control device to operate:

1. Close all doors and lock all doors.
2. Insert the spare key and pull out the key and insert the key again 6 times in 10 seconds.
3. Turn the key to "ACC" position.
4. Open the driver's seat door.

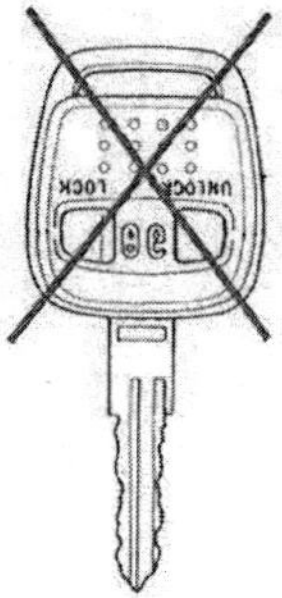

# EMERGENCIES

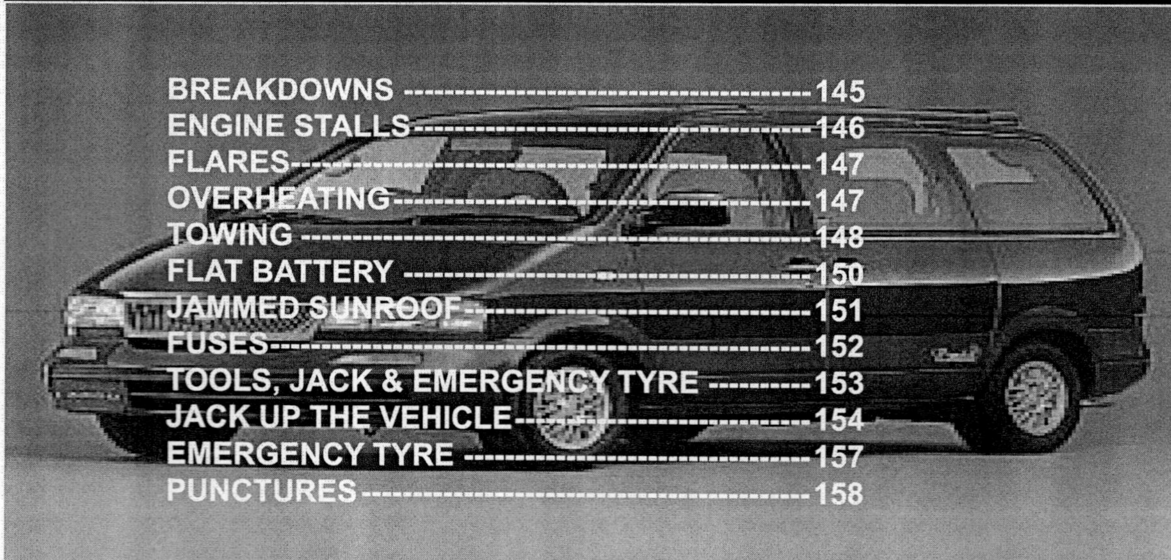



## NISSAN LARGO

## Breakdown on roads

1. Move the vehicle to the side of the road and turn on the hazard light to warn other drivers.

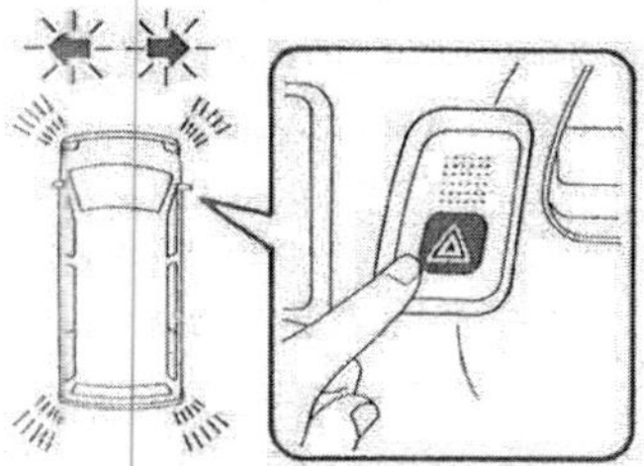

2. On highways or motorways, a hazard sign must be placed at the rear of the vehicle (required by law in Japan).

3. Passengers must not stay in the vehicle. Move to a safe place on the side of the road.

3. After ensuring safety, call for assistance.

## Engine stops while driving

1. Press the brake pedal hard as the break will be less effective because the brake booster is not working.
2. Operate the steering wheel steadily as the power of the power steering will not work.

## If you run out of fuel

(Diesel Vehicles)

After refilling, follow the procedure below to remove air from the fuel system.

1. Pump the priming pump up and down until it becomes stiff to move.
2. Turn the ignition to start the engine.
   If the engine is not rotating smoothly, rev the accelerator once or twice.

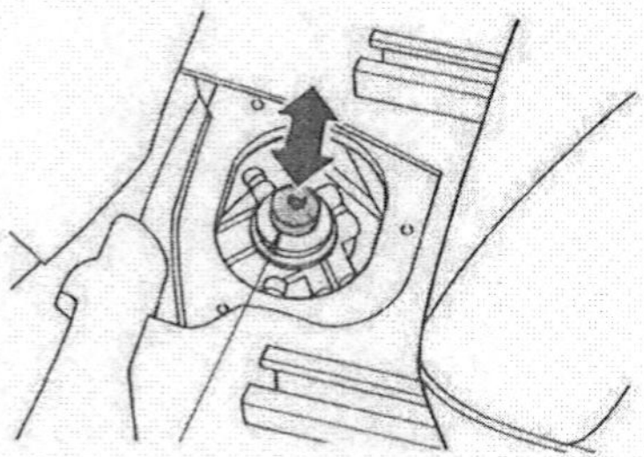

Priming Pump

Note:

If the engine does not start even after following the procedure, have it checked by your Nissan dealer.

## If the engine stalls on a railway crossing or intersection

1. Do not panic. Try to start the engine again.
2. If the engine will not restart, ask passengers or people close by to help push the vehicle to a safe place. Place shift lever in **N**.

If you cannot move the vehicle off the railway crossing, start the flare and let the train know immediately. Push the emergency button of the railway crossing.

# FLARES

1. Remove the flare from its holder under the glove box.

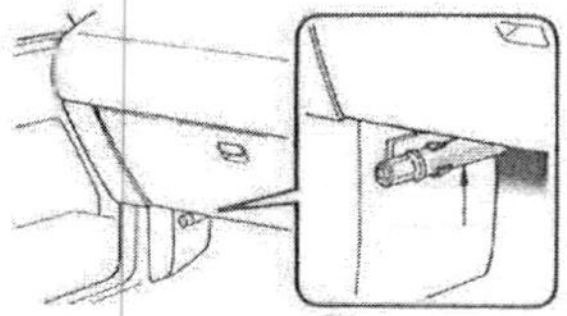


2. Remove the flare from its casting by turning while pulling out

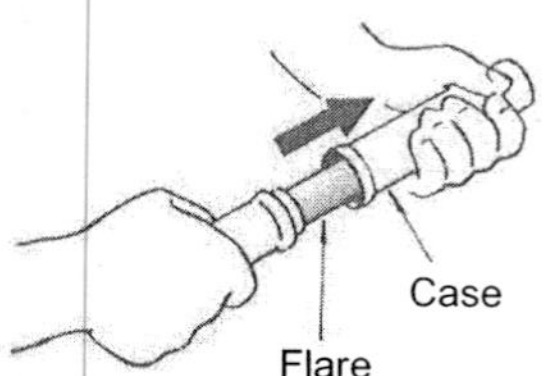


3. Strike the end of the flare with the end of the case to start the flare.

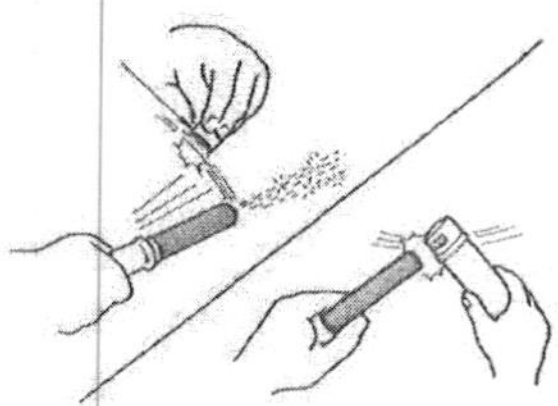

Cautions:

- Do not use a flare in a tunnel as this will reduce vision and may cause other vehicles to collide. Use hazard lights instead.
- Do not use the flare near any flammable materials.
- Purchase a new flare from Nissan before the expiry date displayed on the existing flare expires.

# OVERHEATING

1. If the needle of the water temperature meter goes up to the H zone, the engine is overheating. Stop the vehicle in a safe place immediately.
2. Leave the engine running, and open the bonnet to ventilate the engine. If the radiator fan is not working, turn off the engine immediately.

3. Turn off the engine once the needle of the water temperature meter has dropped. Once the engine has cooled sufficiently, checked the coolant level. Opening the cap when the engine is not cooled sufficiently will allow the hot steam and water to escape, possibly resulting in scalding.

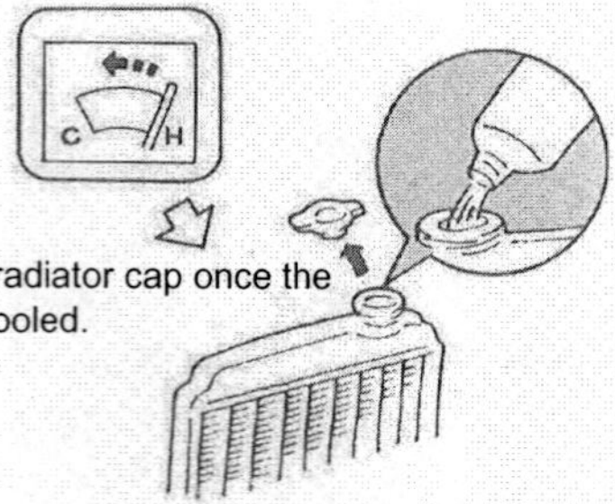


Remove the radiator cap once the engine has cooled.

4. If the coolant is low, refill the radiator tank with coolant.

5. Have the vehicle checked by your Nissan dealer if the vehicle frequently overheats while there is nothing wrong with the coolant or fan belt etc.

# BEING TOWED

1. Attach a rope to the towing hook on both vehicles.

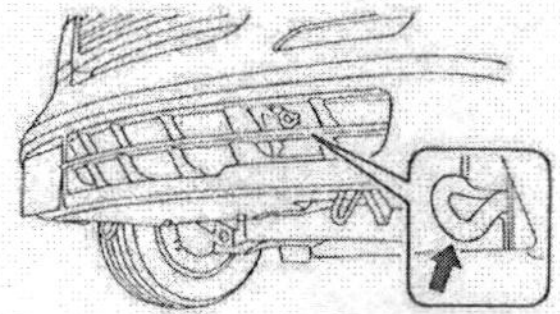

If using a U bend hook, take care not to damage the bumper. Use it as shown in the diagram below.

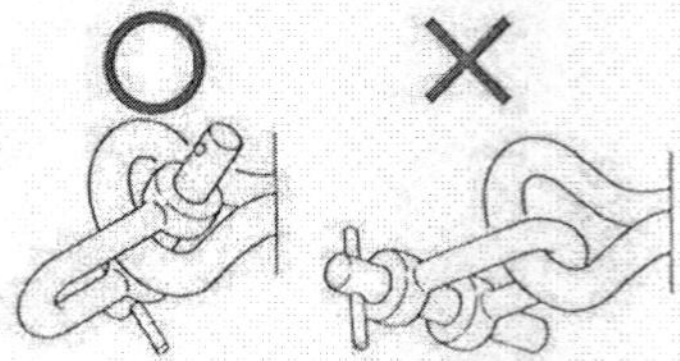

2. Place a white cloth larger than $0.3m^2$ in the centre of the rope.

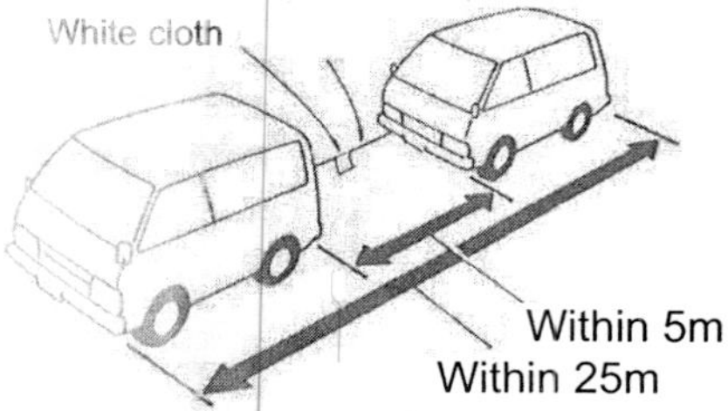


3. Place the shift lever in the **N** position, and turn the ignition to ACC or ON.

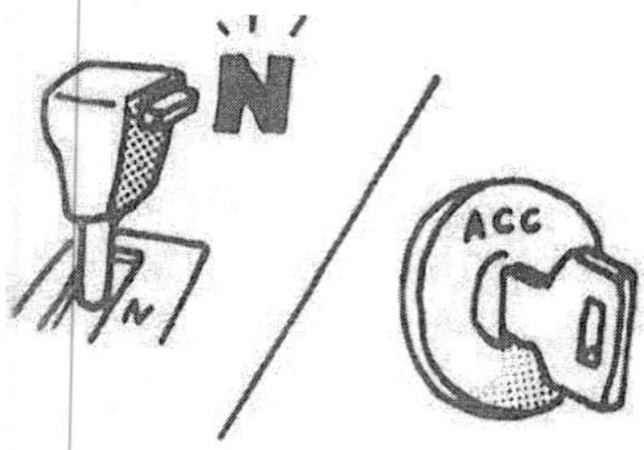


4. While being towed, try to keep the rope tight between the two vehicles (no slack). Pay attention to the brake light of the vehicle in front.

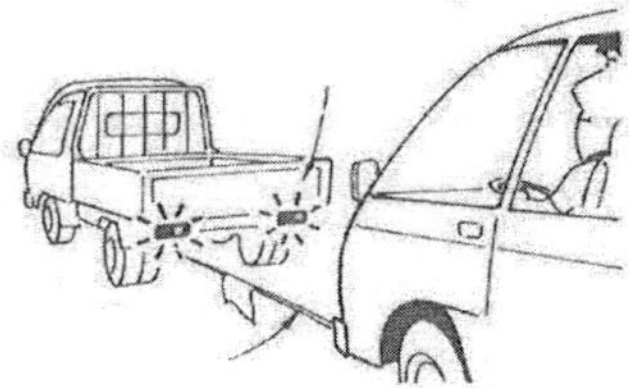

Caution

- When the engine is stopped, the brake booster will not operate and the brakes will not be as effective. Press the brake pedal firmly. Be careful with the steering wheel as it will be very heavy.

## TOWING HOOKS

- Do not attempt to tow a vehicle heavier than your own vehicle.
- Only attache the rope to the towing hook.
- Do not drive the vehicle in a way that will apply a large shock to the towing hook.

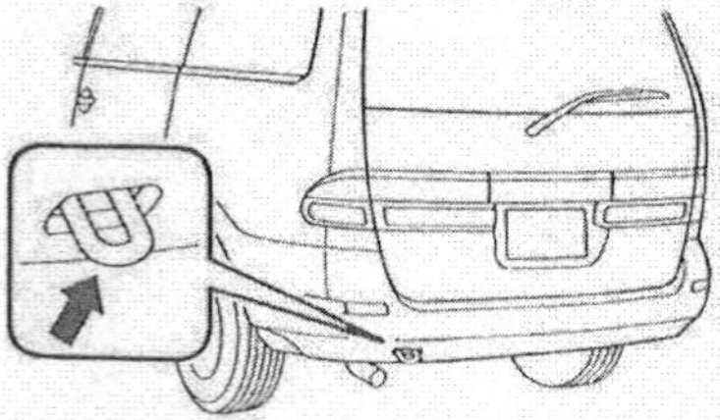

# ELECTRIC SYSTEM PROBLEMS

## Flat battery

A booster cable (sold separately) can be used to connect to another vehicle's battery (12V) to start the engine.

1. Park the other vehicle close enough that the booster cable can reach the battery of both vehicles.

2. Connect the booster cable in the following order. If this order is not followed, a fire may result.

I) Connect the first booster cable to the positive terminal of the flat battery.

II) Connect the first booster cable to the positive terminal of the booster battery.

III) Connect the second booster cable to the negative terminal of the booster battery.
IV) Connect the second booster cable to the engine body (e.g. a bolt).

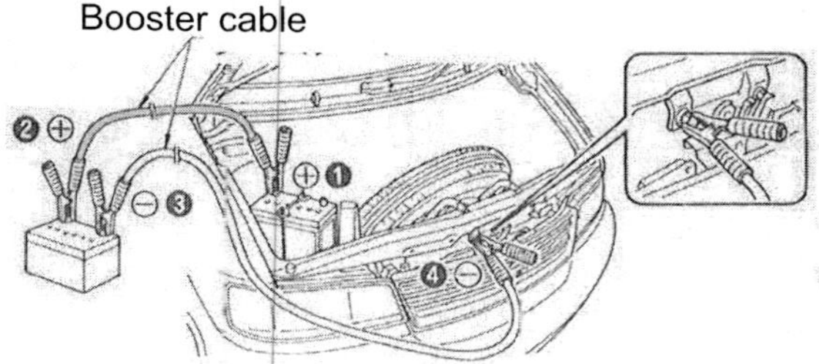


Advice:

- In the IV) step, connect the second booster cable to the engine body (e.g. a bolt) located away from the battery.
- Do not let the booster cable clip touch the vehicle body or any other clips.
- Attach the booster cable clip firmly so it does not come off with the vibrations of the engine when it starts.

3. Start the engine of the booster battery vehicle, and slightly raise engine speed.
4. Turn off the headlights and the air conditioner and start the engine of your vehicle. Remove the booster cable in reverse order.
5. Even after the engine has started, wait a while before using the air conditioner or the audio system.
   Have it checked by your Nissan dealer as soon as possible.

## JAMMED SUNROOF

1. Remove the lens ("a" as shown in the diagram next page).
2. Remove the cap ("c" as shown in the diagram next page). Insert a flat-blade screwdriver between the switch and interior mirror ("d" as shown in the diagram next page) to remove the cap.
3. Remove the switch. Remove the attaching screw (4) ("e" as shown in the diagram next page) with a phillips-head screw driver.

4. Tighten the motor rotor attaching screw. Tighten the motor rotor attaching screw clockwise with a phillips-head screw driver. ("f" as showing in the diagram below)
5. Rotate the motor rotor to close the sunroof. Insert the edge of the crank handle into the motor rotor and turn clockwise to close the front roof. ("g" as showing in the diagram below)

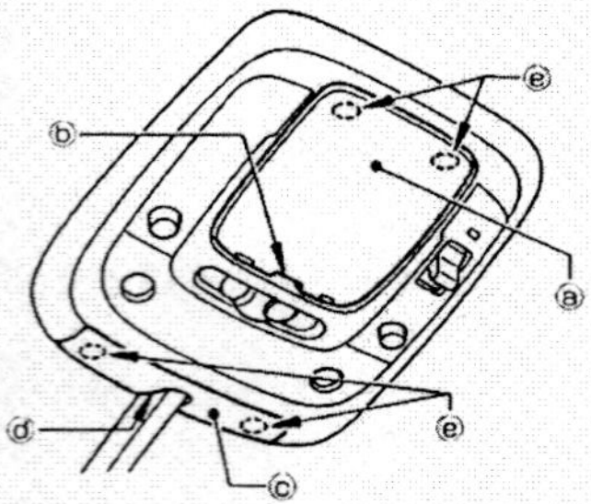


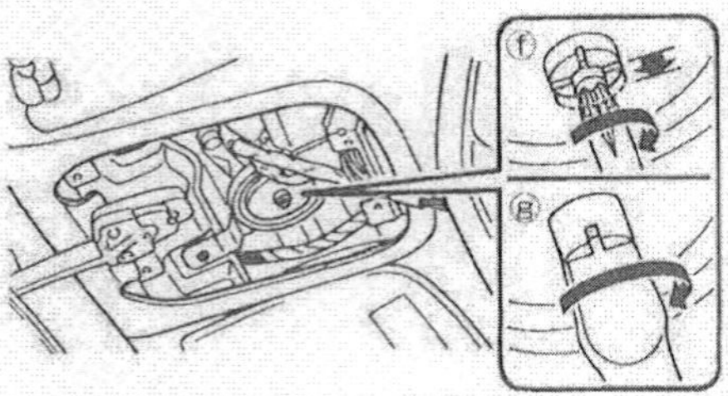


# REPLACING FUSES

When lights will not turn on, or electrical devices will not operate, there may be a blown fuse or bulbs.

1. Place the ignition in the LOCK position. The fuse boxes are located on the bottom right of the meter and in the engine bay.

**The bottom right of the meter**

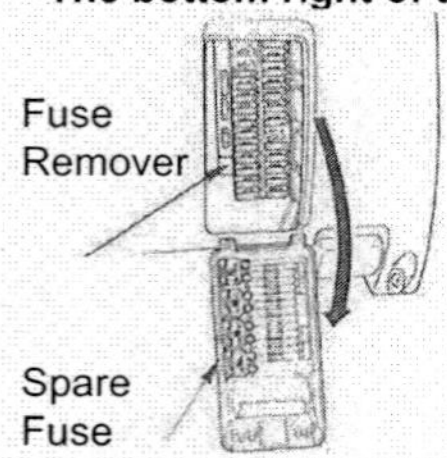


**In the engine bay**

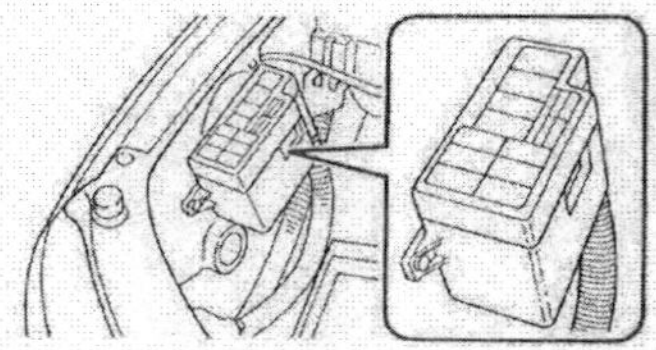

2. Open the fuse box. Remove the fuse with the fuse remover and check whether it is blown.

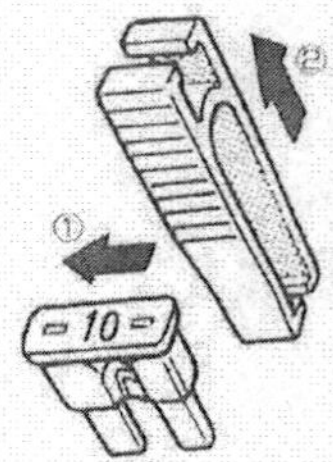

3. If the fuse is blown , replace with a fuse of the same amperage.

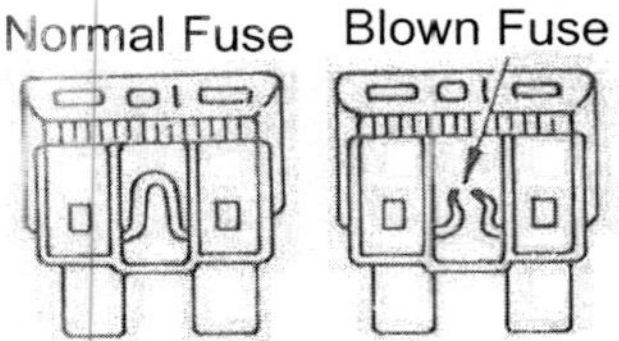


## TYRE PROBLEMS

### Tools, jack & emergency tyre

The tools, jack and emergency tyre are located in the boot. Return the tools and jack to their allocated positions after use.

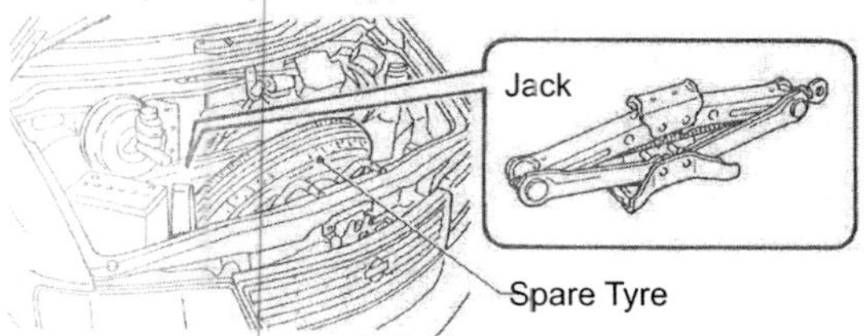


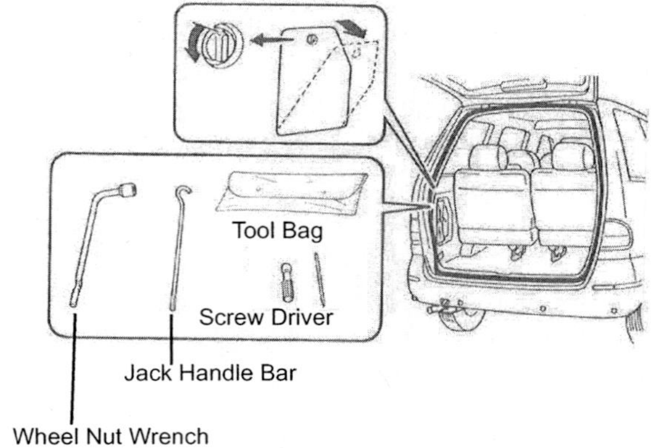


## HAZARD SIGN

There is a space to house the hazard sign located left side of the third seat.

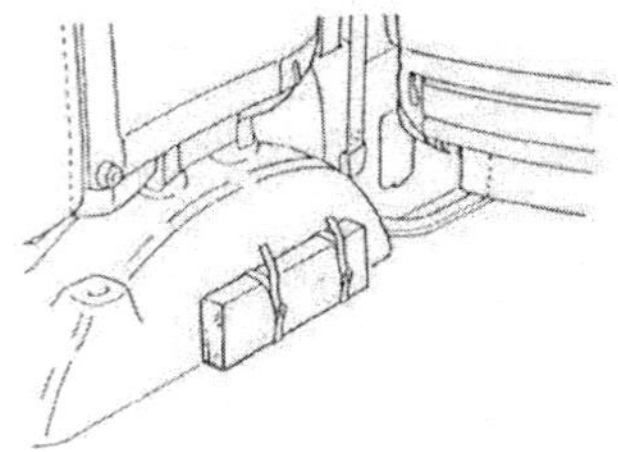

Caution:

- Return the tools and jack to their allocated positions after use.
- Only use the jack supplied with the vehicle for replacing or rotating tyres, or fitting tyre chains.

## Jack up procedure

### To take out the jack

1. Pull out the cover upward to remove it.

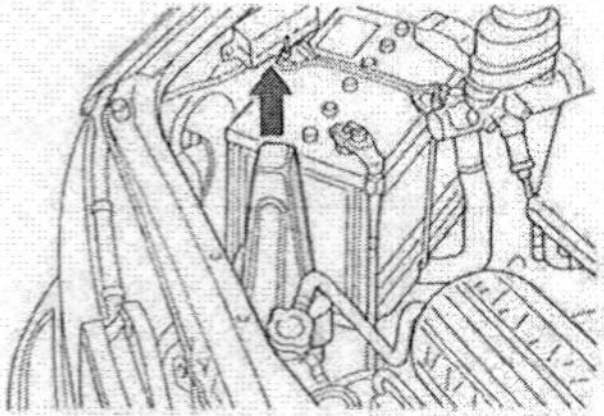

2. Turn the jack to the left to remove it.

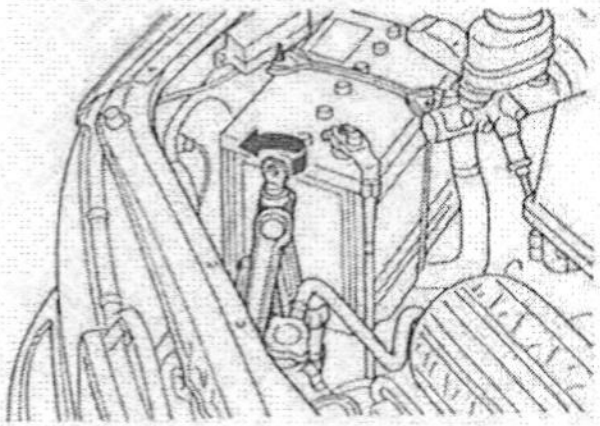

### To house the jack

1. To house the jack into the bracket with the rotating knob facing upward.

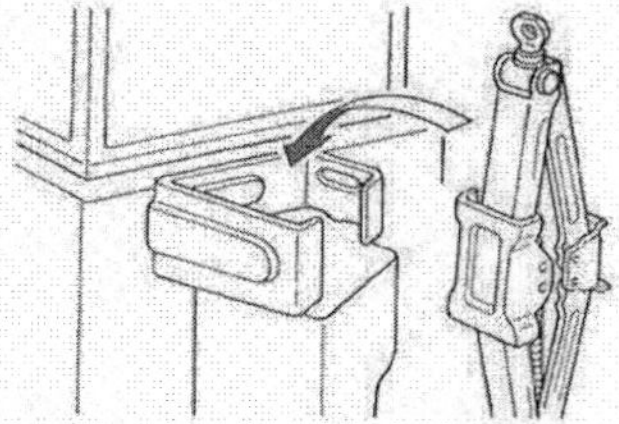

2. Turn the rotating knob to the right to fix the jack.

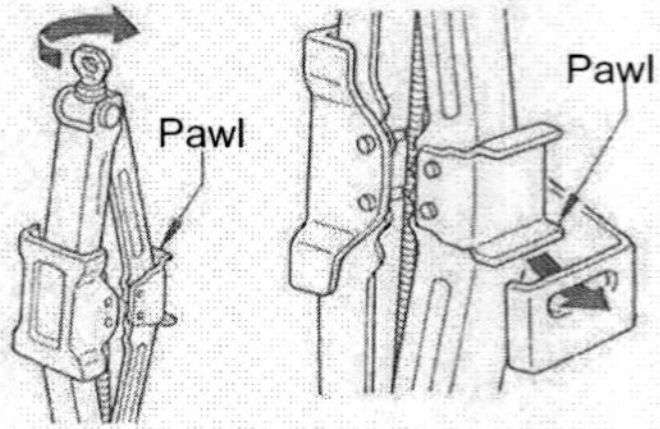


Make sure the bottom pawl is in the hole of the bracket.

3. Cover the jack with the cover. Make sure the "JACK" mark on the cover positions as showing in the diagram below.

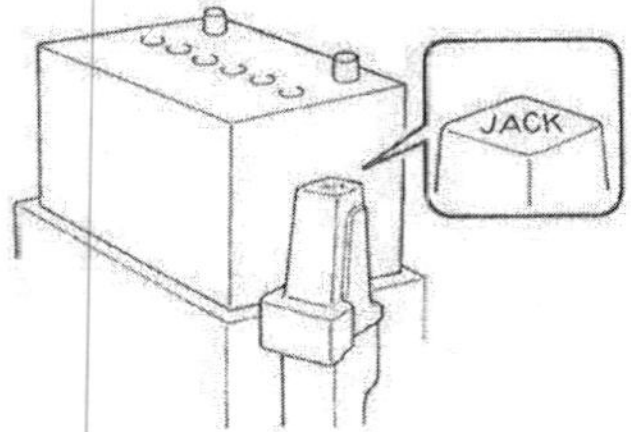


## To set the jack

Attach the jack handle bar and the wheel nut wrench to the jack as shown in the diagram.

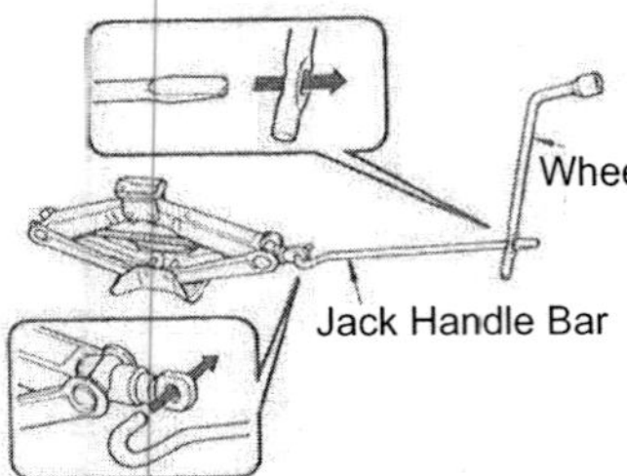


## Jack setting position

Set the jack as showing in the diagram below..

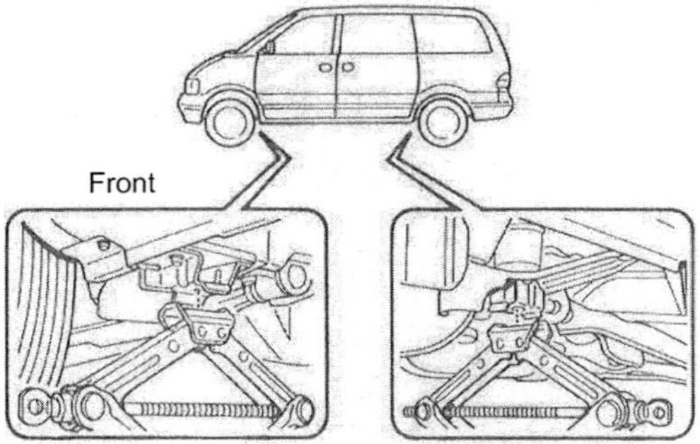


Caution:

- Do not under any circumstance go underneath the vehicle while it is jacked up. If the jack slips serious injuries could result.
- Only use the jack from your own vehicle. Do not use a jack from another vehicle.
- Only use a jack for changing a tyre or fitting tyre chain.
- Do not attempt to jack the vehicle up on soft ground. The jack could fall and cause a serious accident.

- Before jacking up the vehicle, apply the parking brake, and place the shift lever in "P".
- Use a stone or a piece of wood as a wheel stopper to secure the vehicle.
- Do not place anything above or below the jack.

## JACK UP PROCEDURE

1. Stop the engine and apply the parking brake. Place the shift lever in "P". Remove all passengers and luggage from the vehicle.

   Place the jack on the flat and hard ground.

2. Place a wheel stopper under the tyre diagonally opposite to the tyre that is to be jacked up.

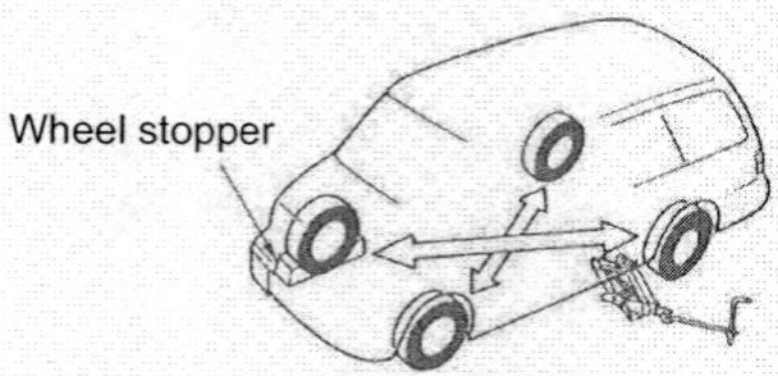


3. Turn the jack with your hand until the flange of the jack reaches the height of the jack groove.

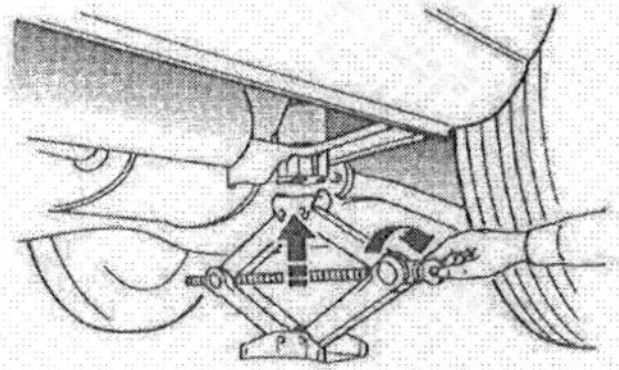

4. Turn the jack handle bar until the tyre lifts off the ground slightly.

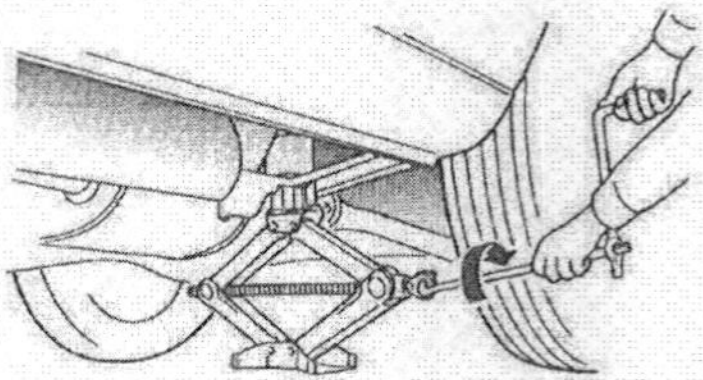

# EMERGENCY TYRE

The emergency tyre is a temporary tyre that is to be used only while the puncture is being fixed. Observe the following points.

- The emergency tyre equipped in your vehicle should only be used for this vehicle. Do not place the emergency tyre from your vehicle on other vehicles, or use emergency tyres from other vehicles on your vehicle.
- When the emergency tyre is fitted to the vehicle, the vehicle should not be driven over 80km/h. The emergency tyre should only be used when one of the standard tyres has a puncture. The punctured tyre should be repaired and replaced as soon as possible.
- Do not fit tyre chains to the emergency tyre. If a front tyre has a puncture in snowy or icy conditions, do not replace the front tyre with the emergency tyre, instead replace the front tyre with a rear tyre, and that rear tyre with the spare tyre.
- Replace the emergency tyre if it is worn.

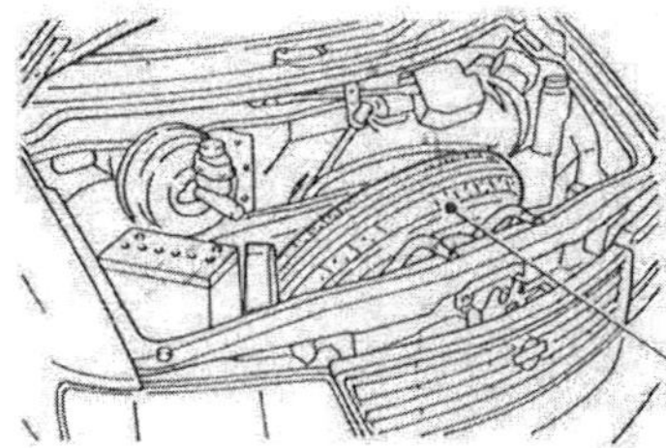


## REMOVING THE EMERGENCY TYRE

1. Insert the bonnet stay into the stay hole to secure the bonnet.

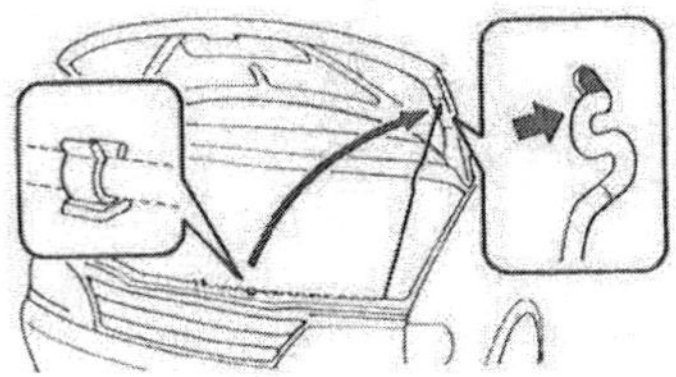

2. Loosen the cramp by turning it to the left. The cramp located the middle part of the tyre. Lift up the tyre to remove it.

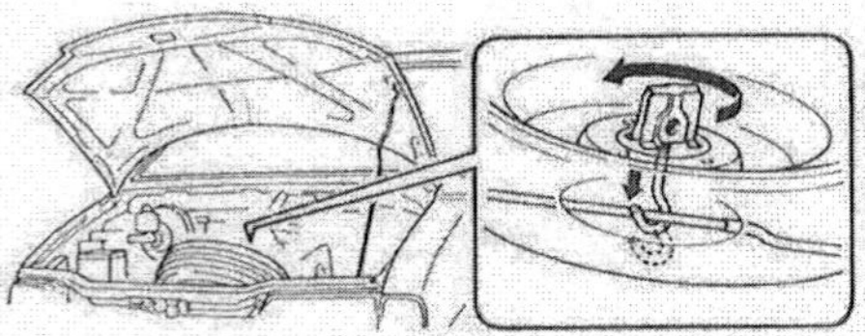

To house the emergency tyre, follow the steps for removing the tyre in reverse order.

# PUNCTURES

## To change the tyre

1. Without creating a traffic hazard, move the vehicle to a safe level place. Remove all passengers and any heavy luggage from the vehicle. Turn on the hazard lights, and if necessary place a hazard sign behind the vehicle.

2. Stop the engine, apply the parking brake and prepare the emergency tyre, tools and jack.

3. Turn the jack with your hand until the jack has reached the height of the jack-up points.

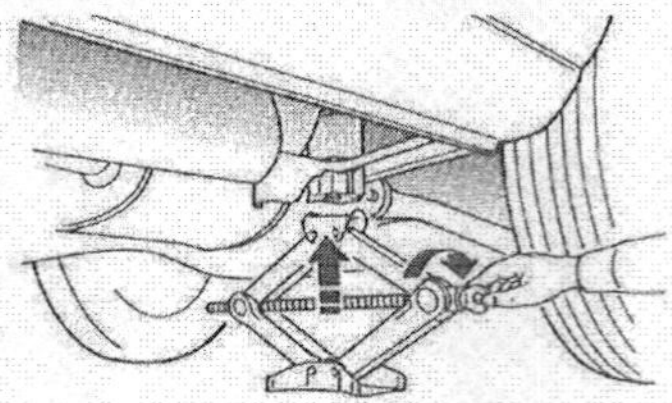

4. Cover the jack handle with a cloth and prise off the wheel cover (centre cap) taking care not to scratch it.

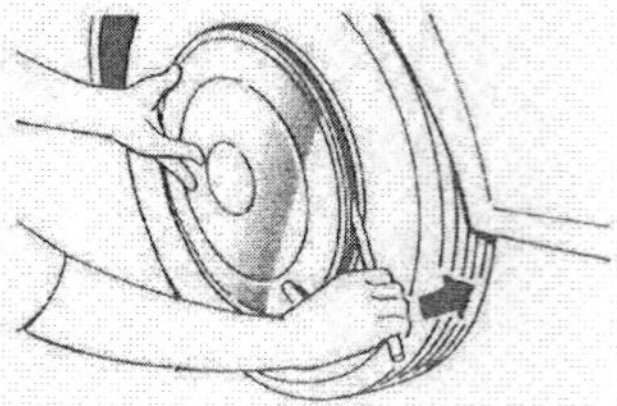

5. Using the wheel nut wrench, turn each nut in an anticlockwise direction once to loosen the nuts.

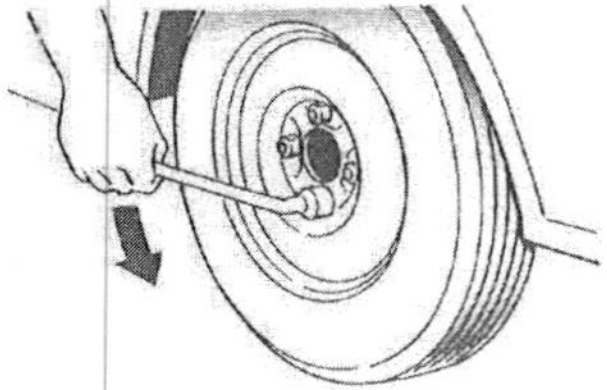

6. Jack up the tyre.

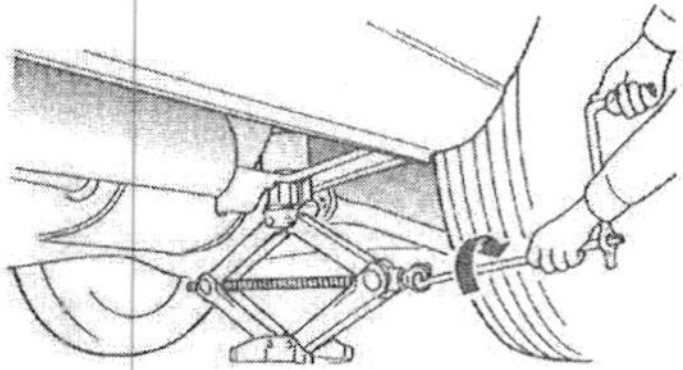

7. Remove the nuts and take off the punctured tyre. Place the tyre on the ground wheel side up.

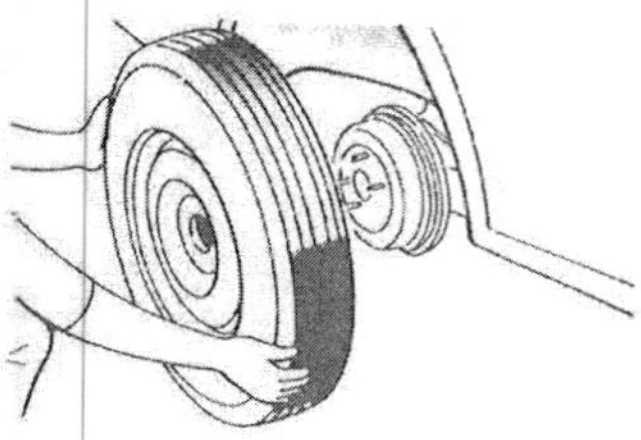

8. Tighten the nuts clockwise until the tapered part of the nut is lightly resting on the wheel hole seat.

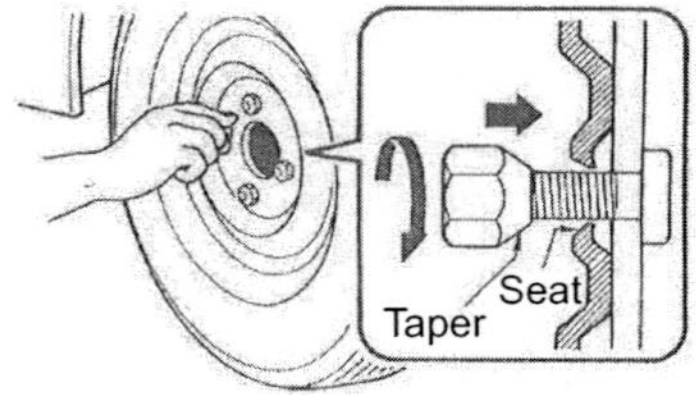


9. Using the wheel nut wrench, tighten the nuts 2-3 times in the order shown in the diagram below.

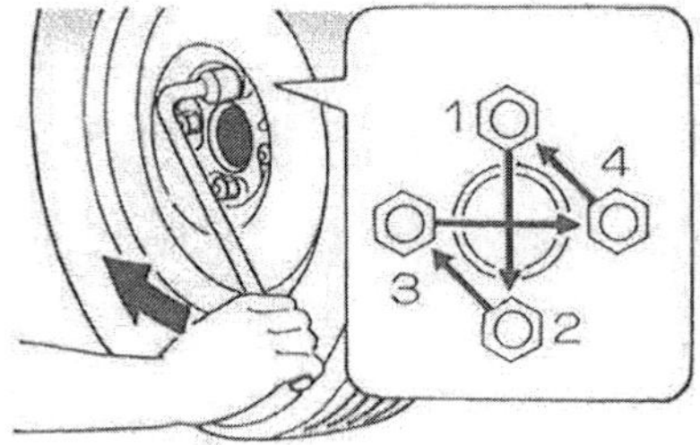

10. Lower the jack. After the tyre has reached the ground, tighten the nuts fully. Tightening torque: 10-12kg-m

Caution:

- When lowering the jack, grip the jack handle and jack handle bar firmly with both hands to prevent them from slipping out and causing an unexpected accident.

Advice:

- Do not depress the wheel nut wrench with your foot to tighten the nuts as this may over tighten the nuts and damage the bolts.

11. Replace the wheel cover (centre cap). Align the wheel cover with the air valve. (The wheel cover can not be fitted onto the emergency tyre).

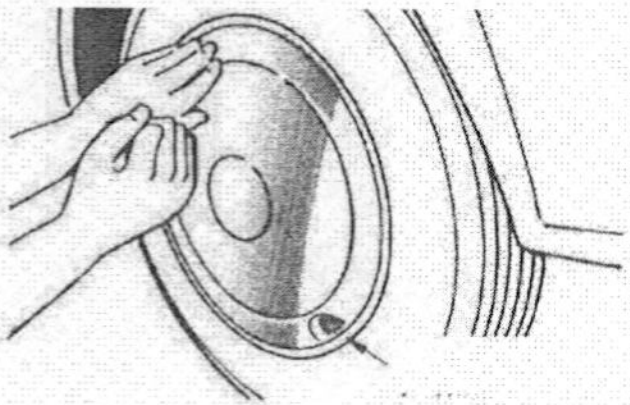

# WET WEATHER DRIVING & WINTER / SUMMER CARE

## NISSAN LARGO

# WET WEATHER DRIVING

## To remove window fogging

1. Turn on the air conditioner.
2. Select or .
3. Select the fresh air option.

## To remove rear window fog

To remove the rear window fog, use the rear window defogger switch.

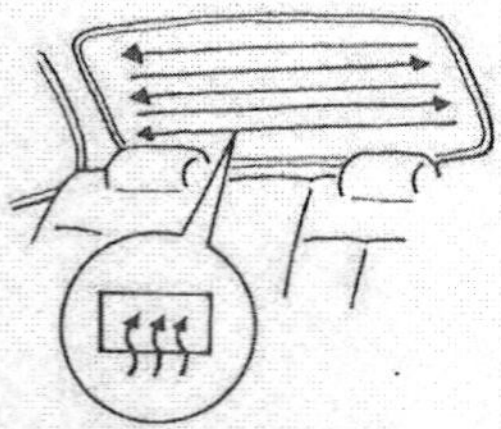

## To clean the windshield

Use glass cleaner to clean the wind shield. If the windshield is greasy, the lights of approaching vehicles may reflect, making it difficult to see clearly.

## When the wiper blades leave marks on the windshield

If the old wiper blades are worn or there is something between the blades and the wind shield, marks will appear on the windshield. Replace with new blades if the old blades are worn.

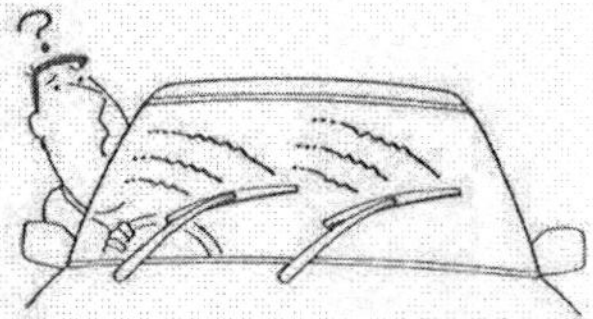

## When raindrops hang on the mirrors

Coat the mirrors with genuine Nissan glass coat and wipe with a dry cloth, so as to keep the mirrors clear in rainy condition.

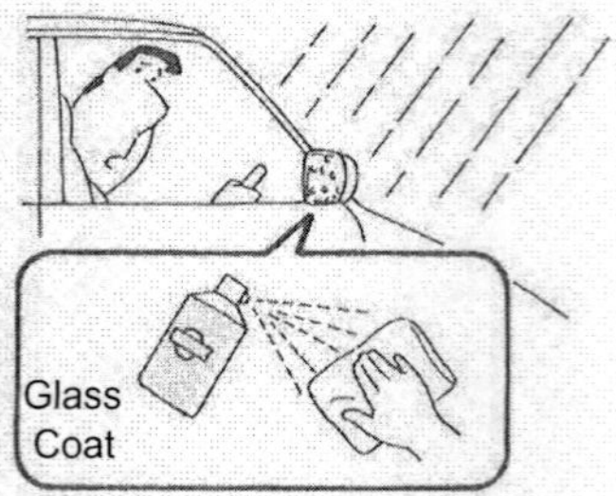

# SUMMER DRIVING

## To prevent overheating

- Check the fluid level in the radiator regularly. If the fluid is used up too soon, have it checked by your Nissan dealer.
- If the needle of the water temperature gauge approaches the H zone, stop the vehicle in a safe place and rest for some time.

## When parking in the sun

- Cover the seat and steering wheel with whitish towels or clothes to prevent the temperature from going up too high.
- Do not leave cassette, camera, video or others inside the vehicle.

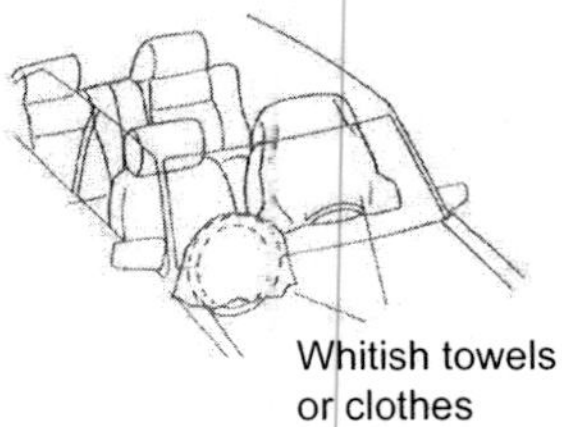


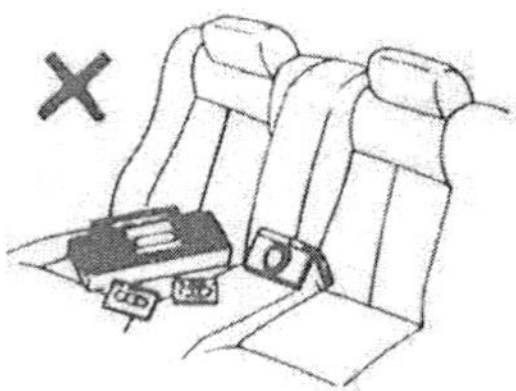

## After driving by seaside

After driving by the seaside, the vehicle is covered with salt. Wash the vehicle as soon as possible to prevent rust. Remember to wash the tyre area

Warning:

- Do not leave children or dependants in the vehicle alone. If the vehicle is parked in direct sunlight for a long time, the inside of the vehicle may overheat and cause heat exhaustion.

Caution:

- If the vehicle is parked in direct sunlight for a long time the resin and metal parts may become very hot and cause burns if they are touched. Be particularly careful with yong children.

- Do not leave cans of soft drinks in a vehicle parked in direct sunlight as they may explode.

## Check Air Conditioner Before Summer

Check that the air conditioner is operating properly before the summer months. The air conditioning will be ineffective if the condenser is blocked or the refrigerant gas is insufficient.

## Let hot air escape from the vehicle

Open the windows and let hot air escape from the vehicle before turning the air conditioning on.

## Avoid over-using the air conditioner

Be careful not to have the air conditioner set too cold. Passengers who find it too cold may need to use a blanket on their knees etc.

## WINTER PREPARATION

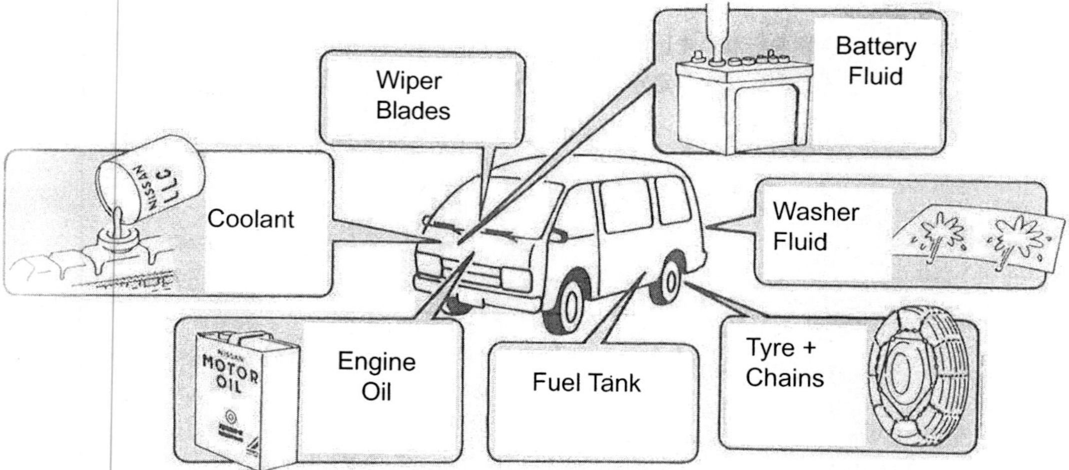

## Engine Oil

Replace the existing engine oil with oil that is suitable to the climate the vehicle is being used in. Refer to the table below.

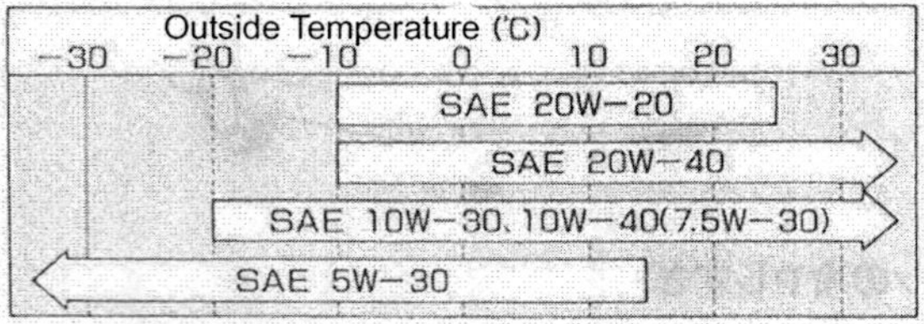


It is recommended to use Nissan genuine engine oil 7.5W-30, 10W-30, 10W-40, 20W-40.

## Coolant Concentration

To prevent the coolant form freezing, change the mixture of antifreeze and coolant to best suit the temperature the vehicle is being used in.

| Antifreeze Concentration | Freezing Temperature |
|---|---|
| 30% | Approx. -15°C |
| 50% | Approx. -35°C |

Advice:

- We recommend you use Nissan Genuine Long Life coolant (LLC).
- Set the coolant concentration at 50%.
- For information on checking the coolant concentration, please ask your Nissan dealer.

## Studless Tyre, Tyre Chains

- When replacing the tyres with studless tyres, ensure that all four tyres are of the same size, brand and pattern.
- We recommend you use Nissan tyre chains that are the correct size for your vehicle.

## Washer Fluid

Dilute the washer fluid in accordance with mixture ratios for the various temperatures shown in the chart below.

| Climate | Dilution | Freezing Temperature |
|---|---|---|
| Normal Climates | 1 part washer fluid / 2 parts water | Approx.-10°C |
| Cold Winter | 1 part washer fluid / 1 part water | Approx.-20°C |
| Extremely Cold Winter | Only washer fluid | Approx.-30°C |

We recommend you use Nissan Genuine window washer fluid.

Advice:

Do not use the washer switch without washer fluid, as this may result in motor failure.

## Fuel Tank

Use Nissan iceproof to drain the fuel tank.

## Cold Climate Wiper Blades

Cold climate wiper blades are equipped with a rubber cover over the metal areas of the blade to prevent it from freezing to the windscreen.

Use Nissan cold climate wiper blades.

## Broken-type Wiper Arm

The broken-type wiper arm can be worked up. Work up the arm while parking outside in winter to prevent the wiper blades from freezing onto the glass.

Caution:

If the bonnet is opened when the wipers are worked up, the bonnet and the wiper may be damaged.

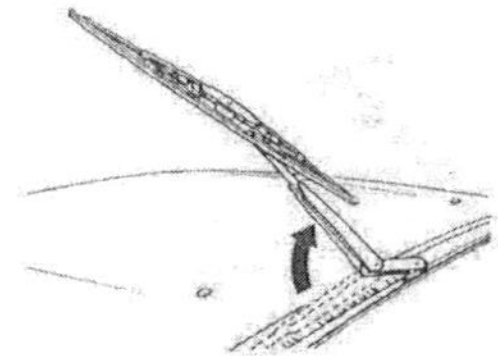

## Battery Fluid

Check the battery fluid to make sure it is between upper and lower limits.

# BEFORE DRIVING

## To Remove Snow

Remove snow from the windscreen before driving. To remove snow, use a plastic scraper. If you try to use the wiper, it will damage the wiper and may scratch the glass.

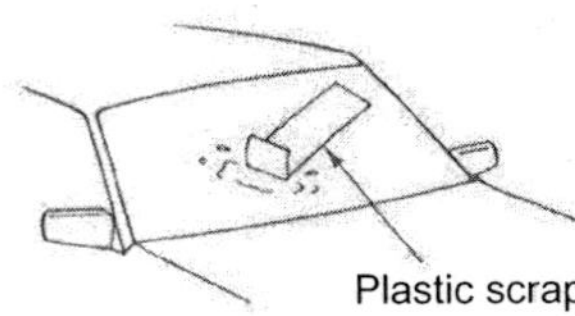

## Ice Buildup around Tyre Area

Ice buildup around the tyre area (brake hose and fender) should be removed carefully without damaging the parts or scratching the vehicle body.

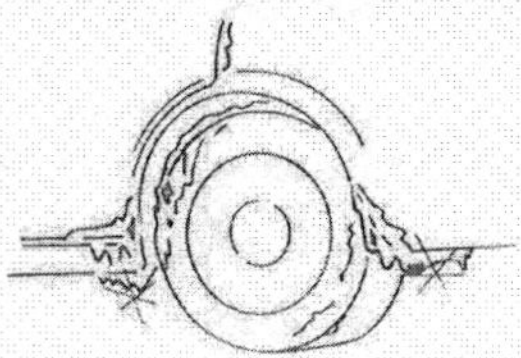

## Frozen Doors

When the doors are frozen shut, the rubber lining around the doors will ripped apart if they are opened by force. It is advised to pour warm water around the frozen areas to melt the ice. The remaining water should be wiped off immediately so that it does not freeze.

## Before Entering the Vehicle

Always wipe off all snow or ice from your shoes to prevent slippery pedals or window fogging.

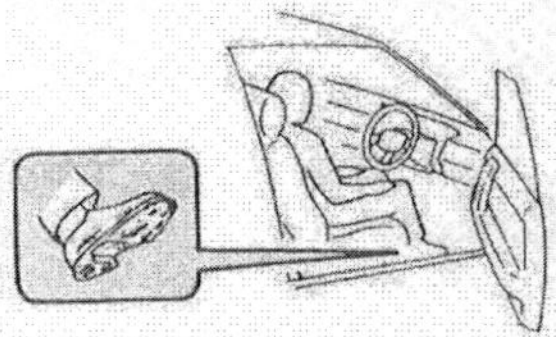

## DRIVING ON SNOWY ROADS

- Drive carefully on snowy roads. Avoid sudden turns, braking and acceleration as these are dangerous.
- If snow accumulated around the brakes freezes, the brakes will not work effectively. From time to time press the brake pedal lightly to check the condition of the brakes and remove any moisture from the brakes.

- If snow that is flicked up while driving builds up behind the fenders, the steering will be negatively affected. Check the ice buildup from time to time so that it does not accumulate to a point where it seriously affects steering in a dangerous way.

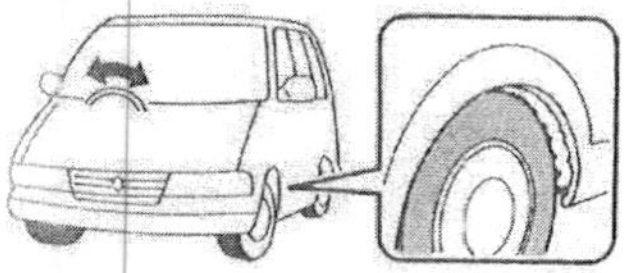

# TYRE CHAINS

## Before Fitting the Tyre Chains

- Fit tyre chains to the front wheels only.
- Always use genuine Nissan tyre chains that fit the size of tyres.
- Stop your vehicle in a safe place on level ground.
- Apply the parking brake and stop the engine. Turn on the hazard lights and if necessary place a hazard sign behind the vehicle.

Advice

- When you have purchased the chains, line them up along the tyre. If they are too long cut them to size.
- Do not drive on roads without snow with chains fitted. The roads may be damaged and the chains will wear quickly and the life-span will be reduced.
- Do not drive a 4WD vehicle on roads without snow with tyre chains fitted. The vehicle mechanic parts may be damages.

## Fitting the Chains

1. To prevent the vehicle from moving, place a wheel stopper or stone behind the rear tyres and jack up the front tyre that you wish to fit the chain to.

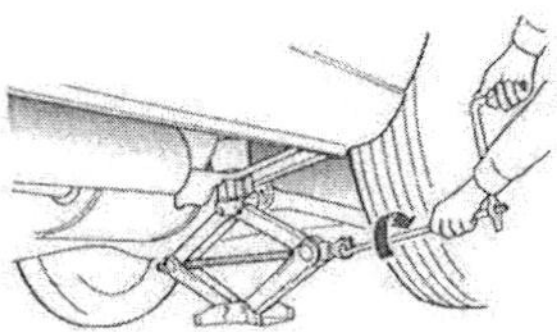

2. Ensure the connector hooks are facing outwards and place the chain over the tyre.

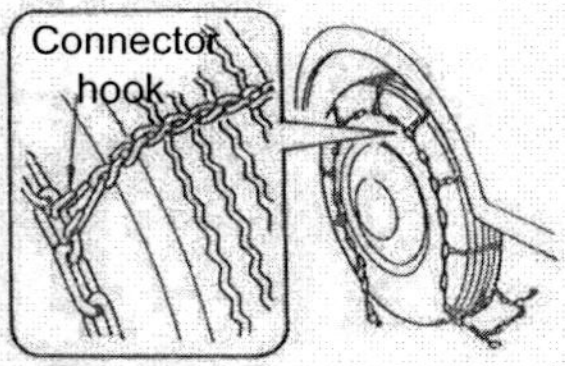


3. Pull both ends of the chain and connect the inside of the chain first , then the outside.

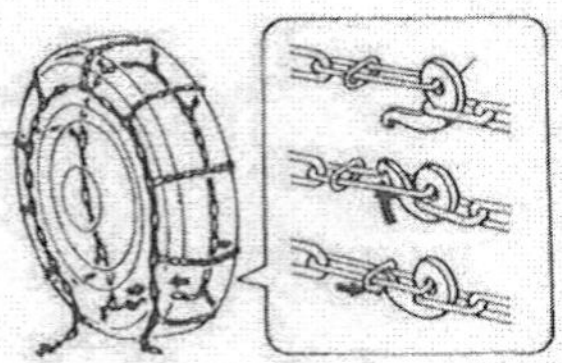


4. Secure the excess chain using wire.

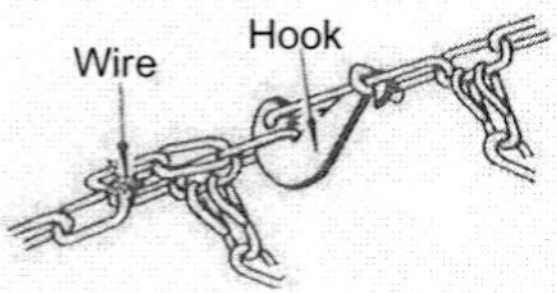


5. Attach the chain band clips to the chain as shown in the diagram below. Ensure the clip is facing outward.

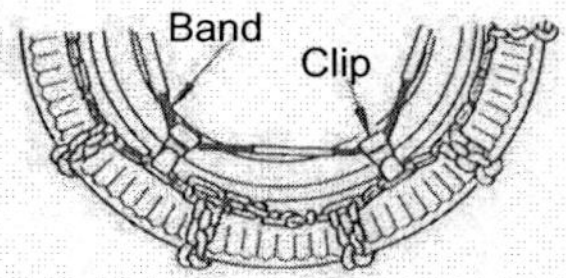


6. After 2-3 minutes of driving, check the tyre chains for slacks. Tighten if necessary. Do not drive over 30km/h with tyre chains fitted.

## Removing the Tyre Chains

1. Remove the chain bands, and remove the hooks from the inside first.
2. Move the vehicle slightly and remove the chains.

## Parking in Snow Country

- When parking for a long time, to prevent the parking brake from freezing, do not apply the parking brake but Place the shift lever in **P** for automatic vehicles, or in **1** or **R** for manual vehicles, and place wheels stoppers under the wheels.

- Do not park with the front of the car against the wind as snow may get into the engine making the engine too cold to start.
- Do not park under eaves or a tree as snow may fall and damage the vehicle.

## After Driving on Snowy Roads

Wash your vehicle, including underneath the vehicle, after driving on roads where ice prevention chemicals are sprayed as those chemicals can corrode your vehicle.

## DIESEL VEHICLE

Diesel freezes at temperatures below -10°C which may block the fuel line. When travelling to cold regions, refuel as soon as possible once you have reached your destination.

| Fuel type | Temperature Range |
|---|---|
| JIS No.2 diesel | -10°C |
| JIS No.3 diesel | -18°C |
| JIS No.3 special diesel | -25°C |

Advice:
JIS No.3 Special diesel should not be used in summer or warm climates as it will cause the engine to stall.

# VEHICLE MAINTENANCE

# NISSAN LARGO

# EXTERIOR CARE

In order to keep the vehicle looking in top condition, the vehicle must be cleaned regularly.

- We recommend you to store the vehicle in a garage or under a roofed area that is well ventilated.
- Wash the vehicle as soon as possible, if it shows so dirt.
- Wax once a month or when the water no longer beads like water droplets on the paint.
- In the following instances, the paint work and the vehicle body or parts could result in damage or corrosion. Clean the vehicle as soon as possible.
  - Driving near the sea.
  - Driving on roads where anti-ice prevention chemicals have been used.
  - When tar, tree sap, bird droppings and dead insects stick to the paint work.
  - Driving in areas where there is a high proportion of soot & smoke, oil, stone, coal and metal particles and chemical substances in the air.
  - When the vehicle is covered in dust or mud etc.

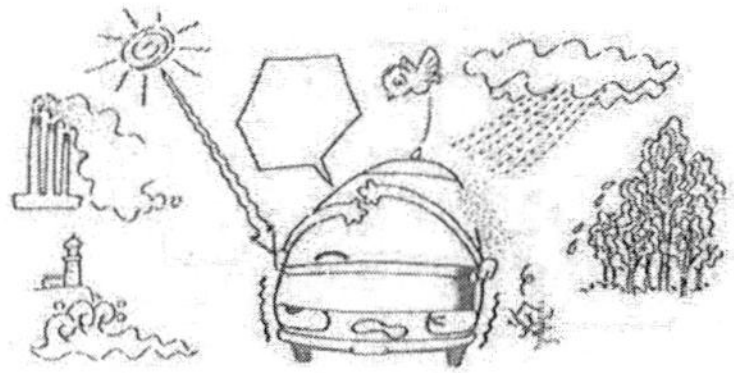

## Washing the Vehicle

1. Spray plenty of water over the vehicle and use a sponge to clean the vehicle, starting first with the upper area of the vehicle, then moving down to the wheel areas and underneath the vehicle to remove dirt and grime.
2. When there is a large amount of dirt and grime on the vehicle body, use body shampoo.
3. Wipe all water droplets off.

Advice

- When washing the vehicle, be careful not to spray water over the electrical areas in the engine bay.
- Do not use wire brushes or other hard brushes that may scratch the paintwork.
- Be careful not to injure hands or fingers when cleaning the underside or wheel areas of the vehicle.

## USING A CAR WASH

### Automatic Car Wash

House door-mirrors and the antenna. The brushes in these car washes are harsh on the paintwork, and may remove the lustre finish.

### High Pressure (Coin) Car Wash

Do not place the nozzle of the hose too close to the windows, as water may be pushed into the vehicle interior.

Advice

- Avoid washing around door glass under high pressure.
- Remove the roof antenna. (GTU-R type vehicles)
- Vehicles with a spoiler may not use car wash, depending on the type of car wash, as the spoiler may hang up on the wash machine.

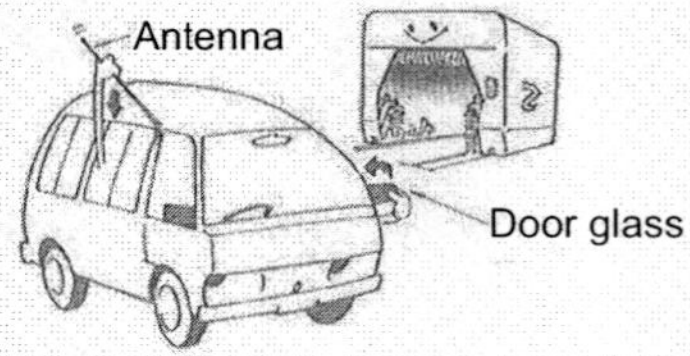


## WAXING

Wax after the vehicle has been cleaned and when it is at a cool temperature.

The bumpers that is painted should use the same wax. Unpainted parts should not be waxed.

Advice

- Do not use any wax that contains abrasive. It will remove the water repellent lustre finish.
- Read the instructions on the wax before using.
- We recommend you use Nissan Genuine Car Wax that does not contain any abrasives.

## TOUCH UPS

Use touch up paint on small scratches to prevent the paint going rusty and to lengthen the life of the paintwork.

Note:

The colour of the touch up paint may differ slightly from the colour of the paintwork.

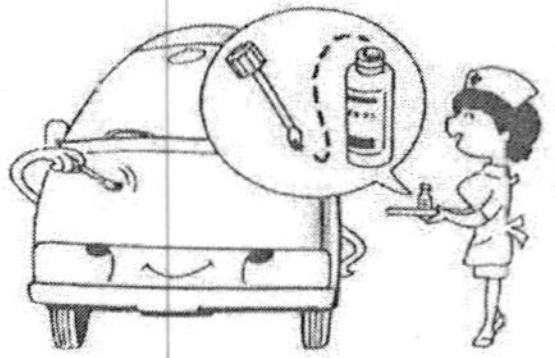

## SUPER FINE COAT

### Normal Cleaning

The vehicle with a super fine coat have a surface that repels water, even when just washed with water to maintain the lustre finish of the vehicle. If the vehicle is very dirty, use a body shampoo and wash off with plenty of water.

### Waxing

We recommend you use a Nissan Genuine Super Fine Coat Wax. If this is not obtainable, use a metallic paintwork wax that does not contain any abrasive.

## INTERIOR CARE

### Carpet

Vacuum clean, then use a dry cleaner to get the dirt out of it.

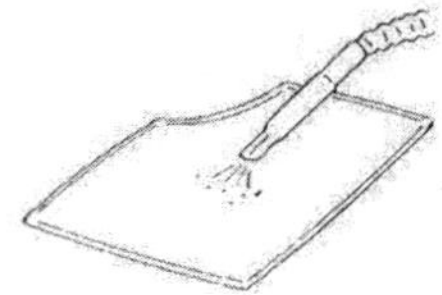

### Cloth and Vinyl Leather

Clean with diluted synthetic detergent using a soft cloth to wipe gently. Wash the cloth in clean water and wring out well, then wipe off the detergent solution.

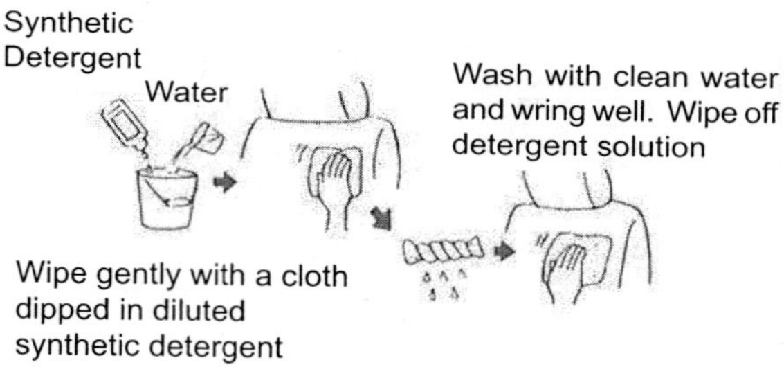

Advice
When very dirty, use Nissan Genuine Room Cleaner. Read the instructions on the product before use.

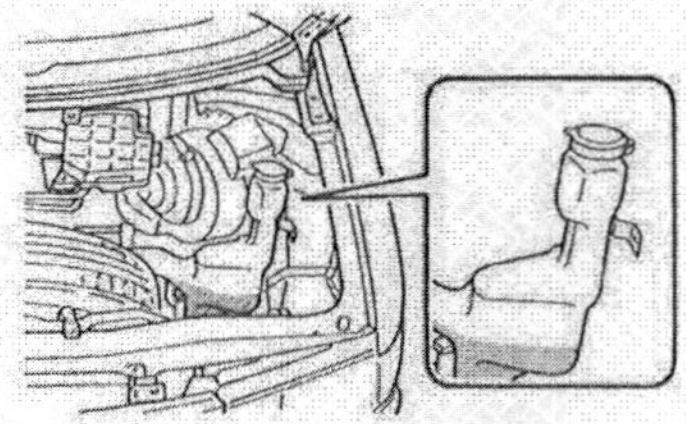

## To Refill Washer Fluid

Refill the washer tank with genuine Nissan window washer fluid
Dilute the washer fluid in accordance with mixture ratios for the various temperatures shown in the chart below.

| Climate | Dilution | Freezing Temperature |
|---|---|---|
| Normal Climates | 1 part washer fluid / 2 parts water | Approx.-10°C |
| Cold Winter | 1 part washer fluid / 1 part water | Approx.-20°C |
| Extremely Cold Winter | Only washer fluid | Approx.-30°C |

Note:

- When there is no washer fluid, do not turn on the washer switch, as this may cause motor failure.
- When you press the cap and pull out the dropper, if there is no washer fluid in the tube, the washer tank is empty. Refill with washer fluid.

## To Replace Wiper Blade

1. Erect the wiper arm and set the blade at an angle of 30°.
2. Press the claw of the blade.

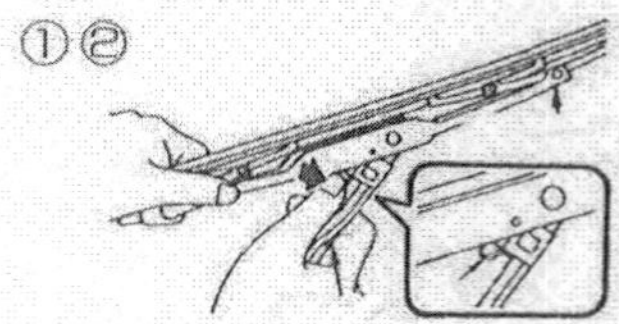

3. When pressing the claw, press the blade in the direction of the arrow.

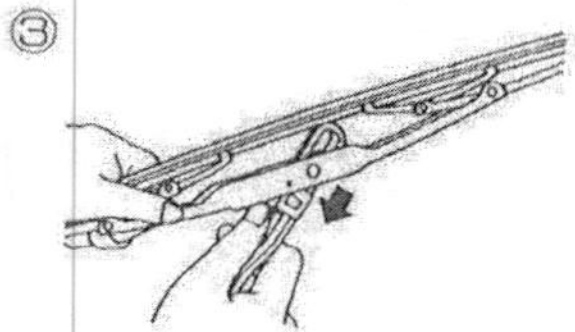

4. Remove the blade from the arm.

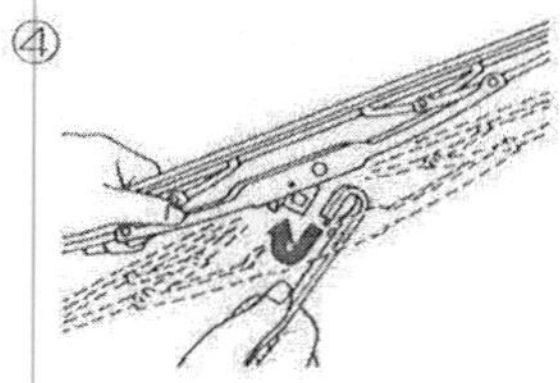

5. Fit in a new blade and reverse the procedure. (No need to press the claw of the blade.) Make sure the blade is securely fixed.

Note:

- Replace the blade when the wiper arm is erected.
- You can replace the gum only. The gum can be purchased from your Nissan dealer.

## Changing the wiper rubber

Push the A section of the blade, and slide the wiper rubber in the direction of the arrow to remove it.

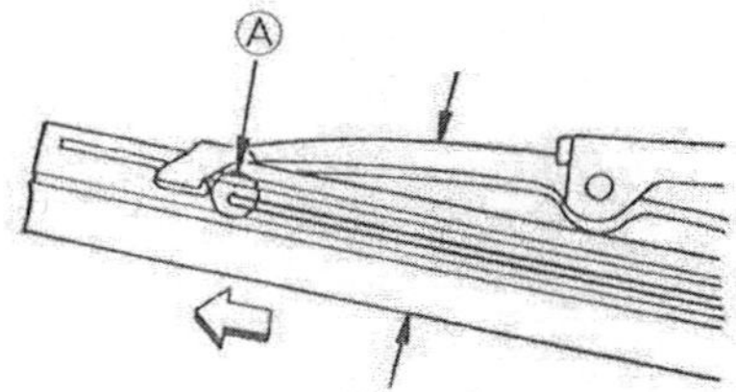


Conversely, to attach a wiper rubber, thread the rubber along the blade, starting with the section of the blade that is NOT the A section. When the A section passes the claw of the blade the rubber will fix in place.

Note:

If the wiper rubber is first wet with soapy water it will be easier to remove. Wiper rubbers can be bought at a Nissan dealer.

# CHANGING TYRES

## To Rotate Tyres

To prevent partial tyre wear and lengthen the life of your tyres, rotate the tyres every 5,000km in the way shown in the diagram.

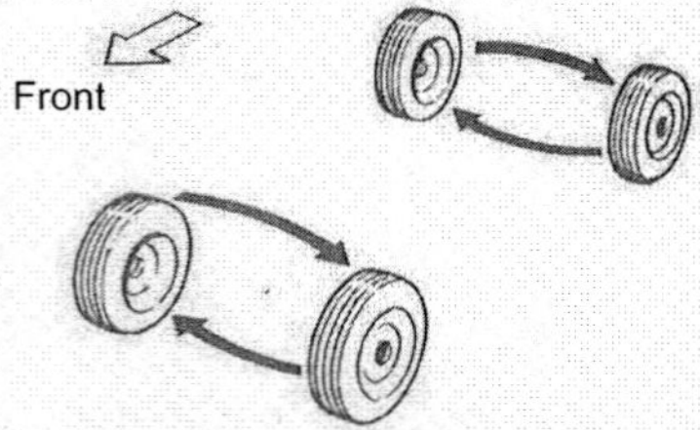


## To Change Tyres

When changing tyres or road wheels, make sure you use the specified size and tyre fit. The installation method differs depending on the vehicle type.

<u>Note:</u>
Road wheels from other vehicles may not be usable even if the rim size and the offset amount are the same. Consult your Nissan dealer before installing such wheels.

| Tyre | Wheel | | |
|---|---|---|---|
| | R in Size | P.C.D. | Offset |
| 195/70R14 91S (front) | 14X5 1/2JJ | 114.3mmX4 (hole) | 30mm |
| 215/65R14 94S (rear) | 14X6JJ | | |

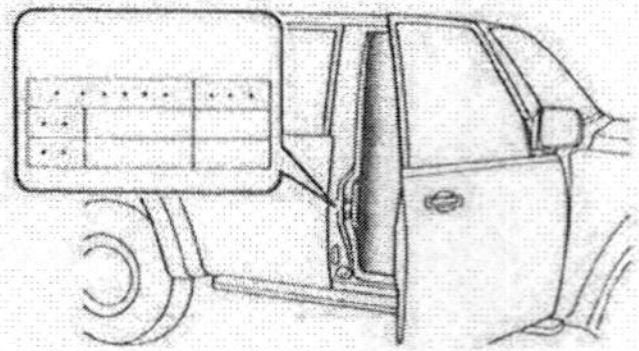

# SERVICE DATA & SPECIFICATION

# NISSAN LARGO

## SERVICE DATA -LARGO

<table>
<tr><th colspan="2">ITEM</th><th colspan="2">SERVICE DATA</th></tr>
<tr><td rowspan="2">FAN BELT</td><td rowspan="2">Deflection (Approx 10kg pressure)</td><td>Gasoline</td><td>7~8mm</td></tr>
<tr><td>Diesel</td><td>13.5~15.5mm</td></tr>
<tr><td rowspan="2">POWER STEERING BELT</td><td rowspan="2">Deflection (Approx 10kg pressure)</td><td>Gasoline</td><td>8~9 (6~7.5)mm</td></tr>
<tr><td>Diesel</td><td>13~15.5mm</td></tr>
<tr><td rowspan="2">BRAKE PEDAL</td><td>Play</td><td colspan="2">3~11mm</td></tr>
<tr><td>Clearance (Approx 50kg pressure)</td><td colspan="2">More than 110mm</td></tr>
<tr><td>PARKING BRAKE</td><td>Engaged Brake (Approx 20kg pressure)</td><td colspan="2">8~9mm notch</td></tr>
</table>

<table>
<tr><th colspan="3">ITEM</th><th>SERVICE DATA</th></tr>
<tr><td rowspan="4">Engine Oil Replacement</td><td rowspan="2">Oil Change</td><td>Gasoline</td><td>Approx 3.1 L</td></tr>
<tr><td>Diesel</td><td>2WD: Approx 5.1 L 4WD: Approx 5.3 L</td></tr>
<tr><td rowspan="2">Oil and Filter Change</td><td>Gasoline</td><td>Approx 3.4 L</td></tr>
<tr><td>Diesel</td><td>2WD: Approx 5.7 L 4WD: Approx 5.9 L</td></tr>
<tr><td colspan="3">Coolant Capacity (Including Reservoir)</td><td>Approx 11 L</td></tr>
<tr><td colspan="3">Fuel Tank Capacity</td><td>Approx 3 L</td></tr>
</table>

# SERVICE DATA -LARGO

| ITEM | | | VOLTAGE (V-W) |
|---|---|---|---|
| Bulbs | Headlight | | 12-60/55 |
| | Fog Light | | 12-55 |
| | Clearance Light | | 12-5/21 |
| | License Plate Light | | 12-5 |
| | Brake Light / Tail Light | | 12-21/5 |
| | High Mount Spotlight | | 12-21 |
| | Reverse Light | | 12-21 |
| | Indicators & Hazard Lights | Front / Rear | 12-18/21 |
| | | Side | 12-5 |

# ENGINE BAY -LARGO

## FRONT ENGINE BAY

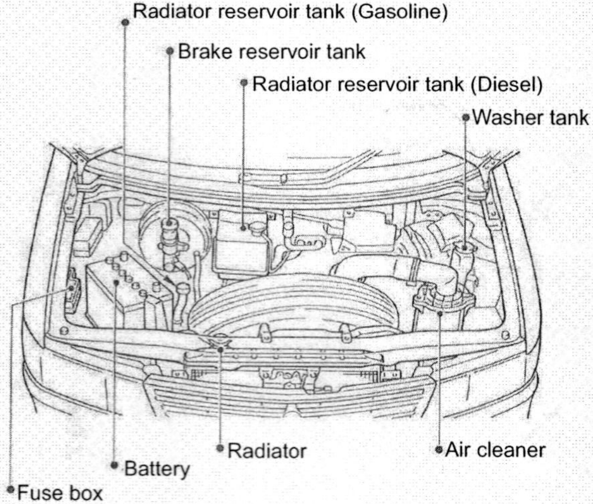


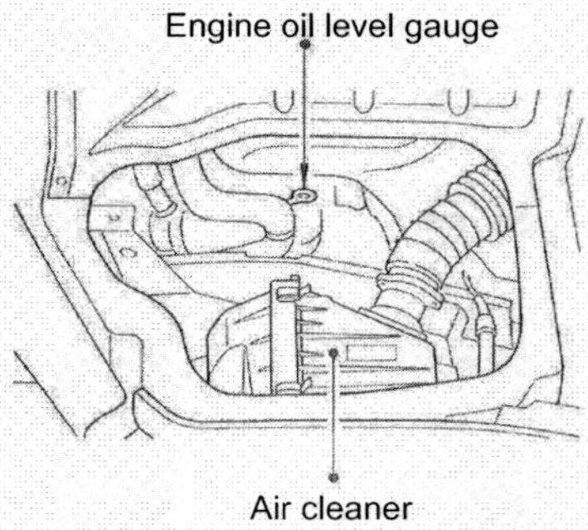


## Side of the engine bay (Diesel)

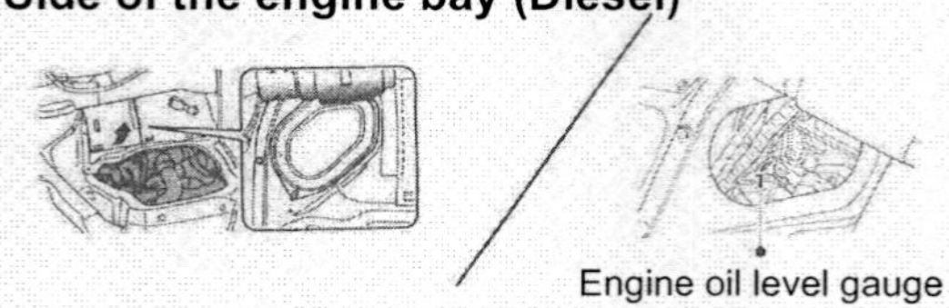


## Backside / under of the driver's seat

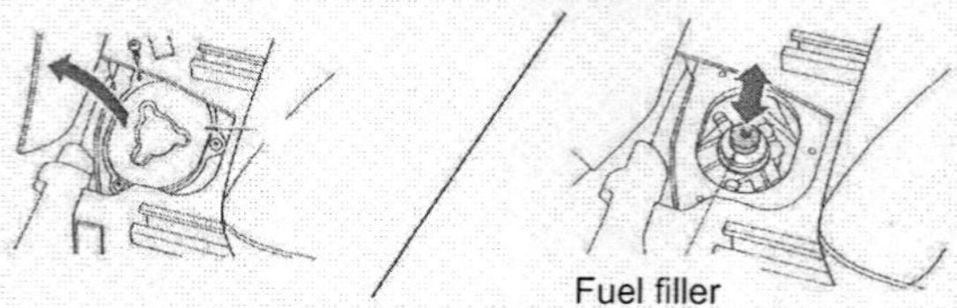

# SPECIFICATIONS - LARGO - 4WD

| Vehicle Model | | Grande_GT Pack_ 4WD(AT_2.4) | Grande _4WD(AT_2.4) | SX-G_GT Pack _4WD(AT_2.4) | SX-G_4WD(AT_2.4) |
|---|---|---|---|---|---|
| Vehicle Type | | E-NCW30 | E-NW30 | E-NCW30 | E-NW30 |
| Drive System | | 4x4 | 4x4 | 4x4 | 4x4 |
| Number of Doors | | 4 | 4 | 4 | 4 |
| Total Length (mm) | | 4585 | 4585 | 4585 | 4585 |
| Total Width (mm) | | 1745 | 1745 | 1745 | 1745 |
| Total Height (mm) | | 1920 | 1990 | 1920 | 1850 |
| Wheel Base (mm) | | 2735 | 2735 | 2735 | 2735 |
| Min Ground Clearance | | 160 | 160 | 160 | 160 |
| Tread (mm) | Front | 1480 | 1480 | 1480 | 1480 |
| | Rear | 1485 | 1485 | 1485 | 1485 |
| Seating Capacity | | 7 | 7 | 7 | 7 |
| Vehicle Weight AT (kg) | | 1590 | 1580 | 1580 | 1580 |
| Vehicle Weight MT (kg) | | - | - | - | - |
| Min Turning Radius (m) | | 5.2 | 5.5 | 5.5 | 5.5 |
| Suspension | Front | Strut | Strut | Strut | Strut |
| | Rear | Multi link | Multi link | Multi link | Multi link |
| Brake | Front | Ventilated Disc | Ventilated Disc | Ventilated Disc | Ventilated Disc |
| | Rear | Leading Trailing | Leading Trailing | Leading Trailing | Leading Trailing |
| Tyre Size | Front | 195/70R14 91S | 195/70R14 91S | 195/70R14 91S | 195/70R14 91S |
| | Rear | 215/65R14 94S | 215/65R14 94S | 215/65R14 94S | 215/65R14 94S |

# SPECIFICATIONS - LARGO - 4WD

| Vehicle Model | | RX-G_4WD(AT_2.4) | Grande _4WD(AT_ 2.0_ Diesel) | SX-G_4WD(AT_2.0_ Diesel) | RX-G_4WD(AT_2.0_ Diesel) |
|---|---|---|---|---|---|
| Vehicle Type | | E-NW30 | Y-VNW30 | Y-VNW30 | Y-VNW30 |
| Drive System | | 4x4 | 4x4 | 4x4 | 4x4 |
| Number of Doors | | 4 | 4 | 4 | 4 |
| Total Length (mm) | | 4585 | 4585 | 4585 | 4585 |
| Total Width (mm) | | 1850 | 1900 | 1850 | 1850 |
| Total Height (mm) | | 1920 | 1990 | 1920 | 1850 |
| Wheel Base (mm) | | 2735 | 2735 | 2735 | 2735 |
| Min Ground Clearance | | 160 | 160 | 160 | 160 |
| Tread (mm) | Front | 1480 | 1480 | 1480 | 1480 |
| | Rear | 1485 | 1485 | 1485 | 1485 |
| Seating Capacity | | 7 | 7 | 7 | 7 |
| Vehicle Weight AT (kg) | | 1630 | 1710 | 1680 | 1670 |
| Vehicle Weight MT (kg) | | - | - | - | - |
| Min Turning Radius (m) | | 5.2 | 5.5 | 5.5 | 5.5 |
| Suspension | Front | Strut | Strut | Strut | Strut |
| | Rear | Multi link | Multi link | Multi link | Multi link |
| Brake | Front | Ventilated Disc | Ventilated Disc | Ventilated Disc | Ventilated Disc |
| | Rear | Leading Trailing | Leading Trailing | Leading Trailing | Leading Trailing |
| Tyre Size | Front | 195/70R14 91S | 195/70R14 91S | 195/70R14 91S | 195/70R14 91S |
| | Rear | 215/65R14 94S | 215/65R14 94S | 215/65R14 94S | 215/65R14 94S |

# SPECIFICATIONS - LARGO - 4WD

| Vehicle Model | Grande_GT Pack_ 4WD(AT_2.4) | Grande _4WD(AT_2.4) | SX-G_GT Pack _4WD(AT_2.4) | SX-G_4WD(AT_2.4) |
|---|---|---|---|---|
| Engine Mode | KA24DE | KA24DE | KA24DE | KA24DE |
| Engine Type | Straight | Straight | Straight | Straight |
| Cylinder Number | 4 | 4 | 4 | 4 |
| Valve Operating System | DOHC | DOHC | DOHC | DOHC |
| Valve Number | 4 | 4 | 4 | 4 |
| Compressor | - | - | - | - |
| Piston Displacement (cc) | 2388 | 2388 | 2388 | 2388 |
| Compression Ratio | 9.5 | 9.5 | 9.5 | 9.5 |
| Max Output (ps/rpm) | 145 / 5200 | 145 / 5200 | 145 / 5200 | 145 / 5200 |
| Max Torque (kgm/rpm) | 22 / 4000 | 22 / 4000 | 22 / 4000 | 22 / 4000 |
| Fuel System | Electronically Controlled | Electronically Controlled | Electronically Controlled | Electronically Controlled |
| Fuel Type | Unleaded Gasoline | Unleaded Gasoline | Unleaded Gasoline | Unleaded Gasoline |
| Tank Capacity | 60 | 60 | 60 | 60 |
| Transmission | 4AT | 4AT | 4AT | 4AT |
| 10•15 Mode Fuel Consumption (km/L) | 7.6 | 7.8 | 7.6 | 7.8 |
| Fuel consumption at 60km/h | - | - | - | - |

# SPECIFICATIONS - LARGO - 4WD

| Vehicle Model | RX-G_4WD(AT_2.4) | Grande _4WD(AT_ 2.0_ Diesel) | SX-G_4WD(AT_2.0_ Diesel) | RX-G_4WD(AT_2.0_ Diesel) |
|---|---|---|---|---|
| Engine Mode | KA24DE | CD20Ti | CD20Ti | CD20Ti |
| Engine Type | Straight | Straight | Straight | Straight |
| Cylinder Number | 4 | 4 | 4 | 4 |
| Valve Operating System | DOHC | SOHC | SOHC | SOHC |
| Valve Number | 4 | 2 | 2 | 2 |
| Compressor | - | Turbo | Turbo | Turbo |
| Piston Displacement (cc) | 2388 | 1973 | 1973 | 1973 |
| Compression Ratio | 9.5 | 22.2 | 22.2 | 22.2 |
| Max Output (ps/rpm) | 145 / 5200 | 100 / 4400 | 100 / 4400 | 100 / 4400 |
| Max Torque (kgm/rpm) | 22 / 4000 | 21 / 2400 | 21 / 2400 | 21 / 2400 |
| Fuel System | Electronically Controlled | Jet Pump | Jet Pump | Jet Pump |
| Fuel Type | Unleaded Gasoline | Diesel Oil | Diesel Oil | Diesel Oil |
| Tank Capacity | 60 | 60 | 60 | 60 |
| Transmission | 4AT | 4AT | 4AT | 4AT |
| 10•15 Mode Fuel Consumption (km/L) | 7.6 | 7.8 | 7.6 | 7.8 |
| Fuel consumption at 60km/h | - | 16.7 | 16.7 | 16.7 |

# SPECIFICATIONS - LARGO - MR (MID ENGINE-REAR DRIVE)

| Vehicle Model | | Grande_GT Pack_AT_2.4) | Grande _(AT_2.4) | SX-G_GT Pack _(AT_2.4) | SX-G_(AT_2.4) |
|---|---|---|---|---|---|
| Vehicle Type | | E-NCW30 | E-NW30 | E-NCW30 | E-NW30 |
| Drive System | | MR | MR | MR | MR |
| Number of Doors | | 4 | 4 | 4 | 4 |
| Total Length (mm) | | 4585 | 4585 | 4585 | 4585 |
| Total Width (mm) | | 1745 | 1745 | 1745 | 1745 |
| Total Height (mm) | | 1920 | 1990 | 1920 | 1850 |
| Wheel Base (mm) | | 2735 | 2735 | 2735 | 2735 |
| Min Ground Clearance | | 165 | 165 | 165 | 165 |
| Tread (mm) | Front | 1485 | 1485 | 1485 | 1485 |
| | Rear | 1480 | 1480 | 1480 | 1480 |
| Seating Capacity | | 7 | 7 | 7 | 7 |
| Vehicle Weight AT (kg) | | 1580 | 1560 | 1580 | 1530 |
| Vehicle Weight MT (kg) | | - | - | - | - |
| Min Turning Radius (m) | | 5.2 | 5.5 | 5.5 | 5.5 |
| Suspension | Front | Strut | Strut | Strut | Strut |
| | Rear | Multi link | Multi link | Multi link | Multi link |
| Brake | Front | Ventilated Disc | Ventilated Disc | Ventilated Disc | Ventilated Disc |
| | Rear | Leading Trailing | Leading Trailing | Leading Trailing | Leading Trailing |
| Tyre Size | Front | 195/70R14 91S | 195/70R14 91S | 195/70R14 91S | 195/70R14 91S |
| | Rear | 215/65R14 94S | 215/65R14 94S | 215/65R14 94S | 215/65R14 94S |

# SPECIFICATIONS - LARGO - MR (MID ENGINE-REAR DRIVE)

| Vehicle Model | | RX-G_(AT_2.4) | Grande _(AT_2.0_ Diesel) | SX-G_(AT_2.0_ Diesel) | RX-G_(AT_2.0_ Diesel) |
|---|---|---|---|---|---|
| Vehicle Type | | E-W30 | Y-VW30 | Y-VW30 | Y-VW30 |
| Drive System | | MR | MR | MR | MR |
| Number of Doors | | 4 | 4 | 4 | 4 |
| Total Length (mm) | | 4585 | 4585 | 4585 | 4585 |
| Total Width (mm) | | 1745 | 1745 | 1745 | 1745 |
| Total Height (mm) | | 1920 | 1990 | 1920 | 1850 |
| Wheel Base (mm) | | 2735 | 2735 | 2735 | 2735 |
| Min Ground Clearance | | 165 | 165 | 165 | 165 |
| Tread (mm) | Front | 1485 | 1485 | 1485 | 1485 |
| | Rear | 1480 | 1480 | 1480 | 1480 |
| Seating Capacity | | 7 | 7 | 7 | 7 |
| Vehicle Weight AT (kg) | | 1520 | 1600 | 1570 | 1560 |
| Vehicle Weight MT (kg) | | - | - | - | - |
| Min Turning Radius (m) | | 5.2 | 5.5 | 5.5 | 5.5 |
| Suspension | Front | Strut | Strut | Strut | Strut |
| | Rear | Multi link | Multi link | Multi link | Multi link |
| Brake | Front | Ventilated Disc | Ventilated Disc | Ventilated Disc | Ventilated Disc |
| | Rear | Leading Trailing | Leading Trailing | Leading Trailing | Leading Trailing |
| Tyre Size | Front | 195/70R14 91S | 195/70R14 91S | 195/70R14 91S | 195/70R14 91S |
| | Rear | 215/65R14 94S | 215/65R14 94S | 215/65R14 94S | 215/65R14 94S |

# SPECIFICATIONS - LARGO - MR (MID ENGINE-REAR DRIVE)

| Vehicle Model | Grande_GT Pack_AT_ 2.4) | Grande _(AT_2.4) | SX-G_GT Pack _(AT_2.4) | SX-G_(AT_2.4) |
|---|---|---|---|---|
| Engine Mode | KA24DE | KA24DE | KA24DE | KA24DE |
| Engine Type | Straight | Straight | Straight | Straight |
| Cylinder Number | 4 | 4 | 4 | 4 |
| Valve Operating System | DOHC | DOHC | DOHC | DOHC |
| Valve Number | 4 | 4 | 4 | 4 |
| Compressor | - | - | - | - |
| Piston Displacement (cc) | 2388 | 2388 | 2388 | 2388 |
| Compression Ratio | 9.5 | 9.5 | 9.5 | 9.5 |
| Max Output (ps/rpm) | 145 / 5200 | 145 / 5200 | 145 / 5200 | 145 / 5200 |
| Max Torque (kgm/rpm) | 22 / 4000 | 22 / 4000 | 22 / 4000 | 22 / 4000 |
| Fuel System | Electronically Controlled | Electronically Controlled | Electronically Controlled | Electronically Controlled |
| Fuel Type | Unleaded Gasoline | Unleaded Gasoline | Unleaded Gasoline | Unleaded Gasoline |
| Tank Capacity | 65 | 65 | 65 | 65 |
| Transmission | 4AT | 4AT | 4AT | 4AT |
| 10-15 Mode Fuel Consumption (km/L) | 8.2 | 8.5 | 8.2 | 8.5 |
| Fuel consumption at 60km/h | - | - | - | - |

# SPECIFICATIONS - LARGO - MR (MID ENGINE-REAR DRIVE)

| Vehicle Model | RX-G_(AT_2.4) | Grande _(AT_2.0_ Diesel) | SX-G_(AT_2.0_ Diesel) | RX-G_(AT_2.0_ Diesel) |
|---|---|---|---|---|
| Engine Mode | KA24DE | CD20Ti | CD20Ti | CD20Ti |
| Engine Type | Straight | Straight | Straight | Straight |
| Cylinder Number | 4 | 4 | 4 | 4 |
| Valve Operating System | DOHC | SOHC | SOHC | SOHC |
| Valve Number | 4 | 2 | 2 | 2 |
| Compressor | - | Turbo | Turbo | Turbo |
| Piston Displacement (cc) | 2388 | 1973 | 1973 | 1973 |
| Compression Ratio | 9.5 | 22.2 | 22.2 | 22.2 |
| Max Output (ps/rpm) | 145 / 5200 | 100 / 4400 | 100 / 4400 | 100 / 4400 |
| Max Torque (kgm/rpm) | 22 / 4000 | 21 / 2400 | 21 / 2400 | 21 / 2400 |
| Fuel System | Electronically Controlled | Jet Pump | Jet Pump | Jet Pump |
| Fuel Type | Unleaded Gasoline | Diesel Oil | Diesel Oil | Diesel Oil |
| Tank Capacity | 65 | 65 | 65 | 65 |
| Transmission | 4AT | 4AT | 4AT | 4AT |
| 10•15 Mode Fuel Consumption (km/L) | 8.5 | - | - | - |
| Fuel consumption at 60km/h | - | 19.8 | 19.8 | 19.8 |

# Index

## F



## G



## H



## I



## J



## K



## L



## M



## O



## P

R



S



T



V



W



UX410-T58